Equality and City Schools

The Open University

Faculty of Educational Studies

The Urban Education Course Team

John Raynor (*Chairman*)
Beryl Crooks
Patricia Farrington
Alec Fleming
Jane Harden
Elizabeth Harris
Donald Holmes
David Jenkins
John Miller
John Oates
Caroline Pick
Gwynn Pritchard
Peter Raggatt
David Seligman
David Zeldin

Consultants

Brian Bates (*University of Sussex*)
Armin Beck (*University of Illinois*)
David Byrne (*University of Durham*)
Maurice Craft (*University of Exeter*)
Brian Holmes (*University of London*)
Eric Midwinter (*'Priority', Liverpool*)
Suzanne Mowat (*OECD*)
John Newson (*University of Nottingham*)
Harry Passow (*Teachers College, Columbia University*)
Bill Williamson (*University of Durham*)

Equality and City Schools

Readings in Urban Education
Volume 2

Edited by

John Raynor and Jane Harden
for the Urban Education Course Team at
The Open University

London

Routledge & Kegan Paul
in association with
The Open University Press

First published 1973
by Routledge & Kegan Paul Ltd,
Broadway House, 68–74 Carter Lane,
London EC4V 5EL
Printed in Great Britain by
Cox & Wyman Ltd,
London, Reading and Fakenham

ISBN 0 7100 7718 1 (c)
ISBN 0 7100 7719 X (p)

Contents

General introduction

Two companion volumes of readings, *Cities, Communities and the Young*, and *Equality and City Schools* have been prepared for the third-level course, 'Urban Education', offered by the Faculty of Educational Studies at The Open University. The starting point for the course is the fact that education is closely connected with the process of urbanization in that both were the product of industrialization. Urban living and its problems is the context against which urban education is set. The course, which is essentially problem-centred, seeks to provide knowledge of and insight into the development, working and problems of urban communities with an appreciation of their effect on individual development and on the processes of education. What effect, for example, do poverty and housing have upon education and on the individual? Which organizational forms of education are most appropriate to the urban setting? To what extent do proposed changes in education involve political considerations about control and participation?

Urban education is a relatively new area in education, even less developed in Britain than in the United States. For this reason many of the articles are either by American authors or by specialists in social sciences other than education. Later, no doubt, as the field develops, other readers will be produced with material drawn mostly from British sources. We have, however, deliberately avoided including material drawn from the prescribed reading list or material sent out as Open University offprints. It is for this reason that certain seminal articles on the subject do not appear. The selection of articles ranges from established viewpoints to contemporary controversial material and is drawn from journals, books and reports.

Taken together, the Readers are designed to provide:

(1) an analysis of some of the main features of urban life;

(2) an illustration of the way in which the urban context affects individual development and education; and

(3) a review of some of the new ideas and strategies for change and intervention at individual and institutional levels.

The Readers form one component of a course which includes correspondence texts, BBC radio and television programmes, student activities, personal tuition and prescribed texts, However, because the Readers have been compiled to provide students with suitable background material from a number of fields which impinge on urban education, they should also prove a valuable source for trainee or in-service teachers, administrators, planners and social workers with a special interest in the urban environment.

The first Reader focuses on the nature of the urban environment and on the individual within it. It establishes an urban perspective in the light of which a variety of educational issues are examined in the second Reader. For example, the concepts of community, community development and community participation are discussed in Reader 1, while in Reader 2 the emphasis is on the potential role of the community in widening the curriculum and the boundaries of the school. Because the Readers are complementary, several issues appear in both volumes but are presented in different ways. For example, compensatory education is discussed in Reader 1 with regard to the individual, and in Reader 2 with regard to educational policy towards achieving educational equality.

Reader 2 is divided into four sections. Section 1 discusses aspects of social inequality and the extent to which education can be the means to obtaining a more equitable society. The concept of equality of educational opportunity is central to this debate, and changes in its interpretation and practice are reviewed, with particular reference to the concept of compensatory education and the strategies of the Educational Priority Areas. In Section 2, some of the factors influencing the distribution of education resources in LEAS* and the relationship between resources and educational attainment are examined.

Sections 3 and 4 look at new ideas for city schools and their curricula. As the articles in Reader 1 showed, social, economic and political inequalities occur in their most concentrated form in

* All references to Local Authorities and LEAS pertain to those in existence before reorganization in 1974.

urban areas. But such a context need not necessarily have a negative effect on education. Cities contain enormous educative potential in terms of both human and material resources. A variety of proposed and actual departures for city schools from traditional forms of education, based on these lines of thought, are presented in Section 3. Changes in curriculum are implicit in these new forms of schooling, and Section 4 looks both at the link between the urban culture and the curriculum, as well as strategies for change in content and teaching style.

Acknowledgments

The Open University and the publishers would like to thank the following for permission to reproduce copyright material. All possible care has been taken to trace ownership of the selections included and to make full acknowledgment for their use.

Reading

1.1 By permission of the British Association for the Advancement of Science, 1969.

1.2, 3.4 Copyright © by President and Fellows of Harvard College, 1968, 1967.

1.3, 1.4 Reproduced with the permission of the Controller of Her Majesty's Stationery Office, 1967, 1972.

1.5, 2.3, 3.8 These articles first appeared in *New Society*, the weekly review of the social sciences, 128 Long Acre, London W.C.2.

1.6 By permission of Martinus Nijhoff's Boekhandel N.V., 1971.

2.1 By permission of Cambridge University Press, 1971.

2.2 This report is taken from *Where*, the monthly magazine that gives information on education, published by the Advisory Centre for Education, Cambridge.

2.4 © 1972 Oxford University Press, reproduced by permission of The Clarendon Press, Oxford.

3.1 Reproduced by arrangement with Holt, Rinehart & Winston, Inc., New York © 1968.

3.2 By permission of Calder and Boyars Ltd, 1971.

3.3 Reprinted by permission of the publisher, Sage Publications, Inc., Beverly Hills, Calif., 1971.

3.5 © The Open University, 1973.

3.6 By permission of Penguin Books Ltd, 1972.

3.7 By permission of Evans/Methuen, 1970.

Introduction to Section 1

Education and social equality

Social inequality is a feature of all societies and exists in a wide variety of forms. Goldthorpe (1.1) examines social inequality in Britain and its manifestations. Inequality in economic reward is the most obvious, but equally important are the inequalities expressed in the social status systems as well as in access to social power, where clearly some can command greater resources to serve their ends than others.[1] Because social inequality is so pervasive it is highly resistant to attempts to reduce it, despite the policies pursued in such fields as incomes, health and education.

However, Goldthorpe argues that prevailing patterns of inequality, although stable, cannot be attributed to 'natural' variation in individuals, functional constraints, or the operation of 'impersonal' market forces. Social inequality can only be explained as a 'man-made structure with important self-perpetuating properties'—and as such, can neither be considered a necessary feature of our society, nor be taken as 'given' when considering social issues.

Education is a major determinant of life-chances in industrial societies, and the remaining papers in this section discuss its effectiveness to date as an agency for social change. Coleman (1.2)[2] traces the evolution of egalitarian principles and strategies in education since public education began to appear in Europe and America in the early nineteenth century. Until the 1950s, the concept of 'equality of educational opportunity' focused on equality of access and resource input to schools. Since then, the growing recognition of non-educational determinants of educational attainment has shifted the emphasis on to equality in the *outcomes* of schooling (i.e. equality of achievement for the average member of non-educationally defined groups).

In the 1950s and 60s the underfunctioning in the school system

1

of children from certain groups in our society (generally from lower social class groups with homes with inadequate material circumstances) was widely attributed to a supposed deprivation of access to and stimulation from the mainstream culture. Such a culture is defined as that dominated by the values of the more powerful groups in advanced societies, which find their expression in, among other things, the institutional orders of the society. This led to a belief that such children were deprived in experience and in learning, particularly in language.

Within this context, the strategy of compensatory education for the deprived was developed, notably in the USA, in an attempt to prevent the growth of these so-called deficits and hence create equality of educational achievement between social groups.[3]

Morton and Watson (1.3) consider the development of compensatory education in the United States within the context of 'the liberal ideology', a view of society they believe to be widely held by dominant social groups in both the USA and Britain. They describe it as essentially conservative, advocating piecemeal social change within the existing framework of social institutions, but denying the need for basic institutional reorganization. Thus compensatory education, based on the assumption that problems are rooted in the individual, rather than the overall social order, can be seen as a specific expression of this ideology. They consider that a fundamental shortcoming of both the liberal ideology and compensatory education is the failure to take into account diversity of life experiences and values.

In Britain the Plowden Report (1967) proposed the strategy of Educational Priority Areas as a means of giving extra educational help to children in socially deprived neighbourhoods. The Report advocated 'positive discrimination' for such areas in terms of educational resources (1.4) and also stressed the need for parental involvement in education. The implications, however, of positive discrimination can go far beyond education itself; but essentially the EPA strategy is a form of compensatory education, and as such is open to the criticisms of Morton and Watson (1.3), Bernstein (1.5) as well as many others.

Bernstein (1.5) argues that many of the children towards whom compensatory education is directed have not yet been offered an adequate education environment. The notion of the family and child as deficit systems to be filled out diverts attention from the inadequacies of schools and, moreover, is reinforced by research which rarely challenges the dominant groups' assumptions about what constitutes valid knowledge or skills. Bernstein emphasizes the need to recognize and work within the child's own existing culture, instead of continually measuring him against the mainstream culture and finding him wanting.

This positive recognition of different cultures underlies the concept of community education—different educational formats for differing areas—which grew out of the 1968–71 EPA Programme.[4] Halsey, National Director of the Programme, summarizes the equality debate and then extends it by introducing community education as a more radical means of achieving social equality through education (1.6).

Notes

1 See also the article in *Cities, Communities and the Young: Readings in Urban Education*, vol. 1, Section 1, in particular 1.7 to 1.11, for discussion of these issues.

2 Author of the US survey *Equality of Educational Opportunity* (Office of Education, OE – 38001; US Government Printing Office, 1966).

3 See also the articles in *Cities, Communities and the Young: Readings in Urban Education*, vol. 1, Section 3, in particular 3.8, for discussion of these issues. Halsey gives an overview of American compensatory education in chapter 2 of *Educational Priority*, vol. I (HMSO, 1972; E351 set book).

4 See sections 3 and 4 for further discussion of community education; *Educational Priority*, vol. I for an account of the EPA Programme.

1.1 Social inequality and social integration in modern Britain[1]

John H. Goldthorpe

The overall extent and pattern of social inequality in modern Britain has been recently reviewed by a number of writers[2] and research is providing a steady flow of new information on particular aspects of this inequality. I shall not attempt here to add to this detailed knowledge, nor to produce any new synthesis of the information that exists. I wish simply to make three points about the general nature of social inequality before turning to the problem with which my paper will be centrally concerned: that is, the problem of the *implications* of inequality for social integration. The three points are the following.

(i) Social inequality, in societies such as ours, is manifested in a very wide variety of ways—wider than is usually recognized in public discussion of the matter. For example, inequalities in economic resources tend, relatively speaking, to receive a fair amount of attention. The finding reported by Meade that 5 per cent of the population own 75 per cent of all personal wealth[3] has figured quite frequently in recent political argument, as have data on the number of households whose members could be regarded as living in poverty—on incomes, say, below the 'National Assistance' level.[4] But far less is heard of the further marked inequalities that are involved in the ways in which economic rewards are actually gained—most importantly, in the content of work tasks and roles. There is, however, by now ample evidence to show that wide differences exist between occupations and jobs in the extent to which they offer possibilities of *intrinsic* satisfaction to the individuals engaged in them or, on the other hand, are a source of psychological or social deprivation.[5] To take an obvious contrast, the inequalities in reward between professional employment and factory work are clearly not confined to the differences in their income levels.

Source: *Advancement of Science* (1969,) 26 (128), 190–202.

Again, one aspect of inequality in work which it *has* of late been somewhat fashionable to point to, and to decry, is that of the status differences which operate among different categories of employee in most industrial organizations; for instance, in such matters as methods of payment, 'clocking-in' and lateness rules, toilet, canteen or car-parking arrangements, and so on. But discussion of these questions has usually been carried on without any reference to the far more basic inequality represented by the steep gradient of *authority* within such organizations—which, in fact, status distinctions serve largely to symbolize.

The tendency here illustrated to conceive of inequality in a piecemeal manner, rather than as a multiform and pervasive phenomenon, results, I would argue, from a failure to appreciate in what, fundamentally, social inequality consists. This leads me to my second point.

(ii) Social inequality in all its manifestations can be thought of as involving differences in social power and advantage: power being defined as the capacity to mobilize resources (human and non-human) in order to bring about a desired state of affairs; and advantage as the possession of, or control over, whatever in society is valued and scarce. Power and advantage are thus closely related. Power can be used to secure advantage, while certain advantages constitute the resources that are used in the exercise of power. Moreover, different forms of power and advantage tend in their very nature to be convertible: economic resources can be used to gain status or to establish authority; status can help to reinforce authority or to create economic opportunities; positions of authority usually confer status and command high economic rewards, and so on.

In this perspective, then, the way in which inequality structures virtually the whole of social life can be readily understood. Differences in social power and advantage, simply because they imply differences across the whole range of life-chances, always tend, other things being equal, to become generalized differences. Furthermore, it is important to add that this effect operates not only from one area of social life to another but also through time. Inequalities of condition at any one point in time create inequalities of opportunity for future achievement. For example, the intergenerational aspects of this phenomenon could be said to constitute the central problem thus far for the sociology of education. The results of research in this field provide impressive evidence of how, notably through the agency of the family, the stability of social strata tends to be maintained—despite the growing importance of education to career chances and the development of policies aimed at reducing non-academic influences on educational attainment.[6]

(iii) It has, therefore, to be recognized that structures of social inequality of both condition and opportunity—or, in other words, systems of social stratification—are inherently highly resistant to change. The members of higher strata have the motivation and in general the resources to hold on to their position and to transmit it to their children, while the members of lower strata are often caught up in vicious circles of deprivation. This is not, of course, to suggest that change in stratification systems cannot, or does not, occur; but rather that any significant reduction in the degree of inequality will require purposive, well-designed and politically forceful action to this end—that it is unlikely to come about simply as the unsought for consequence of technological advance, economic growth, or any such like secular trends.[7] Such developments may well modify certain forms of inequality; but they appear just as likely to accentuate others.

Indeed, far from industrial societies having 'built-in' processes which steadily diminish inequality—as some writers have claimed —what is striking, at least in the British case, is the frequently very limited effect of even the deliberate pursuit of equality through governmental action. For example, as already implied, the egalitarian aspects of educational policy over the last half century or so have resulted in only a very slight lessening in class differentials in educational opportunity—despite the fact that over the same period an enormous expansion of educational facilities has occurred.[8] In a similar way, major improvements in medical services and general standards of health have failed over a long period to produce any appreciable reduction in relative class differentials in infant mortality and in many kinds of morbidity.[9] And finally in this respect it may be noted that inequalities in incomes, after being somewhat diminished in the war and immediate post-war period, subsequently stabilized and then from around 1950 appear, if anything, to have widened again.[10]

In sum, one may say that social inequality, as observed in present-day Britain, takes the general form of a substantially self-maintaining structure of social groupings differentiated multifariously and often extremely in terms of the power and advantage that their members enjoy. What, then, are the consequences of this inequality for the integration of British society; that is to say, for the extent to which the actions of individuals and groups tend regularly to comply with recognized norms, and to be thus consistent with, rather than in conflict with or unrelated to, the expectations and actions of other individuals and groups?[11]

This question, in certain of its aspects, has in fact been examined by a number of recent writers, who have adopted a similar initial approach. They have started from the observation that in Britain considerable and abiding inequality does not apparently give rise to deeply divisive conflicts in which the existing social structure, political institutions included, is frequently and fundamentally called into question. They have then gone on to infer from this, not unreasonably, that the resentment of inequality among the less favoured sections of the population is neither particularly widespread nor particularly militant—and especially if comparisons are made with the situation in certain other societies. Thus, the somewhat more specific problem which emerges from this approach is the following: why is it that, given the prevailing degree of social inequality, there is no widely supported and radical opposition to the existing socio-political order, and that at all levels of the stratification hierarchy attitudes of acceptance, if not of approval, are those most commonly found? At this point, analyses tend to divide into two main types which one might conveniently label 'social psychological' and 'culturalist'. The first type is best displayed in the work of Runciman.[12]

Briefly, Runciman's argument is that to account for the discrepancy between the objective degree of inequality in British society and the actual awareness and resentment of this inequality, we must consider the 'reference groups' in terms of which individuals in the lower social strata assess their position. That is to say, we must consider the other groups in society—real or imagined—with which members of less favoured groups habitually *compare* themselves in evaluating their rewards, opportunities and social deserts generally, and in relation to which their expectations and aspirations are formed. If, for instance, the reference groups adopted by a certain membership group are located fairly closely in the stratification hierarchy to the membership group's own position, then the degree of felt inequality is likely to be quite slight, no matter what the overall range of factual inequality may be. A strong sense of grievance is only to be expected if reference groups are selected in a more 'ambitious' way so that considerable inequality is perceived and is then, on the basis of the comparison made, regarded as illegitimate and unjust. In other words, the degree of *relative* deprivation—deprivation which is subjectively experienced and which may thus influence political behaviour—is primarily determined *by the structure of reference groups* rather than by the structure of inequality itself as the sociologist might describe it.

Runciman's own research, using both historical and survey methods, indicates that among the British working class reference groups are, and generally have been, restricted in scope; and that while some variation in this respect can be traced over time and from one form of inequality to another, no consistent trend is evident towards wider-ranging comparisons. Consequently, the disruptive potential that social inequality might be thought to hold remains in fact suppressed: social integration is furthered through perceptual and conceptual limitations.

Turning secondly to the 'culturalist' type of analysis, it should be said that this has been chiefly elaborated by American social scientists interested in the question of the social bases of stable and effective democracy.[13] In treating Britain as one of the relatively few countries whose polity might be thus described, these investigators have been led to examine—with differing degrees of directness—such issues as the following: Why among lower social strata in Britain is there not far more alienation from a political system which is élitist in itself and under which many other forms of inequality persist? Why is there no longer in Britain, if indeed there ever was, a powerful class-based social movement seeking radical structural changes of an egalitarian kind, and prepared if necessary to challenge existing political institutions in pursuit of its objectives?

In the explanations that are offered for the absence of these possible threats to stable democracy, major emphasis is laid on the nature of British 'political culture'; that is, on the pattern or 'mix' of attitudes which research has shown to exist in British society towards political institutions and political life in general. Like other countries in which democracy flourishes, the argument runs, Britain has, in the course of her historical development, built up a political culture of a distinctive type. It is one characterized primarily by the *balance* that holds, even across lines of class and party, between participant, activist attitudes on the one hand and acquiescent, passive attitudes on the other; between emotional commitment to political principle and cool pragmatism; between consensus on matters of procedure and conflict over particular issues.

Through their socialization into this culture from childhood onwards, it is held that the majority of citizens come to feel a sense of unfanatical, but generally unquestioning, allegiance to the established political order, and one that is unlikely to be seriously disturbed by any grievances they may have over the distribution of social power and advantage. Such grievances do not lead to alienation from the political system since there is wide acceptance of the 'democratic myth'—the myth that the individual can influence political decisions and outcomes—and the system itself is not therefore seen as exploitive. Moreover, attitudes towards the political élite tend to be ones of trust, if not of deference, and the exercise of government authority is generally accepted as legitimate. For example, in one study survey data are presented to show that manual workers who believe that there are inordinately powerful groups in British society (such as 'big business') are as much prepared to allow government a wide sphere of authority as are workers who do not share in this belief.[14] In other words, grievances arising out of inequality do not tend to become so highly politicized that established political institutions and processes are themselves challenged. Political awareness is in any case at only a moderate level, and politics is only rarely a central life interest. Consequently, the availability of the ordinary citizen for involvement in 'unstabilizing' mass movements is low; the political culture effectively inhibits the radical political action which marked social inequality might otherwise be expected to generate.

Clearly, social psychological and culturalist points of view on the issue in question are not incompatible: they could, rather, be represented as complementary and mutually supportive on the following lines. Because the reference groups of lower strata have remained generally restricted, political issues stemming from social inequality have tended to be relatively 'mild' and capable of being resolved or accommodated by existing political arrangements. This has, therefore, helped a basically 'allegiant' political culture to form. Reciprocally, the development of such a culture has been inimical to the spread of ideological thinking—

as, say, on the matter of social justice—which could lead both to a heightened awareness of inequality and deprivation, and to greater recognition of their political dimensions.[15] In short social psychological processes of the kind examined by Runciman could be seen as a necessary condition of the political culture of British democracy, while this culture in turn, once established, favours the persistence of these processes.

Despite the various criticisms with which they have met, the analyses I have reviewed do, in my opinion, go some important part of the way to explaining why the consequences of inequality in Britain are not socially divisive in an extreme degree. But what has to be kept in mind, and what I wish here to emphasize, is that for the most part these analyses treat the problem of inequality and integration only from one particular angle. As I earlier noted, the focus of interest is on the possible *political* implications of inequality; and what is in effect illumined is chiefly the question of why among the British working class there is found no significant support for political ideas and movements of a revolutionary cast, nor even the widespread *incivisme* which characterizes sections of, say, the French or Italian working class. However, there are other major aspects of the problem which may be distinguished, and ones which have been curiously neglected. In particular, I would advance the view—as the central thesis of this paper—that the most far-reaching implications of inequality for the integration of British society occur not in the political sphere but rather in that of economic life; and that they are manifested not in a situation of fundamental class struggle but rather in a situation of anomie; that is, in a situation in which, to stay close to the original Durkheimian notion, there is a lack of *moral* regulation over the wants and goals that individuals hold. This contention can best be elaborated by reference to two closely related topics of current public concern: industrial relations and incomes policy.

In a recent paper—entitled 'The Reform of Collective Bargaining: from Donovan to Durkheim'—two leading authorities, Fox and Flanders, have in fact argued explicitly and at length that the British system of industrial relations is now in an anomic state.[16] In the post-war period, these authors observe, the wants, expectations and aspirations of industrial workers have expanded notably, and not only in regard to wage levels but also in such matters as security of employment, job rights and control over work organization. At the same time, generally high levels of employment have given many groups of workers the power to pursue their new goals with some effectiveness. A frequent outcome has then been that such groups have broken through the regulation of work relationships imposed by collective agreements at a national level and have secured agreements of a more favourable kind at company, plant or shop level. Thus, Fox and Flanders argue, industrial relations have become disordered in two main ways: first, as a result of the problems involved in developing new normative systems, capable of accommodating the new issues of industrial conflict which now arise; and second, and more seriously, because the solutions arrived at have tended to be *ad hoc* and piecemeal ones of only limited, local application. This tendency has therefore given rise to a proliferation of normative systems based on often unrelated or divergent principles; and such a situation is one rife with anomalies, frustrations and rivalries which constantly generate new tensions and conflicts both between employers and workers and between different sets of workers: 'Disorder feeds upon disorder.' The consequences of this anomic state are then to be seen not simply in strikes and other dislocations of the productive process, but further 'in such things as chaotic pay differentials and uncontrolled movements of earnings and labour costs'. Thus, it is claimed, threats are posed to the long-term development of the economy (apart from the aggravation of short-term balance of payments problems) and there could, furthermore, be serious political implications: increasing disorder might generate popular demands for state intervention of an authoritarian kind which would mark the end of the present pluralistic and voluntary basis of industrial relations.

The analysis offered by Fox and Flanders is insightful and important. However, I would suggest that it is one that does not go far enough in revealing just how deeply rooted in the structure of British society is the 'disorderly' situation with which it is concerned; and, further, that this limitation results precisely from the fact that Fox and Flanders do not follow Durkheim in relating the problem of anomie to the problem of inequality. This argument can best be illustrated by reference to their recommendations for reform in industrial relations—that is, for the 'reconstruction of normative order'. Briefly, what they stress is the continuing need for an incomes policy, accompanied by the regularizing and rationalizing of collective bargaining from plant and company level upwards. In this latter respect, they point to the availability and usefulness of such techniques as productivity bargaining and job evaluation and other means of measuring and rewarding different kinds of work. Through a programme of reform on the lines in question, they see the possibility of achieving a more logical wages structure, greater control over earnings and labour costs, and industrial relations institutions which, through being more adaptable to change themselves, will be better able to manage the conflicts that change inevitably produces.

Fox and Flanders recognize that there is no guarantee that such objectives will in fact be achieved, and they refer to the 'Promethean character' of the task of reform. None the less, I would argue that they still under-estimate the difficulties that are involved: in particular, in creating an area of relatively rational and orderly inequality in place of the present 'wages jungle' *when this jungle is simply part of a wider structure of inequality which has no rationale whatsoever*—other, perhaps, than the principle of 'to them that have shall more be given'. For example, at one point in their paper Fox and Flanders remark that 'The debate on incomes policy is often conducted within the trade union movement as if collective bargaining were simply a mechanism for pursuing social justice as between capital and labour, and its function of determining the relative fortunes of different groups of labour is ignored.' This may be fair comment, but it is still highly questionable if an incomes policy of the kind they favour can be effective in establishing a less chaotic and more equitable pattern of earnings *within* the working class in the context of the *overall* degree of economic inequality which statistics on the distribution of income and wealth reveal. An industrial worker seeking a wage increase might be prepared to recognize that his claim was weak in comparison with that of, say, certain of his lower-paid workmates; but he would have no difficulty in finding other groups, possibly outside the working class, in relation to whom his claim could be much better justified—even assuming that his range of reference groups was not extensive. Moreover, it should be emphasized here that while restricted reference groups may inhibit feelings of grievance over inequalities, this is not to say that they actually motivate individuals to *hold back* from attempting to improve their position, especially economically: limited social horizons are not, as Durkheim might have put it, a source of moral restraint.[17]

Now it must be said that Fox and Flanders are well aware—

indeed, they emphasize—that the normative regulation resulting from collective bargaining is unlikely ever to rest purely upon consensus; it will also be a product of the balance of power between the parties concerned and of their calculation of what for the time being, is the most advantageous position they can achieve. What may further be involved, at least in initiating any reform, is some kind of third party intervention—'the forceful articulation of common norms by some authoritative source'. However, to follow Durkheim's argument closely here, one has to insist that in so far as the normative order in economic life is *not* based upon consensus, but is rather founded upon coercion or expediency, then the threat of anomie and of chronic malinte-gration remains—no matter what degree of internal logic or coherence normative systems may be given. For as Durkheim stresses, unless in modern society the regulation of economic life— and, crucially, the regulation of inequality—*does* have some accepted moral basis, then it is unlikely to be effective in any continuing way. To the extent that the normative order is imposed by superior power, fundamental discontent and unrest persist if only in latent form; to the extent that it results from the calcula-tion of advantage under given (non-moral) constraints, it is likely to be called into question as soon as these constraints vary.[18]

Thus, while proposals for reform of the kind that Fox and Flanders put forward might well endow collective bargaining institutions and procedures with a good deal more formal rationality than they at present possess, I find it difficult to believe that such measures could go very far towards ensuring *stable* normative systems, of either a substantive or a procedural kind, at any level of industrial relations. The absence of an accepted moral basis for economic life as a whole in our kind of society must always render precarious the norms which at any time prevail in any specific area—a plant, company, industry, etc. As but one illustration of this point, taken from Durkheim's own discussion of the problem, one may consider the implications of inequalities of opportunity for attitudes towards inequalities of condition. If the former are extreme and without effective legitimation, little consensus can be expected on the latter—even supposing that some hierarchy of social positions and roles is generally acknow-ledged. For, as Durkheim argued, 'it would be of little avail for everyone to recognize the justice of the hierarchy of functions as established by public opinion, if they did not also consider just the way in which individuals are recruited to these functions'.[19] While ever, then, British society is characterized by the present marked degree of inequality in educational and occupational opportunity, it is difficult to see that there is any basis for the achievement of what Fox and Flanders regard as the ultimate objective of industrial relations reform; namely, 'agreed normative codes regulating the production and distribution of wealth in modern industrial society'—or, at all events, agreement will for the majority remain highly qualified, reluctant or uncertain, and thus inherently *un*stable. One need not assume that rank-and-file industrial employees resent the inferior life-chances they have been accorded as keenly as the facts might warrant in ord claim that few will feel *morally* bound by the normative codes which govern their working lives. It is sufficient to ask from what source, given the nature of the British social order, such a sense of moral commitment might stem.[20]

My conclusion must then be that the reconstruction of normative order in British industrial relations which Fox and Flanders pursue is something of an *ignis fatuus*. Within a society in which inequality exists as brute fact—largely without moral legitimation—'disorderly' industrial relations cannot, I think, be understood as a particular pathological development which will yield to particular remedies: rather, to maintain a Durkheimian perspective, this disorder must be seen as 'normal'—as a generalized characteristic of societies of the type in question.[21]

The structural features of British society which stand in the way of the reform of industrial relations are at the same time obstructive, as the foregoing discussion would imply, to the effective administration of an incomes policy. The aim of incomes policy, within a market economy such as our own, is usually stated to be that of controlling the growth of incomes so that inflationary tendencies may be kept in check while still preserving relatively high levels of employment and utilized capacity.[22] However, it is essential to appreciate that an incomes policy is not, and cannot be, just another economic instrument—despite the attempt of certain technocratically minded economists to present it in this guise. Once a government attempts to regulate incomes, in no matter how piecemeal or partial a fashion, it is forced into the position of arbiter on particular wage levels or wage changes, and issues of social justice thus inevitably arise and have in some way or other to be resolved. Indeed, government spokesmen in Britain have been generally prepared to acknowledge this situation and even to claim that an incomes policy is, or could be, a means of enhancing social justice; for example, by ensuring a better deal for the lowest-paid workers. But, I would argue, it is basically on account of this normative aspect of incomes policy that its administration runs into serious problems, which have not as yet been overcome, and which may, for reasons I shall shortly suggest, be self-aggravating ones.

At the root of the difficulty is again the fact that not only is the existing distribution of income and wealth in British society unprincipled—in the strict sense of the word—but further that there appears to be little consensus on the principles which *ought* to apply when it is a question of maintaining or altering any specific income level or relativity. Survey data are of some relevance to this argument,[23] but more significant is the great variety of frequently conflicting considerations which are actually invoked when pay issues are debated. Some criteria, for example, would entail at least the possibility of significant change in the existing pay structure—increased productivity, job evaluation ratings, 'absolutely' low wages or persisting manpower shortages: but others, such as increases in the cost of living, the need to preserve a differential or maintain the social status of a particular group, are essentially conservative in their implications. Moreover, as Professor (now Lady) Wootton has pointed out, claims for more pay based on *any* of these often conflicting criteria can be, and usually are, couched in moral terms, or at any rate the economic arguments are related back to moral premises.[24] Thus, one is again forced to the conclusion that little basis for moral *restraint* is currently to be found in British society—that, in other words, a condition of anomie prevails. Given the diversity of moral positions that are tenable in the existing state of public opinion, virtually any occupational group seeking a pay increase is likely to be able to find some kind of legitimation for pressing its case.[25]

From this standpoint, then, it is to be expected that the amount of 'voluntary' support for an incomes policy will be insufficient to enable it to achieve its ends; and such an expectation seems to be generally in accord with British (and other) experience. Furthermore, even when control over incomes is in some way or other 'imposed', it still appears difficult, at least within the constraints on governmental authority that liberal democracy entails, for such control to be very effective for very long. A 'norm' for pay increases may hold up for a short-run period and even a complete 'freeze' may work under crisis conditions—as in Britain, in 1966-7. But in the longer term control seems invariably to break down, most notably at the level at which coercive methods are least feasible—that is, at the grass-roots level of the individual enterprise.[26] A tendency for the actual earnings of many groups of workers to rise above the intended norm, as a result of collective agreements or other less formal arrangements locally made, has to be reckoned as the besetting problem of incomes policy administration—and even, it seems, in 'centrally planned' economies such as that of the USSR.[27]

Thus, as one economist, John Corina, has recently pointed out, 'the unpalatable facts of wage drift', once recognized, pose a hard dilemma so far at any rate as Britain is concerned. Either an attempt must be made to extend the range and increase the stringency of income control, to the point at which voluntary collective bargaining ceases to exist, and at risk of building up a considerable pressure of opposition; or it must be accepted that, under existing conditions, incomes policy initiatives are inherently *unstable* in their effects, and that their progressive breakdown is to be anticipated as a matter of course. Unlike some of his colleagues, Corina is prepared to recognize that 'at bottom, the crucial tangles of incomes policy stem from the intangible concept of "social justice" in income distribution', and are inseparable from issues raised both by the existing structure of inequality and by the lack of accord on what form this structure should possess. As he pertinently asks, '. . . how can incomes policy create consent where social valuations of incomes, within a given incomes distribution, are confused and often obscure?'[28]

Moreover, one point which Corina does not consider is that attempts to implement incomes policy may have quite unforeseen consequences which in fact tend to build up the difficulties involved. It is not simply that a 'freeze' or period of tight control over incomes may be followed by heightened militancy in wage demands, threatening greater inflationary problems than before.[29] There is a further, yet more awkward, possibility: namely, that through increasing information about, and interest in, differences between occupational rewards and conditions, the actual operation of an incomes policy will serve to broaden comparative reference groups among the mass of the population, and at the same time bring issues of equity and fairness into greater subjective salience.[30] Thus, following Runciman's analysis, one would expect, in the case of the working class at least, a growing sense of resentment and grievance over the *status quo* and, in turn, a yet greater unwillingness to accept 'restraint' or to hold back in any way from the direct pursuit of their own maximum advantage. In other words, what are sometimes called the 'educative' functions of incomes policy may well have the effect of undermining the viability of such policy. To the extent that evaluations of income and other economic differences do become less confused and obscure, there is little reason to suppose that what will emerge will be greater consensus from one group or stratum to another: the far more likely outcome, given the prevailing degree of inequality, is that conflicts will become more clearly defined and more widely recognized—that the anomic state of economic life will be made increasingly manifest.

To recapitulate, then, my two central arguments have been the following: first, that social inequality in Britain appears to pose no direct threat to the stability of the political order—because this is, as it were, 'insulated' from the potentially disruptive consequences of inequality by a combination of social-psychological and cultural influences; but second, that the existence of inequality, of an extreme, unyielding and largely illegitimate kind, does militate seriously against any stable normative regulation in the economic sphere—because it militates against the possibility of effective value consensus on the distribution of economic, and other, resources and rewards.

Of these two arguments, it is, I imagine, the latter that will be the more likely to provoke dissent, and chiefly perhaps among social scientists with 'applied' interests in the field of industrial and economic policy; for it obviously suggests that much of their present endeavour will meet with relatively little success. However, as a way both of rounding off this argument and leading on to my own, concluding, observations on policy issues, I would like to draw attention to one further point—somewhat obvious but often neglected—with implications that may be still more unwelcome to those colleagues in question. This is the point that, in spite of frequent attempts, it has not proved possible to give a satisfactory explanation of the persisting degree and form of inequality, in Britain or in any advanced society, by reference primarily to 'external' constraints, and without reference to the purposive exercise of their power and advantage by more privileged groups and strata. In other words, it has not proved possible to explain social inequality otherwise than as a structure with important self-maintaining properties.

For example, attempts to relate social inequality or particular aspects of it—say, in incomes—to differences in the so-called 'natural' attributes of individuals have repeatedly failed; and chiefly because social variation is regularly found to be of a different order of magnitude from natural variation. In advanced societies the dispersion of even earned income has a proportionate range of as wide as 50 or perhaps 100 to 1: no conceivably relevant natural attribute has been shown to vary to such an extent.[31] Again, it is by now evident enough that established structures of inequality yield little to explanation in terms simply of the operation of 'impersonal' market forces—in terms, that is, of the interaction of supply and demand in regard to different types of labour service. Labour economists themselves, as much as educational sociologists, have demonstrated the considerable restrictions that occur on the 'supply' side, as a result of various forms of inequality of opportunity. Consequently, the existence of the essentially 'non-competing groups' which social strata form distorts the labour market into a highly imperfect condition; and the 'imperfections' themselves lie outside the scope of pure economic analysis.[32] Finally, one should note, attempts by sociologists to revamp classical economics in the guise of 'functional' theories of social stratification have scarcely been convincing. Even if one leaves aside the basic problems of how to determine the functional exigencies of a social system or the relative functional importance of positions and roles within it, a logical limitation of such theories must still be stressed: that is, they are adequate only to explaining why *some degree* of social inequality should occur—not why the actual pattern of inequality is as it is.[33]

In short, then, one may assert that attempts to account for observable social inequality in terms simply of constraints, whether stemming from genetics, economics or 'societal' imperatives, are at best of very limited value. Through their very inadequacies, such attempts point to the degree to which the phenomenon of social stratification must be seen as an autonomous one: as a phenomenon which has to be explained largely as the outcome of social action and interaction in the form of competition and conflict, the basis for which being always the inequality in power and advantage previously existing.

This being so, there are, I think, two implications of note. First, since prevailing patterns of inequality cannot be represented as the direct consequence of ineluctable exigencies, it is hard to see how they can be 'scientifically' legitimated as *necessary* features, either of the human condition in general or of the functioning of a particular type of society. In itself, of course, this fact is unlikely to be of much significance for the attitudes towards social inequality which are actually held among the population at large: it seems probable that inequality is indeed quite widely accepted as deriving either from 'natural' differences or from (what sociologists would call) 'functional imperatives'.[34] But this situation then points to the second implication which I see as important. Namely, that when concerned with problems arising out of competition and conflict, such as those found in economic life, applied social scientists must seriously ask themselves whether they do not have an obligation to state, clearly and insistently, that the context of inequality in which these problems typically exist is neither unalterable nor indisputably desirable, and need not, therefore, be taken as a 'given'. In other words, they must consider whether they are not obliged to emphasize what they know about the nature of social inequality, including its self-perpetuating but 'man-made' characteristics, and thus try to redress a situation in which, as Runciman has put it, 'from the moment almost of birth, attitudes to the social structure are conditioned by pressures in which the ideal of social justice plays little if any part.'[35]

If applied social scientists do act in this way, they may well of course make their task of piecemeal social reconstruction even more difficult than I have already suggested; that is, by increasing awareness and resentment of inequality, especially among disadvantaged groups and strata, and thus reducing further the likelihood of their willing cooperation. But if, on the other hand, our social and economic engineers keep silent on the matter of inequality—if they attempt rather to build on the fact that the full extent of inequality is often unrealized and its sources misunderstood—then they are, willy-nilly, applying their knowledge and expertise in a partial way. And on this account, whatever their intentions may be, they lay themselves open to the charge of acting as 'the servants of power'.

I am, then, arguing not only that attempts at reconstituting normative order in economic life have small chances of success under existing conditions of inequality, but further that these chances will be still smaller if social scientists acknowledge an obligation to propagate the findings of examinations of this inequality and to relate these findings to the issues in which they seek to intervene. For it can scarcely be denied that such knowledge is likely to be corrosive of those beliefs and attitudes which, it seems, contain grievances arising out of inequality to a level that is 'manageable' at all.

This, I recognize, may be thought a very negative position to adopt, and in certain respects it obviously is. However, I should like to observe that there is one conclusion with constructive possibilities to which my analysis does lead on directly; that is, that if the problem of anomie in economic life is to be attacked effectively, then the problem of social inequality must be attacked simultaneously. It can, I think, be argued, as a matter of sociology rather than ideology, that in a society that is both industrial and democratic relatively stable normative order in economic life can *only* be created through norms being underpinned by some minimum degree of value consensus—as opposed to merely customary limitations on wants and goals. And such consensus in turn cannot be achieved without the distribution of economic resources and rewards, and indeed the entire structure of power and advantage, becoming in some sense 'principled'—becoming, that is, more capable of being given consistent rational and moral justification. In other words, the advancement of social justice has to be seen not as some lofty and rather impractical ideal, the further pursuit of which must wait upon the attainment of such basic objectives as 'getting the economy right', but rather as an important *precondition* of mitigating current economic difficulties. Such a lesson had to be learnt once in the nineteenth and earlier twentieth centuries, when governments were forced to recognize, as one historian has remarked, that social welfare policies were not 'mere sweeteners of the hard rigours of a system of individualist compulsions' but represented rather 'social provision against waste of life and resources and against social inefficiency—not concessions.'[36] Governments now apparently need to learn that in a society with a highly complex division of labour, in which the possibilities of malintegration are correspondingly great, social inequality which is extreme and without legitimation will continually frustrate the orderly and efficient conduct of industrial and economic affairs generally: or, as Durkheim more succinctly put it, that 'all external inequality compromises organic solidarity'.[37]

This is not the place to spell out in detail how the normative reconstruction of economic life and the reduction of social inequality might proceed together. But certain general possibilities are evident enough. For example, several writers have already observed that attempts to regularize industrial relations at enterprise level, so as to facilitate grievance procedures and checks on wage movements, inevitably raise afresh issues of industrial democracy: issues of the right of employees to participate in management and economic decision-making going beyond the scope of collective bargaining. And at least one economist has been prepared to recognize that effective answers to the key 'micro' problems of incomes policy may well entail 'changes in concepts of managerial structure, authority and control'.[38] Again, as regards incomes policy in 'macro' terms, Professor Wootton more than a decade ago argued the need for such a policy to be *expressly related* to egalitarian objectives, in order to counteract the self-reinforcing character of social inequality and to give the structure of earnings a clearer moral basis; otherwise, the support of large sections of the population could neither be asked for nor expected. Professor Wootton in fact points to the genuinely radical conception of an incomes policy addressed not simply to problems in inflation, but, more basically, to those of social integration and the furtherance of democracy. Such a policy, rather than being devised as an essentially economic instrument, would be framed as part of an overall social policy, with economic considerations being admissible only as and when their imperative nature could be actually demonstrated.[39]

In adumbrating such possibilities, there are two things I should make quite clear. First, I do not for a moment underestimate the difficulties that would be involved in realizing them—not least as a result of the direct opposition which could be safely predicted from those whose power and advantage would be diminished. Second, I am not attempting here to argue for the desirability of developments of the kind in question in any absolute sense— though such a case might no doubt be made. What I am trying to establish is that these possibilities exist, and that unless and until something on these lines is accomplished, then the present anomic character of economic life will remain. I recognize that from a number of value positions the goal of greater equality may be given only low priority, or that inequality may even be regarded as a good in itself. Moreover, I do not believe that the sociologist *qua* sociologist is able to impugn such positions directly. But what *can* be argued sociologically is that those who are prepared to accept social inequality more or less as it presently exists must *also* be prepared to accept 'disorderly' industrial relations, the 'wages jungle' and general economic 'free for all' more or less as *they* now exist—or, as the one remaining possibility, to support attempts at entirely authoritarian solutions to these problems. This last course of action, however, would be perhaps the most effective way of breaking down the insulation of the British political system from issues and grievances stemming from inequality—the insulation which the national political culture has hitherto provided. In other words, it would carry the very real threat of extending economic into political instability.[40]

Finally, to turn from possibilities to probabilities, one has, I think, to accept that for the foreseeable future by far the most likely outcome is the continuance of the present state of affairs; that is, of a situation of persisting, marked inequality and also of chronic industrial unrest and of general economic in-fighting between interest groups under the rules mainly of 'catch as catch can'. Such a forecast is indicated by the fact that the egalitarian restructuring of our society, which could only be achieved as a work of political will, expertise and force, does not now appear to be even on the agenda of any major political party. For those who find this situation an unacceptable one, the main hope, at this stage at least, must lie in attempts at analysis and persuasion; in attempts, that is, to demonstrate, as cogently and as widely as possible, just what the concomitants of existing social inequality are, and how they block the aspirations found in many groups and strata—and not only among the less privileged—for a society in which resources are more rationally and co-operatively used. The highest degree of optimism that egalitarians can permit themselves—the belief that the *need* for greatest equality will eventually prevail—is aptly expressed in one further passage which I take from Durkheim, from near the end of *The Division of Labour*:[41]

> The task of the most advanced societies is then, one could say, a work of justice . . . Just as the ideal of less developed societies was to create or maintain as intense a common life as possible, in which the individual was absorbed, so our ideal is to invest our social relationships with ever greater equity in order to ensure the free development of all socially useful potentialities. When one thinks, though, that for

centuries men have been content with a much less perfect justice, one begins to ask if these aspirations might not perhaps be due to fits of gratuitous impatience; if they do not represent a deviation from the normal state of affairs rather than an anticipation of the normal state of the future; in short, whether the way of curing the disorder they make manifest is through satisfying them or rejecting them. What we have already established . . . enables us to answer this question precisely. There are no needs more firmly grounded than these impulsions, for they are a necessary consequence of the changes that have occurred in the structure of societies . . . In the same way as earlier peoples needed, above all, a common faith to live by, we ourselves need justice; and we can be sure that this need will become increasingly exigent if, as seems in every way likely, the conditions that govern social evolution remain unchanged.

Notes

1 Presidential Address delivered to Section N (Sociology) on 8 September 1969 at the Exeter Meeting of the British Association.
2 See, for example the Introduction by R. M. Titmuss to the recent republication of R. H. Tawney's classic study, *Equality* (5th ed., London, 1964).
3 J. E. Meade, *Efficiency, Equality and the Ownership of Property* (London, 1964), p. 27.
4 See, for example, Brian Abel-Smith and Peter Townsend, *The Poor and the Poorest* (London, 1965).
5 For useful reviews of relevant literature, see Robert Blaunder, 'Work satisfaction and industrial trends in modern society' in W. Galenson and S. M. Lipset (eds), *Labor and Trade Unionism* (New York, 1960), and John Child, *The Business Enterprise in Modern Industrial Society* (London, 1969), pp. 64–76.
6 See the research findings and discussion presented in A. H. Halsey, Jean Floud, and C. A. Anderson, *Education, Economy and Society* (London and New York, 1961), Parts II, III, IV; and Olive Banks, *The Sociology of Education* (London, 1968) Chs 3 to 5.
7 It is also, of course, important that changes in the structure of social inequality should be distinguished from the processes of individual, or group, mobility within a given structure. Such mobility can occur without strata losing their identity as collectivities or 'quasi-groups'. Cf. Walter Buckley, 'Social stratification and the functional theory of social differentiation', *American Sociological Review*, 23 (1958).
8 Alan Little and John Westergaard, 'The trend of class differentials in educational opportunity in England and Wales', *British Journal of Sociology*, 15, 4 (1964).
9 J. N. Morris and J. A. Heady, 'Social and biological factors in infant mortality: V. Mortality in relation to the father's occupation 1911–1950', *Lancet*, i (1955), p. 554; and Morris, *Uses of Epidemiology* (2nd ed., Edinburgh, 1964) pp. 52–64.

10 John A. Brittain, 'Some neglected features of Britain's income leveling', *American Economic Review*, 50 (2) (1960).

11 I am thus concerned here specifically with 'social' as opposed to 'system' integration – to apply the important distinction made by David Lockwood. See his paper, 'Social integration and system integration' in George K. Zollschan and Walter Hirsch (eds), *Explorations in Social Change* (New York, 1964). It should further be noted that social integration is not taken as *implying* actors' moral commitment to the norms they observe. As Cohen stresses, 'there is a *fundamental difference between the recognition of a normative expectation and a commitment to uphold the norm.*') Percy S. Cohen, *Modern Social Theory* (London, 1968), p. 113.) However, what will emerge as a central contention is that a state of social integration will be more *stable*, the greater the degree to which compliance with norms does derive from moral consensus rather than from calculation, coercion, or custom; i.e. the greater the relative importance of 'internal' as opposed to 'external' constraints.

12 W. G. Runciman, *Relative Deprivation and Social Justice: a study of attitudes to social inequality in twentieth-century England* (London, 1966).

13 The most important studies are Harry Eckstein, 'The British political system' in Samuel H. Beer and Adam B. Ulam (eds), *Patterns of Government* (New York, 1962); Gabriel A. Almond and Sidney Verba, *The Civic Culture* (Princeton, 1963) and Eric A. Nordlinger, *The Working Class Tories: Authority, Deference and Stable Democracy* (London, 1967).

14 Nordlinger, *op. cit.*, pp. 107–8. The effect in question was the same among Labour and Conservative voters.

15 In summing up his findings on the relationship between social inequalities and the feeling of relative deprivation, Runciman notes that 'of all its various determinants, one of the least powerful is the abstract ideal of social justice' even though 'the notion of social justice is somewhere implicit in every account of how people feel about social inequality' (*op. cit,* p. 247). He is further aware of the way in which dominant modes of political socialization within British society are inimical to a developed awareness of issues of social justice (pp. 292–4).

16 *British Journal of Industrial Relations*, 7 (2) (1969).

17 At one point at least Durkheim makes a quite explicit distinction between a 'moral discipline' and one maintained by 'custom', and stresses the greater effectiveness of the former. See *Le Suicide* (new ed., Paris, 1930), p. 278. Moreover, the distinction seems to me to be always implicit in, and crucial to, his analyses of the problems of the integration of economically advanced societies, in comparison with those having a less developed division of labour. The most frequent function of comparative reference groups in industrial negotiations would seem to be to help support claims that an improvement in pay or conditions is necessary in order for a particular group to *maintain* its relative position. See the discussion in S. M. Lipset and Martin Trow, 'Reference group theory and trade union wage policy' in Mirra Komarovsky (ed.), *Common Frontiers of the Social Sciences* (Chicago, 1957). Lipset and Trow in fact advance the view that the extent to which workers feel that wage relationships are morally right will determine the comparative reference groups they adopt – rather than *vice versa* (pp. 400–1).

18 Cf. *De la Division du travail social* (7th ed., Paris, 1960), pp. 356–7; *Le Suicide*, pp. 278–9; and *Leçons de sociologie: Physique des moeurs et du droit* (Paris, 1950), ch. 1. Further, as already observed, consensus which reflects moral commitment to norms is in turn seen as more durable, in the context of modern societies, than that which reflects simply the customary observance of norms. Durkheim in fact makes it clear that to increase the integration of such societies and overcome the problems arising from anomie in economic life, it is *not* sufficient simply to have norms or rules articulated: the question of their basis is quite crucial. '... ce n'est pas assez qu'il y ait des règles; car parfois, ce sont ces règles mêmes qui sont la cause du mal.'

19 *Le Suicide*, p. 277. All translations from Durkheim are my own and differ, sometimes significantly, from published versions.

20 The one possible source would seem to be in the close and highly personalized relations between workers, and between workers and the employer, which may prevail in very small scale establishments. Cf. G. K. Ingham, 'Organizational Size Orientation to Work and Industrial Behaviour', University of Cambridge Ph.D. thesis, 1968. Durkheim himself noted how small enterprises might in this way escape the consequences of an anomic division of labour. *De la Division du travail social*, pp. 344–6. The major objective of the 'human relations industry' movement might in fact be described as that of recreating the characteristic quality of interpersonal relations in small establishments in the context of large scale, bureaucratized concerns. It has yet to demonstrate any widespread and lasting success.

21 Cf. *Les Règles de la mèthode sociologique* (Paris, 1895), ch. III. Fox and Flanders argue that at the present day industrial relations are more disorderly than at any time since Britain became an industrial society. This claim is, I think, debatable; but in any case their explanation of why disorder was not greater in earlier periods is essentially in terms of 'custom' or imbalances of power, i.e. 'coercion'; and order thus based cannot be regarded as the converse of anomie. What Durkheim contrasted with the anomie of economic life in modern societies was the idea of a 'moral economy' such as was pursued, and in some measure realized, in pre-industrial Europe.

22 Cf. National Board for Prices and Incomes, *Third General Report. August 1967 to July 1968*, Cmnd 3715 (HMSO, 1968) pp. 6–7.

23 For example, results from an Opinion Research Centre study (February, 1967) showed that when members of a quota sample of electors were asked to choose the one most important objective of an incomes policy out of three suggested, significant differences emerged on class lines, and especially between 'AB' and 'DE' respondents: 71 per cent of the former selected 'that people with special skills are fully rewarded' while 52 per cent of the latter selected 'that lowest paid workers get a reasonable wage' and a further 10 per cent 'that incomes become more equal'. For a report on the survey, see R. P. Kelvin, 'What sort of incomes policy', *New Society*, 6 April 1967.

24 *The Social Foundations of Wage Policy* (2nd ed., London, 1962), Chs IV and V.

25 Nor can it be thought likely that many individuals will support control

over incomes on a purely calculative basis – i.e. on the basis of understanding, or supposed understanding, of the interrelationships between money incomes, costs and prices, and thus of the nature of inflation. Survey research has demonstrated the not very surprising fact that the bulk of the population has little grasp of macro-economics. See Hilde Behrend, 'Price images, inflation and national incomes policy', *Scottish Journal of Political Economy*, 13 (November 1966), and Behrend *et al.*, *A National Survey of Attitudes to Inflation and Incomes Policy*, Edutext Publications, Occasional Papers in Social and Economic Administrations, no. 7 (London, 1966). In any case, no amount of macro-economic understanding could ensure general consensus on the actual application of an incomes policy, the crucial problems of which concern what shall happen to *particular groups* rather than to the aggregate of incomes.

26 See the recent valuable review of the working of incomes policies provided by John Corina, 'Can an incomes policy be administered?' in B. C. Roberts (ed.), *Industrial Relations: Contemporary Issues* (London, 1968).

27 See A. Nove, 'Wages in the Soviet Union: a comment on recently published statistics', *British Journal of Industrial Relations*, 4 (2) (1966).

28 'Can an incomes policy be administered?', pp. 284–8, 290–1. It may be noted that an earlier review of incomes policies in western societies arrived in effect at the conclusion that an essential condition of controlling wage drift was some measure of moral restraint: '. . . a willingness on the part of individual trade unions, groups of workers, and employers to sacrifice some autonomy in matters of wage fixing under circumstances which may be particularly favourable or conducive to their exercise of it'. H. A. Turner and H. Zoeteweij, *Prices, Wages, and Incomes Policies* (ILO, Geneva, 1966), p. 142.

29 *Ibid.*, pp. 135–6.

30 Cf. Lipset and Trow, *art. cit.*, pp. 397–400; also the comments by Bob Rowthorn, 'Unions and the economy' in Robin Blackburn and Alexander Cockburn (eds), *The Incompatibles: Trade Union Militancy and the Consensus* (London, 1967), pp. 221–2.

31 See Wootton, *op. cit.*, pp. 51–4; and Harold Lydall, *The Structure of Earnings* (Oxford, 1968). pp. 68–88. It should of course be said that *all* human attributes that might be treated as 'abilities' or 'capacities' are determined by *both* genetic *and* environmental influences. Cf. J. M. Thoday, 'Geneticism and environmentalism' in J. E. Meade and A. S. Parkes (eds), *Biological Aspects of Social Problems* (Edinburgh, 1965).

32 Cf. Guy Routh, *Occupation and Pay in Great Britain 1906–60* (Cambridge, 1965); A. H. Halsey (ed.), *Ability and Educational Opportunity* (OECD, Paris, 1961); and J. W. B. Douglas *et al.*, *All Our Future* (London, 1968).

33 For a relevant collection of papers, see Reinhard Bendix and S. M. Lipset (eds), *Class, Status and Power* (2nd ed., New York, 1966), Part I: 'The Continuing Debate on Equality'. Also the paper by Buckley earlier cited.

34 Cf. the data referred to by John H. Goldthorpe, David Lockwood, Frank Bechhofer and Jennifer Platt, in *The Affluent Worker in the Class Structure* (Cambridge, 1969), pp. 154–5.

35 *Op. cit.*, p. 294.

36 H. L. Beales, 'The Making of Social Policy', Hobhouse Memorial Lecture, 1945, p. 9.

37 *De la Division du travail social*, p. 373. By '*inégalité exterieure*' Durkheim refers to all inequality resulting from sources other than differences in individual potentialities. Cf. also *Leçons de sociologie*, ch. XVIII.

38 Corina, *art. cit.*, p. 286.

39 *Op. cit.*, ch. VI especially. Particularly pertinent here, for example, would be the requirement that arguments on the functions of economic inequalities as work incentives should be precisely stated and empirically tested, rather than being merely asserted in the form of vague generalities.

40 Cf. Turner and Zoeteweij, *op. cit.*, p. 147.

41 *De la Division du travail social*, pp. 381–2.

1.2 The concept of equality of educational opportunity[1]

James Coleman

The concept of 'equality of educational opportunity' as held by members of society has had a varied past. It has changed radically in recent years, and is likely to undergo further change in the future. This lack of stability in the concept leads to several questions. What has it meant in the past, what does it mean now, and what will it mean in the future? Whose obligation is it to provide such equality? Is the concept a fundamentally sound one, or does it have inherent contradiction or conflicts with social organization? But first of all, and above all, what is and has been meant in society by the ideal of equality of education opportunity?

To answer this question, it is necessary to consider how the child's position in society has been conceived in different historical periods. In pre-industrial Europe, the child's horizons were largely limited by his family. His station in life was likely to be the same as his father's. If his father was a serf, he would likely live his own life as a serf; if his father was a shoemaker, he would likely become a shoemaker. But even this immobility was not the crux of the matter; he was a part of the family production enterprise and would likely remain within this enterprise throughout his life. The extended family, as the basic unit of social organization, had complete authority over the child, and complete responsibility for him. This responsibility ordinarily did not end when the child became an adult because he remained a part of the same economic unit and carried on this tradition of responsibility into the next generation. Despite some mobility out of the family, the general pattern was family continuity through a patriarchal kinship system.

There are two elements of critical importance here. First, the family carried responsibility for its members' welfare from cradle to grave. It was a 'welfare society', with each extended family

Source: *Harvard Educational Review*, special issue (winter 1968), 38 (1), 7–22.

serving as a welfare organization for its own members. Thus it was to the family's interest to see that its members became productive. Conversely, a family took relatively small interest in whether someone in *another* family became productive or not—merely because the mobility of productive labor between family economic units was relatively low. If the son of a neighbor was allowed to become a ne'er-do-well, it had little real effect on families other than his own.

The second important element is that the family, as a unit of economic production, provided an appropriate context in which the child could learn the things he needed to know. The craftsman's shop or the farmer's fields were appropriate training grounds for sons, and the household was an appropriate training ground for daughters.

In this kind of society, the concept of equality of educational opportunity had no relevance at all. The child and adult were embedded within the extended family, and the child's education or training was merely whatever seemed necessary to maintain the family's productivity. The fixed stations in life which most families occupied precluded any idea of 'opportunity' and, even less, equality of opportunity.

With the industrial revolution, changes occurred in both the family's function as a self-perpetuating economic unit and as a training ground. As economic organizations developed outside the household, children began to be occupationally mobile outside their families. As families lost their economic production activities, they also began to lose their welfare functions, and the poor or ill or incapacitated became more nearly a community responsibility. Thus the training which a child received came to be of interest to all in the community, either as his potential employers or as his potential economic supports if he became dependent. During this stage of development in eighteenth-century England, for instance, communities had laws preventing immigration from another community because of the potential economic burden of immigrants.

Further, as men came to employ their own labor outside the family in the new factories, their families became less useful as economic training grounds for their children. These changes paved the way for public education. Families needed a context within which their children could learn some general skills which would be useful for gaining work outside the family; and men of influence in the community began to be interested in the potential productivity of other men's children.

It was in the early nineteenth century that public education began to appear in Europe and America. Before that time, private education had grown with the expansion of the mercantile class. This class had both the need and resources to have its children educated outside the home, either for professional occupations or for occupations in the developing world of commerce. But the idea of general educational opportunity for all children arose only in the nineteenth century.

The emergence of public, tax-supported education was not solely a function of the stage of industrial development. It was also a function of the class structure in the society. In the United States, without a strong traditional class structure, universal education in publicly-supported free schools became widespread in the early nineteenth century; in England, the 'voluntary schools', run and organized by churches with some instances of state support, were not supplemented by a state-supported system until the Education Act of 1870. Even more, the character of educational opportunity reflected the class structure. In the United States, the public schools quickly became the common school, attended by representatives of all classes; these schools provided a common educational experience for most American children—excluding only those upper-class children in private schools, those poor who went to no schools, and Indians and Southern Negroes who were without schools. In England, however, the class system directly manifested itself through the schools. The state-supported, or 'board schools' as they were called, became the schools of the laboring lower classes with a sharply different curriculum from those voluntary schools which served the middle and upper classes. The division was so sharp that two government departments, the Education Department and the Science and Art Department, administered external examinations, the first for the products of the board schools, and the second for the products of the voluntary schools as they progressed into secondary education. It was only the latter curricula and examinations that provided admission to higher education.

What is most striking is the duration of influence of such a dual structure. Even today in England, a century later (and in different forms in most European countries), there exists a dual structure of public secondary education with only one of the branches providing the curriculum for college admission. In England, this branch includes the remaining voluntary schools which, though retaining their individual identities, have become part of the state-supported system.

This comparison of England and the United States shows clearly the impact of the class structure in society upon the concept of educational opportunity in that society. In nineteenth-century England, the idea of *equality* of educational opportunity was hardly considered; the system was designed to provide *differentiated* educational opportunity appropriate to one's station in life. In the United States as well, the absence of educational opportunity for Negroes in the South arose from the caste and feudal structure of the largely rural society. The idea of differentiated educational opportunity, implicit in the Education Act of 1870 in England, seems to derive from dual needs: the needs arising from industrialization for a basic education for the labor force, and the interests of parents in having one's own child receive a good education. The middle classes could meet both these needs by providing a free system for the children of laboring classes, and a tuition system (which soon came to be supplemented by state grants) for their own. The long survival of this differentiated system depended not only on the historical fact that the voluntary schools existed before a public system came into existence but on the fact that it allows both of these needs to be met: the community's collective need for a trained labor force, and the middle-class individual's interest in a better education for his own child. It served a third need as well: that of maintaining the existing social order—a system of stratification that was a step removed from a feudal system of fixed estates, but designed to prevent a wholesale challenge by the children of the working class to the positions held for children of the middle classes.

The similarity of this system to that which existed in the South to provide differential opportunity to Negroes and whites is striking, just as is the similarity of class structures in the second half of nineteenth century England to the white–Negro caste structure of the southern United States in the first half of the twentieth century.

In the United States, nearly from the beginning, the concept of educational opportunity had a special meaning which focused on equality. This meaning included the following elements:

1 Providing a *free* education up to a given level which constituted the principal entry point to the labor force.

2 Providing a *common curriculum* for all children, regardless of background.

3 Partly by design and partly because of low population density, providing that children from diverse backgrounds attend the *same school*.

4 Providing equality within a given *locality*, since local taxes provided the source of support for schools.

This conception of equality of opportunity is still held by many persons; but there are some assumptions in it which are not obvious. First, it implicitly assumes that the existence of free schools eliminates economic sources of inequality of opportunity. Free schools, however, do not mean that the costs of a child's education become reduced to zero for families at all economic levels. When free education was introduced, many families could not afford to allow the child to attend school beyond an early age. His labor was necessary to the family—whether in rural or urban areas. Even after the passage of child labor laws, this remained true on the farm. These economic sources of inequality of opportunity have become small indeed (up through secondary education); but at one time they were a major source of inequality. In some countries they remain so; and certainly for higher education they remain so.

Apart from the economic needs of the family problems inherent in the social structure raised even more fundamental questions about equality of educational opportunity. Continued school attendance prevented a boy from being trained in his father's trade. Thus, in taking advantage of 'equal educational opportunity', the son of a craftsman or small tradesman would lose the opportunity to enter those occupations he would most likely fill. The family inheritance of occupation at all social levels was still strong enough, and the age of entry into the labor force was still early enough, that secondary education interfered with opportunity for working-class children; while it opened up opportunities at higher social levels, it closed them at lower ones.

Since residue of this social structure remains in present American society, the dilemma cannot be totally ignored. The idea of a common educational experience implies that this experience has only the effect of widening the range of opportunity, never the effect of excluding opportunities. But clearly this is never precisely true so long as this experience prevents a child from pursuing certain occupational paths. This question still arises with the differentiated secondary curriculum: an academic program in high school has the effect not only of keeping open the opportunities which arise through continued education, but also of closing off opportunities which a vocational program keeps open.

A second assumption implied by this concept of equality of opportunity is that opportunity lies in *exposure* to a given curriculum. The amount of opportunity is then measured in terms of the level of curriculum to which the child is exposed. The higher the curriculum made available to a given set of children, the greater their opportunity.

The most interesting point about this assumption is the relatively passive role of the school and community, relative to the child's role. The school's obligation is to 'provide an opportunity' by being available, within easy geographic access of the child, free of cost (beyond the value of the child's time), and with a curriculum that would not exclude him from higher education. The obligation to 'use the opportunity' is on the child or the family, so that his role is defined as the active one: the responsibility for achievement rests with him. Despite the fact that the school's role was the relatively passive one and the child's or family's role the active one, the use of this social service soon came to be no longer a choice of the parent or child, but that of the state. Since compulsory attendance laws appeared in the nineteenth century, the age of required attendance has been periodically moved upward.

This concept of equality of educational opportunity is one that has been implicit in most educational practice throughout most of the period of public education in the nineteenth and twentieth centuries. However, there have been several challenges to it; serious questions have been raised by new conditions in public education. The first of these in the United States was a challenge to assumption two, the common curriculum. This challenge first occurred in the early years of the twentieth century with the expansion of secondary education. Until the report of the committee of the National Education Association, issued in 1918, the standard curriculum in secondary schools was primarily a classical one appropriate for college entrance. The greater influx of non-college-bound adolescents into the high school made it necessary that this curriculum be changed into one more appropriate to the new majority. This is not to say that the curriculum changed immediately in the schools, nor that all schools changed equally, but rather that the seven 'cardinal principles' of the NEA report became a powerful influence in the movement towards a less academically rigid curriculum. The introduction of the new non-classical curriculum was seldom if ever couched in terms of a conflict between those for whom high school was college preparation, and those for whom it was terminal education; nevertheless, that was the case. 'The inequality' was seen as the use of a curriculum that served a minority and was not designed to fit the needs of the majority; and the shift of curriculum was intended to to fit the curriculum to the needs of the new majority in the schools.

In many schools, this shift took the form of *diversifying* the curriculum, rather than supplanting one by another; the college-preparatory curriculum remained though watered down. Thus the kind of equality of opportunity that emerged from the newly-designed secondary school curriculum was radically different from the elementary-school concept that had emerged earlier. The idea inherent in the new secondary school curriculum appears to have been to take as given the diverse occupational paths into which adolescents will go after secondary school, and to say (implicitly): there is greater equality of educational opportunity for a boy who is not going to attend college if he has a specially-designed curriculum than if he must take a curriculum designed for college entrance.

There is only one difficulty with this definition: it takes as *given* what should be problematic—that a given boy is going into a given post-secondary occupational or educational path. It is one thing to take as given that approximately 70 per cent of an entering high school freshman class will not attend college; but to assign a *particular child* to a curriculum designed for that 70 per cent closes off for that child the opportunity to attend college. Yet to assign all children to a curriculum designed for the 30 per cent who will attend college creates inequality for those who, at the end of high school, fall among the 70 per cent who do not attend college. This is a true dilemma, and one which no educational system has fully solved. It is more general than the college/non-college dichotomy, for there is a wide variety of different paths that adolescents take on the completion of secondary school. In England, for example, a student planning to attend a university must specialize in the arts or the sciences in the later years of secondary school. Similar specialization occurs in the German *Gymnasium*; and this is wholly within the group planning to attend university. Even greater specialization can be found among noncollege curricula, especially in the vocational, technical, and commercial high schools.

The distinguishing characteristic of this concept of equality of educational opportunity is that it accepts as given the child's expected future. While the concept discussed earlier left the child's future wholly open, this concept of differentiated curricula uses the expected future to match child and curriculum. It should be noted that the first and simpler concept is easier to apply in elementary schools where fundamental tools of reading and arithmetic are being learned by all children; it is only in secondary school that the problem of diverse futures arises. It should also be noted that the dilemma is directly due to the social structure itself: if there were a virtual absence of social mobility with everyone occupying a fixed estate in life, then such curricula that take the future as given would provide equality of opportunity relative to that structure. It is only because of the high degree of occupational mobility between generations—that is, the greater degree of equality of *occupational* opportunity—that the dilemma arises.

The first stage in the evolution of the concept of equality of educational opportunity was the notion that all children must be exposed to the same curriculum in the same school. A second stage in the evolution of the concept assumed that different children would have different occupational futures and that equality of opportunity required providing different curricula for each type of student. The third and fourth stages in this evolution came as a result of challenges to the basic idea of equality of educational opportunity from opposing directions. The third stage can be seen at least as far back as 1896 when the Supreme Court upheld the southern states' notion of 'separate but equal' facilities. This stage ended in 1954 when the Supreme Court ruled that legal separation by race inherently constitutes inequality of opportunity. By adopting the 'separate but equal' doctrine, the southern states rejected assumption three of the original concept, the assumption that equality depended on the opportunity to attend the same school. This rejection was, however, consistent with the overall logic of the original concept, since attendance at the same school was an inherent part of that logic. The underlying idea was that opportunity resided in exposure to a curriculum;

the community's responsibility was to provide that exposure, the child's to take advantage of it.

It was the pervasiveness of this underlying idea which created the difficulty for the Supreme Court. For it was evident that even when identical facilities and identical teacher salaries existed for racially separate schools, 'equality of educational opportunity' in some sense did not exist. This had also long been evident to Englishmen as well, in a different context, for with the simultaneous existence of the 'common school' and the 'voluntary school', no one was under the illusion that full equality of education opportunity existed. But the source of this inequality remained an unarticulated feeling. In the decision of the Supreme Court, this unarticulated feeling began to take more precise form. The essence of it was that the *effects* of such separate schools were, or were likely to be, different. Thus a concept of equality of opportunity which focused on *effects* of schooling began to take form. The actual decision of the Court was in fact a confusion of two unrelated premises: this new concept, which looked at results of schooling, and the legal premise that the use of race as a basis for school assignment violates fundamental freedoms. But what is important for the evolution of the concept of equality of opportunity is that a new and different assumption was introduced, the assumption that equality of opportunity depends in some fashion upon effects of schooling. I believe the decision would have been more soundly based had it not depended on the effects of schooling, but only on the violation of freedom; but by introducing the question of effects of schooling, the Court brought into the open implicit goals of equality of educational opportunity—that is, goals having to do with the *results* of school—to which the original concept was somewhat awkwardly directed.

That these goals were in fact behind the concept can be verified by a simple mental experiment. Suppose the early schools had operated for only one hour a week and had been attended by children of all social classes. This would have met the explicit assumptions of the early concept of equality of opportunity since the school is free, with a common curriculum, and attended by all children in the locality. But it obviously would not have been accepted, even at that time, as providing equality of opportunity, because its effects would have been so minimal. The additional educational resources provided by middle- and upper-class families, whether in the home, by tutoring, or in private supplementary schools, would have created severe inequalities in results.

Thus the dependence of the concept upon results or effects of schooling, which had remained hidden until 1954, came partially into the open with the Supreme Court decision. Yet this was not the end, for it created more problems than it solved. It might allow one to assess gross inequalities, such as that created by dual school systems in the South, or by a system like that in the mental experiment I just described. But it allows nothing beyond that. Even more confounding, because the decision did not use effects of schooling as a criterion of inequality but only as justification for a criterion of racial integration, integration itself emerged as the basis for still a new concept of equality of educational opportunity. Thus the idea of effects of schooling as an element in the concept was introduced but immediately overshadowed by another, the criterion of racial integration.

The next stage in the evolution of this concept was, in my judgment, the Office of Education Survey of Equality of Educational Opportunity. This survey was carried out under a mandate in the Civil Rights Act of 1964 to the Commissioner of Education to assess the 'lack of equality of educational opportunity' among racial and other groups in the United States. The evolution of this concept, and the conceptual disarray which this evolution had created, made the very definition of the task exceedingly difficult. The original concept could be examined by determining the degree to which all children in a locality had access to the same schools and the same curriculum, free of charge. The existence of diverse secondary curricula appropriate to different futures could be assessed relatively easily. But the very assignment of a child to a specific curriculum implies acceptance of the concept of equality which takes futures as given. And the introduction of the new interpretations, equality as measured by results of schooling and equality defined by racial integration, confounded the issue even further.

As a consequence, in planning the survey it was obvious that no single concept of equality of educational opportunity existed and that the survey must give information relevant to a variety of concepts. The basis on which this was done can be seen by reproducing a portion of an internal memorandum that determined the design of the survey:

The point of second importance in design [second to the point of discovering the intent of Congress, which was taken to be that the survey was not for the purpose of locating willful discrimination, but to determine educational inequality without regard to intention of those in authority] follows from the first and concerns the definition of inequality. One type of inequality may be defined in terms of differences of the community's input to the school, such as per-pupil expenditure, school plants, libraries, quality of teachers, and other similar quantities.

A second type of inequality may be defined in terms of the racial composition of the school, following the Supreme Court's decision that segregated schooling is inherently unequal. By the former definition, the question of inequality through segregation is excluded, while by the latter, there is inequality of education within a school system so long as the schools within the system have different racial composition.

A third type of inequality would include various intangible characteristics of the school as well as the factors directly traceable to the community inputs to the school. These intangibles are such things as teacher morale, teachers' expectations of students, level of interest of the student body in learning, or others. Any of these factors may affect the impact of the school upon a given student within it. Yet such a definition gives no suggestion of where to stop, or just how relevant these factors might be for school quality.

Consequently, a fourth type of inequality may be defined in terms of consequences of the school for individuals with equal backgrounds and abilities. In this definition, equality of educational opportunity is equality of results, given the same individual input. With such a definition, inequality might come about from differences in the school inputs and/or racial composition and/or from more intangible things as described above. Such a definition obviously would require that two steps be taken in the determination of inequality. First, it is necessary to determine the effect of these various factors upon educational results (conceiving of results quite broadly, including not only achievement but attitudes towards learning, self-image, and perhaps other variables). This provides various measures of the school's quality in terms of its effect upon its students. Second, it is necessary to take these measures of quality, once determined, and determine the differential exposure of Negroes (or other groups) and whites to schools of high and low quality.

A fifth type of inequality may be defined in terms of consequences of the school for individuals of unequal backgrounds and abilities. In this definition, equality of educational opportunity is equality of results given *different* individual inputs. The most striking examples of inequality here would be children from households in which a language other than English, such as Spanish or Navaho, is spoken. Other examples would be low-achieving children from homes in which there is a poverty of verbal expression or an absence of experiences which lead to conceptual facility.

Such a definition taken in the extreme would imply that educational equality is reached only when the results of schooling (achievement and attitudes) are the same for racial and religious minorities as for the dominant group.

The basis for the design of the survey is indicated by another segment of this memorandum:

> Thus, the study will focus its principal effort on the fourth definition, but will also provide information relevant to all five possible definitions. This insures the pluralism which is obviously necessary with respect to a definition of inequality. The major justification for this focus is that the results of this approach can best be translated into policy which will improve education's effects. The results of the first two approaches (tangible inputs to the school, and segregation) can certainly be translated into policy, but there is no good evidence that these policies will improve education's effects; and while policies to implement the fifth would certainly improve education's effects, it seems hardly possible that the study could provide information that would direct such policies.
>
> Altogether, it has become evident that it is not our role to define what constitutes equality for policy-making purposes. Such a definition will be an outcome of the interplay of a variety of interests, and will certainly differ from time to time as these interests differ. It should be our role to cast light on the state of inequality defined in the variety of ways which appear reasonable at this time.

The survey, then, was conceived as a pluralistic instrument, given the variety of concepts of equality of opportunity in education. Yet I suggest that despite the avowed intention of not adjudicating between these different ideas, the survey has brought a new stage in the evolution of the concept. For the definitions of equality which the survey was designed to serve split sharply into two groups. The first three definitions concerned input resources: first, those brought to the school by the actions of the school administration (facilities, curriculum, teachers); second, those brought to the school by the other students, in the educational backgrounds which their presence contributed to the school; and third, the intangible characteristics such as 'morale' that result from the interaction of all these factors. The fourth and fifth definitions were concerned with the effects of schooling. Thus the five definitions were divided into three concerned with inputs to school and two concerned with effects of schooling. When the Report emerged, it did not give five different measures of equality, one for each of these definitions; but it did focus sharply on this dichotomy, giving in chapter 2 information on inequalities of input relevant to definitions one and two, and in chapter 3 information on inequalities of results relevant to definitions four and five, and also in chapter 3 information on the relation of input to results again relevant to definitions four and five.

Although not central to our discussion here, it is interesting to note that this examination of the relation of school inputs to effects on achievement showed that those input characteristics of schools that are most alike for Negroes and whites have least effect on their achievement. The magnitudes of differences between schools attended by Negroes and those attended by whites were as follows: least, facilities and curriculum; next, teacher quality; and greatest, educational backgrounds of fellow students. The order of importance of these inputs on the achievement of Negro students is precisely the same: facilities and curriculum least, teacher quality next, and backgrounds of fellow students, most.

By making the dichotomy between inputs and results explicit, and by focusing attention not only on inputs but on results, the Report brought into the open what had been underlying all the concepts of equality of educational opportunity but had remained largely hidden: that the concept implied *effective* equality of opportunity, that is, equality in those elements that are effective for learning. The reason this had remained half-hidden, obscured by definitions that involve inputs, is, I suspect, because educational research has been until recently unprepared to demonstrate what elements are effective. The controversy that has surrounded the Report indicates that measurement of effects is still subject to sharp disagreement; but the crucial point is that *effects* of inputs have come to constitute the basis for assessment of school quality (and thus equality of opportunity) in place of using certain inputs by definition as measures of quality (e.g. small classes are better than large, higher-paid teachers are better than lower-paid ones, by definition).

It would be fortunate indeed if the matter could be left to rest there—if merely by using effects of school rather than inputs as the basis for the concept, the problem were solved. But that is not the case at all. The conflict between definitions four and five given above shows this. The conflict can be illustrated by resorting again to the mental experiment discussed earlier—providing a standard education of one hour per week, under identical conditions, for all children. By definition four, controlling all background difference of the children, results for Negroes and whites would be equal, and thus by this definition equality of opportunity would exist. But because such minimal schooling would have minimal effect, those children from educationally strong families would enjoy educational opportunity far surpassing that of others. And because such educationally strong backgrounds are found more often among whites than among Negroes, there would be very large overall Negro–white achievement differences—and thus inequality of opportunity by definition five.

It is clear from this hypothetical experiment that the problem the results of what constitutes equality of opportunity is not solved. The problem will become even clearer by showing graphs with some of the results of the Office of Education Survey. The highest line in Figure 1 shows the achievement in verbal skills by whites in the urban Northeast at grades 1, 3, 6, 9 and 12. The second line shows the

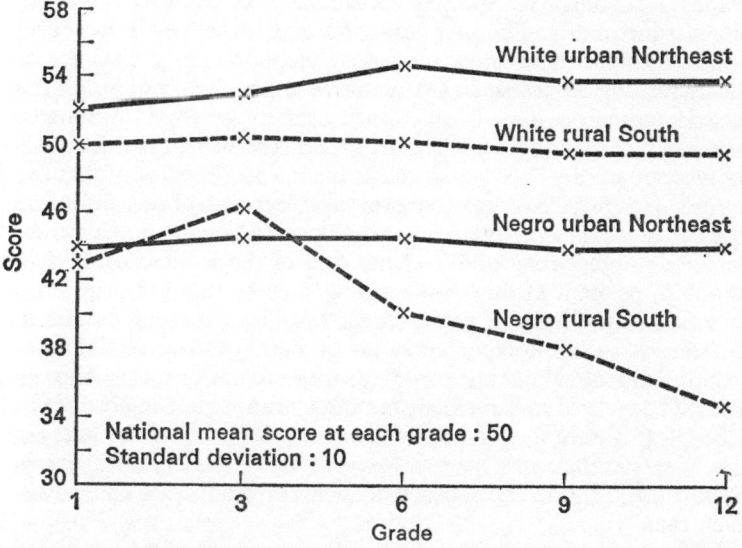

Figure 1 Patterns of achievement in verbal skills at various grade levels by race and region.

achievement at each of these grades by whites in the rural South-east. The third shows the achievement of Negroes in the urban Northeast. The fourth shows the achievement of Negroes in the rural Southeast.

When compared to the whites in the urban Northeast, each of the other three groups shows a different pattern. The comparison with whites in the rural South shows the two groups beginning near the same point in the first grade, and diverging over the years of school. The comparison with Negroes in the urban Northeast shows the two groups beginning farther apart at the first grade and remaining about the same distance apart. The comparison with Negroes in the rural South shows the two groups beginning far apart and moving much farther apart over the years of school.

Which of these, if any, shows equality of educational opportunity between regional and racial groups? Which shows greatest inequality of opportunity? I think the second question is easier to answer than the first. The last comparison showing both initial difference and the greatest increase in difference over grades 1 through 12 appears to be the best candidate for the greatest inequality. The first comparison, with whites in the rural South, also seems to show inequality of opportunity, because of the increasing difference over the twelve years. But what about the second comparison, with an approximately constant difference between Negroes and whites in the urban Northeast? Is this equality of opportunity? I suggest not. It means, in effect, only that the period of school has left the average Negro at about the same level of achievement relative to whites as he began—in this case, achieving higher than about 15 per cent of the whites, lower than about 85 per cent of the whites. It may well be that in the absence of school those lines of achievement would have diverged due to differences in home environments; or perhaps they would have remained an equal distance apart, as they are in this graph (though at lower levels of achievement for both groups, in the absence of school). If it were the former, we could say that school, by keeping the lines parallel, has been a force towards the equalization of opportunity. But in the absence of such knowledge, we cannot say even that.

What would full equality of educational opportunity look like in such graphs? One might persuasively argue that it should show a convergence, so that even though two population groups begin school with different levels of skills on the average, the average of the group that begins lower moves up to coincide with that of the group that begins higher. Parenthetically, I should note that this does *not* imply that all students' achievement comes to be identical, but only that the *averages* for two population groups that begin at different levels come to be identical. The diversity of individual scores could be as great as, or greater than, the diversity at grade 1.

Yet there are serious questions about this definition of equality of opportunity. It implies that over the period of school there are no other influences, such as the family environment, which affect achievement over the twelve years of school, even though these influences may differ greatly for the two population groups. Concretely, it implies that white family environments, predominantly middle class, and Negro family environments, predominantly lower class, will produce no effects on achievement that would keep these averages apart. Such an assumption seems highly unrealistic, especially in view of the general importance of family background for achievement.

However, if such possibilities are acknowledged, then how far can they go before there is inequality of educational opportunity? Constant difference over school? Increasing differences? The unanswerability of such questions begins to give a sense of a new stage in the evolution of the concept of equality of educational opportunity. These questions concern the *relative intensity* of two sets of influences: those which are alike for the two groups, principally in school, and those which are different, principally in the home or neighborhood. If the school's influences are not only alike for the two groups, but very strong relative to the divergent influences, then the two groups will move together. If school influences are very weak, then the two groups will move apart. Or more generally, the relative intensity of the convergent school influences and the divergent out-of-school influences determines the effectiveness of the educational system in providing equality of educational opportunity. In this perspective complete equality of opportunity can be reached only if all the divergent out-of-school influences vanish, a condition that would arise only in the advent of boarding schools; given the existing divergent influences, equality of opportunity can only be approached and never fully reached. The concept becomes one of degree of proximity to equality of opportunity. This proximity is determined, then, not merely by the *equality* of education inputs, but by the *intensity* of the school's influences relative to the external divergent influences. That is, equality of output is not so much determined by equality of the resource inputs, but by the power of these resources in bringing about achievement.

Here, then, is where the concept of equality of educational opportunity presently stands. We have observed an evolution which might have been anticipated a century and a half ago when the first such concepts arose, yet one which is very different from the concept as it first developed. This difference is sharpened if we examine a further implication of the current concept as I have described it. In describing the original concept, I indicated that the role of the community and the educational institution was relatively passive; they were expected to provide a set of free public resources. The responsibility for profitable use of those resources lay with the child and his family. But the evolution of the concept has reversed these roles. The implication of the most recent concept, as I have described it, is that the responsibility to create achievement lies with the educational institution, not the child. The difference in achievement at grade 12 between the average Negro and the average white is, in effect, the degree of inequality of opportunity, and the reduction of that inequality is a responsibility of the school. This shift in responsibility follows logically from the change in the concept of equality of educational opportunity from school resource inputs to effects of schooling. When that change occurred, as it has in the past few years, the school's responsibility shifted from increasing and distributing equally its 'quality' to increasing the quality of its *students'* achievements. This is a notable shift, and one which should have strong consequences for the practice of education in future years.

Note

1 This paper was delivered at the conference on the *Equality of Educational Opportunity* report sponsored by the Colloquium Board of the Harvard Graduate School of Education, 21 October 1967.

1.3 Compensatory education and contemporary liberalism in the United States: a sociological view[1]

D. C. Morton and D. R. Watson

The greater the degree of internal structural and cultural differentiation of a society, the less likely it is that educational institutions will promote all groups' values 'equivalently'. As an established empirical generalisation, it seems that in modern societies some groups' values and skills predominate over those of other groups. These groups, who have a consequent advantage in school, are those which have an economic and power advantage in modern society, i.e. the dominant groups.[2] This paper constitutes an attempt to demonstrate sociologically the full significance of this empirical generalisation for the education of children from subordinate groups. First, we examine the concepts of 'compensatory education' and 'liberalism'.

What is compensatory education?[3]

During the past decade, increasing emphasis has been placed by educationists and applied social scientists upon the 'disadvantage' and 'deprivation' of children from certain socio-economic groups. This emphasis has been particularly marked in the USA, but is also increasingly noticeable in Britain. The concepts of 'disadvantage' and 'deprivation' are often ill defined and diffuse, but seem to centre upon an alleged lack of 'language development' in these children. Educational programmes have been developed to 'compensate' for these perceived 'deficits'.[4] Most such 'compensatory programmes' are related to the pre-school education of children, being rooted in psychological research into 'early childhood development'. In general, the emphasis upon linguistic and perceptual deficits in compensatory education programmes seems to have developed from the interests of psychologists, who sometimes came into this field of research from that of remedial

Source: *International Review of Education* (1971), 17 (3), 289–307.

education for mentally-handicapped children. The programmes generally aim at 'compensating' children through pre-empting the growth of deficits by exposing the children to an 'enriched', stimulating, pre-school environment. The main objective is to equip such children to compete with more 'privileged' groups of children in the school system, from the earliest possible age. These programmes feed into dominant psychological theories of the development of skills and 'intelligence' and their relatedness to success within the educational system, which in turn is supposed[5] to be causally related to success in the 'wider society'.

The liberal ideology

This ideology implies a view of society, as well as being a set of explicit political beliefs and directives, which we believe to be widespread in both the USA and Britain.[6] We shall be primarily concerned with the former aspect. The liberal ideology advocates social change in piecemeal fashion, within the existing framework of social institutions. It denies the need for basic institutional reorganisation, upheaval or revolution. Thus the liberal ideology is in a sense a variety of conservative ideology rather than of radical-socialist ideology, although recognising the 'need' for limited institutional change. In the case of increasing claims for civil rights in the USA,[7] the extreme conservative argues that Negroes are in their present situation vis-à-vis other groups of Americans, because they 'deserve to be', by virtue of their alleged inferiority, laziness, apathy and lax morality. The radical socialist claims that Negroes are in their present position because American social institutions are fundamentally racist, and that their plight is inevitable, given that type of social structure. His implied ameliorative action involves basic structural changes, such as the setting up of a separate black state founded upon Negro institutions and culture. The liberal adopts the position of the 'reasonable man' by taking an allegedly middle path, which assumes the fundamental adequacy of American institutions and denies the need for radical change, but acknowledges that 'something needs to be done' if the system is to function equitably.

The liberal ideology is epitomised by non-violent, constitutional, legal and administrative 'solutions', whereas radical ideologies are often associated with violent and revolutionary 'solutions'. Thus Samuel Lubell[8] has claimed that 'in the South the first need has long been to end all discrimination *by law*'. Karl Mannheim[9] has shown how the liberal perspective involves an identification with bourgeois groups, a humanistic morality (see Dr M. L. King Jr's statement below) and stresses individualism and the import-ance of rationality in social problem-solving—a rationality embodied in bureaucratic action and administrative routine.[10] Liberal solutions tend to avoid those sectors of society which are 'emotionally-charged' or constituted of so many 'contradictions' as to be unmanageable by bureaucratic-administrative rationality.

In the mid-1960s *laissez-faire* conservatives and segregationists in Congress were finally overcome by the liberals on the civil rights and poverty issues. During the first half of the decade, poverty and related problems became more visible to the public.[11] Urban poverty in particular was increasingly viewed as a threat to the established social order. In Conant's dramatic words: 'We are allowing social dynamite to accumulate in our large cities.'[12] The civil rights movement came to be perceived, rightly or wrongly, as one of the primary sources of pressure for rapid social change. Civil rights commentators, protesters, and others stressed not only the high levels of poverty and unemployment of the largely Negro, urban centres, but also the part played by educational institutions in perpetuating such problems. Thus education became a prime concern of civil rights groups in the northern cities as well as in the segregated South.

In the light of growing public concern, more and more govern-mental officials came to see the institutions of education not only as a primary focus of civil rights workers' demands but also as the means of redressing many grievances through breaking 'the cycle of poverty'. P. Meranto[13] reports the then Secretary of Health, Education and Welfare as linking poverty, unemployment and poor education with rising crime and delinquency (that is with growing social disorder)[14] and as expressing the hope that better education would break these links. In this context, the 1965 Elementary and Secondary Education Act, which embodied the liberal ideology, provided Congress with a vehicle for at least partially satisfying the needs of the poor 'without appearing to "knuckle-under" to the demands of civil rights groups', and led to a dramatic increase in Federal aid to primary and secondary schools, from about $500 million in 1965 to $1,800 million in 1966.[15]

As part of this movement towards accommodating these threats to order through adjusting the institutions of education, the function of compensatory education became more clearly and explicitly defined. As already indicated, the liberal accepts the legitimacy of the existing social order and defines those groups who implicitly or explicitly challenge the adequacy of the social system by their non-conformity to dominant norms and values, as being ill equipped to maximise the advantages supposed to be available to them within the present system. Such non-conformity and expressions of discontent are often 'explained' as being symptoms of maladjustment.[16] John Horton lucidly elaborates these criteria of maladjustment and points to their political implications.[17]

Because the liberal accepts the general inviolability of the social order, he often regards problems as being moral in nature, as in this passage by Martin Luther King, Jr:[18]

> By non-violent resistance the Negro can also enlist all men of goodwill in his struggle for equality. The problem is not a purely racial one, with Negroes set against whites. In the end it is not a struggle between people at all, but a tension between justice and injustice. Non-violent resistance is not aimed against oppressors but against oppression. Under its banner, consciences, not racial groups, are enlisted. . . . The way of non-violence means a willingness to suffer and sacrifice. It may mean going to jail . . . it may even mean physical death. But if physical death is the price a man must pay to free his children and his white brethren from a permanent death of the spirit, then nothing could be more redemptive.

The liberal maintains his ideology with its implicit emphasis on the essential morality of the social order by adopting individualism as a sufficient mode of both understanding and solving the 'social problems' and 'social evils' which he perceives. Thus Samuel Lubell[19] asks: 'What are the conditions that are needed for racial peace to become attainable? The key requirement, I believe, is to replace racialism with individualism. What is indispensable is . . . that we restructure our own thinking to be able to treat each Negro as a recognizable individual and not as an anonymous black face . . . Until that comes to pass, the social framework for orderly evolutionary racial progress will be missing.'

Morality and individualism are combined in the liberal's belief in the God-given or constitutionally-guaranteed 'rights of the individual', and in his moral condemnation of those in the dominant group, such as some employers and landlords, who visibly deny such rights to members of minority groups. He regards all men as being created equal, with equal rights, but also extends this belief to the assumption that all men are similar. Thus he assumes that all Americans, whether Negro, Jewish, Puerto Rican, or Sioux Indian can come to conform to and identify with the so-called 'American Dream' of achievement and success. Since the liberal identifies himself with the image of social order embodied in the American Dream, he easily assumes that all men not only can, but should, so conform and identify.

The relation of liberalism to compensatory education

It is our contention that the ideology of compensatory education is a specific expression of the liberal ideology. From this standpoint the formulation of social problems in psychological terms such as 'maladjustment', 'linguistic or sensory deprivation' and 'poor motivation' can be seen as the scientific counterpart of the individualistic approach to social problems which characterises the liberal perspective. The technical terminology of psychology thus reflects the liberal's conviction that problems are rooted in individuals rather than in the overall social order.

Liberal convictions that the social order is both legitimate and right are buttressed by several other concepts which focus attention elsewhere. A common 'ameliorative' policy advocated by liberals is the 'special areas approach'. By implying that 'the problem', whether that of poverty or educational disadvantage, is limited to certain areas and to a small minority of the total population, such an approach tends to deflect attention from the full extent of the problem and its roots in the overall social system. This approach is exemplified by such concepts as 'the inner city' and 'educational priority areas', which together focus attention away from rural and small-town problems and the educational disadvantages encountered by working-class children everywhere.[20]

As a variant of conservative ideology, the liberal perspective involves an implicit identification with the dominant, privileged strata of society,[21] commonly referred to as 'the Establishment'.[22] For example, Bayard Rustin's address[23] to the Center for the Study of Democratic Institutions contains many transparent and explicit indications of his identification with 'the leadership group', whom he distinguishes from 'the simple people on the street'.

Such identification usually leads to the liberal's implicit acceptance of the dominant group's values and skills as those of society as a whole. The ethic of professionalism, which includes ideals of vocation, service and selflessness that are part of the moral position of liberalism, represents a major example of a dominant group value. Horton suggests that professionals under the guise of 'scientific neutrality' or 'professional detachment' assume that their own particular group values and perspectives constitute the core values and perspectives of the majority of Americans. In particular, it is reasonable to assume that social workers and educators increasingly construe professional/upper-middle-class values as the core values of society as a whole.[24] This general orientation is expressed in the use of such phrases as 'culturally deprived'.[25] In C. Wright Mills's parlance, the vocabulary and assumptions of social pathologists are socially 'situated' in the dominant groups of society.[26]

An important instance of the tendency of professionals to assume a widespread consensus with their own 'establishment values' is the fact, noted by many observers, that seemingly objective and scientific IQ tests are far more 'culture-bound' than 'culture-fair'.[27] Alfred Binet,[28] who developed the first scale of IQ tests in 1905, made it perfectly clear that by 1908 he was aware that his tests measured the effects of cultural training upon 'intelligence' rather than 'intellectual capacity', despite his efforts to avoid this danger. Professor F. L. Goodenough of the University of Minnesota, who in 1926 herself devised a widely-used performance test which she believed to be 'culture-fair' has since admitted to being mistaken. Writing with D. B. Harris[29] in 1950 she stated: 'the search for a culture-free test, whether of intelligence, artistic ability, personal-social characteristics, or any other measurable trait is illusory, and . . the naive assumption that the mere freedom from verbal requirements renders a test equally suitable for all groups is no longer tenable.' She even apologised for her own earlier study.

In effect, such tests implicitly over-generalise in that they assume that the norms, values, orientations and skills which constitute the intelligence of middle-class people are the only valid measurer of the intelligence of people of all groups in the society and therefore provide an 'objective' basis for comparing all people. Professor Allison Davis[30] aptly crystallises this issue as follows:

The lifelong process by which culture helps to guide, develop, limit and evaluate all mental problem-solving has not received sufficiently serious attention from either test-makers or educators. They continually make the error of regarding middle-class culture, and even more narrowly, middle-class school culture, as the 'true' culture, or the 'best' culture. More than 95 per cent of our teachers and professors are middle-class in their socio-economic status. Like all other cultural groups, teachers and professors regard that particular version of culture (those mores, emotional patterns, and social values) which they have learned from their own families, friends, and teachers, as the 'best' and only 'true' culture. This attitude is powerfully reflected in school curriculums, in intelligence tests, and in teachers' judgments of their pupils.[31] It is an attitude which is fatal to the development of the full mental capacity of either the teacher or the pupil.

In what ways do the values and other elements of the culture of the middle class become expressed in supposedly objective and fair tests? Among many general predisposing factors mentioned by Eells and his collaborators is the nature of the vocabulary and grammar taught and used in schools, which is that commonly used within middle-class groups, including the teaching profession, and which may be unfamiliar to the children of non-middle-class parents, amongst whom different 'codes' and orientations to the use of language predominate. The work of Bernstein and his colleagues seems to substantiate this point.[32]

In spite of Binet's failure and Professor Goodenough's assertion, many testers continue to construct what they claim to be culture-free or culture-fair tests.[33] Many items which supposedly test apprehension of spatial relationships are often claimed to be culture-fair even when they rely heavily upon language in giving directions pertaining to the item. Eells points out that such directions often utilise abstractions with which a middle-class child is likely to be more familiar.[34] One such item, intended for nine-year-old children, is:

Mark the group of three letters that has the most loops:

BTB DWD FMF HFL

Eells reports that proportionally twice as many low status group children made errors in answering this item, and gives scores of examples of similarly biased items. We suggest that the concepts and grammatical structure in the directions would be more familiar to a higher status nine-year-old.

Another test item which contains cultural bias is referred to by Klineberg.[35] In one portion of the National Intelligence Test the subject must supply the missing word in the following sentence: '. . . should prevail in churches and libraries'; the correct answer being 'silence'. As Klineberg points out: 'Anyone who has visited an American Negro church in the south of the United States, knows however, that silence is neither the rule nor the idea.' On the basis of their experience, Negro children would be less likely than others to answer this item 'correctly'.

Bernstein's research into social class differences in the use of language and toys, during early childhood, indicates differences in the cultural meanings which are realised through language by different socio-economic groups. These differences favour the middle-class child, since the meanings and modes of realisation employed in school are those most familiar to the middle classes. Bernstein also claims that experiments and tests which lead to 'unfavourable' comparisons of working-class with middle-class children tend to compare the groups solely in terms of the presence or absence of middle-class cultural elements. This gives rise to a 'deficit-system' view of working-class children and the notion that they are in need of 'compensation'.[36] Bernstein finally attacks the concepts of compensatory education of focusing attention upon the child's home and 'sub-culture' as the source of his educational 'disadvantages', thereby distracting analytical and practical attention from the intrinsic bias of the school in favour of middle-class children.

Possible unforeseen consequences of the implementation of liberal policies

This variety of 'liberalism' may well contain many limitations. Let us trace what may be the wider social repercussions if compensatory education programmes advocated by liberals are successfully implemented. We can also draw some parallels with liberal policies outside education. Liberal educationists tend to overlook social institutions outside the bounds of formal education in their explanations of and solutions for the problems they address.[37] Other liberals, whilst still considering only formal institutions, often discuss a wider range of them.

As Rustin points out, the 'technological revolution' in the USA, as shaped in part by the dominant groups,[38] is evidently leading to a general contraction of the labour force. At the same time, compensatory education programmes have the manifest aim of equipping people to compete more successfully for these contracting opportunities. Hence, it may well be that such programmes, if successful in increasing the numbers of qualified and highly motivated school-leavers, will also succeed in intensifying the struggle for increasingly scarce job opportunities. Robert K. Merton has pointed out, in his essay on anomie, the unforeseen consequences of limited opportunity structures in society. They engender large numbers of people whose aspirations have been 'blocked', leading to various forms of crime, delinquency and rebellion, which, of course, are directly counter to the *manifest* aims of education as embodied in liberal ideology.

This increased competition for jobs may lead to the development of new patterns of racial prejudice and discrimination, or new adaptations of existing patterns.[39] As Merton and others have indicated, to imbue different groups of the population with the same qualities (e.g. the skills, and motivation to compete for jobs), is not necessarily to remove intolerance, discrimination and other 'irrational' barriers to equality.[40] It has been pointed out by the Political and Economic Planning Report on 'Racial Discrimination in Britain' that discriminatory practices in employment tend to be greatest in the case of *highly-qualified* minority group members. Thus, what are, in the case of white Anglo-Saxon Protestants regarded as virtues ('ambition', 'willingness to compete', 'determination to make good', 'self-confidence') became perceived vices when displayed by, say, Jews ('self-seeking', 'cut-throat', 'ruthlessness', 'over-confidence', 'superciliousness'). In this, and other more basic ways, the liberal 'solutions' of assimilation and acculturation may not only leave white prejudice untouched, but also leave the Negro's hatred of the white man and the oft-postulated autonomous social and cultural identity of the Negro out of account.[41]

In many respects, therefore, the liberal educator's solution unwittingly implies many changes of a fundamental (or radical) nature in many institutional arrangements, such as the occupational structure and the provision for leisure, which fall outside the framework of formal educational institutions. For instance, if everyone is to 'make good' occupationally within a context of full employment, then each individual's working week would have to be shortened and his leisure time increased, given the declining total demand for labour. Thus, liberal policies which purportedly tread a middle-path in social change, ultimately imply many derivative changes which have been characterised as 'radical' and recommended by such radicals as Paul Goodman— changes which the middle path is designed to avoid. Needless to say, liberals do not follow through these implications.[42] Without these derivative changes, the 'liberal solution' alone is little more than an articulated tokenism, the long-term shortcomings of which have been attested to by Killian and Grigg:[43]

> White liberals may regard each token step as a gain for which all Americans should be thankful. But in the context of intergroup relations, each of these steps will be a victory for Negroes, and a defeat for the dominant white group. But such small symbolic victories will not signify the termination of the power struggle, either in the communities in which they occur, or in the larger American Society. In spite of temporary victories or temporary defeats, the drive of Negroes for identity will continue for a long time. There will be respites following periods of struggle and stress. Token victories will not eliminate the substratum of dissatisfaction which underlies the Negro's struggle, but they will encourage renewal of the struggle.

Hence, liberal values in education may not only be doomed to failure (in their own terms) but may actively produce results which liberals would regard as problems.

Some liberals, largely outside the field of education, perceive a need for the creation of jobs, and suggest that governmental agencies should assume this function. But many of these recommendations, when examined in detail, would, if implemented, merely tend to reinforce occupational stratification on ethnic group lines. For example, Bayard Rustin[44] suggests that young Negroes, who he alleges are sitting in Central Park, smoking marihuana and drinking wine, could be put to work by City Hall, renovating and maintaining the park. He also suggests employing Negroes as 'assistant teachers', to take over the disciplinary, supervisory and custodial duties of the qualified professional teacher. This is only one step removed from the table-waiting, shoe-shining, Redcap image of the Negroes' place in society.

Perhaps the most telling limitation of the liberal position is that members of subordinate groups may, as Horton puts it, 'have difficulty in recognising themselves in the role in which they are cast by the liberal story'. It may be that even Rustin's position, where he speaks of his solving the problems of 'the simple people on the streets' denotes a lack of rapport with his less privileged fellow Negroes' own perception of their plight. As Horton says:[45] '[The liberal sociologist] probably speaks least of all for the Negro. The liberal sociologist will have some difficulty describing the world from the view-point of Negro "rioters" in Los Angeles and other cities.[46] In any case, he will not agree with anyone who believes (in fact or in ideology) that the Negro may have a separate and self-determining identity.' Similarly, as Carmichael and Hamilton put it: 'The white liberal must view the racial scene through a drastically different lens from the black man's.'[47] As an example of this, Silberman quotes an East Harlem Negro adolescent's attitude towards the social workers who attempt to implement the liberal's point of view: 'They're all around the neighbourhood, and most of them are rat fink types. They act like they think we're not human. They think they've got all there is, and all they've got to do is convert us to think and do whatever they think and do.' If the Negroes or lower-class people do not endorse the liberal's view of their dilemma, it follows that there is little probability of their long-term cooperation with white liberal policies. 'Because of the middle-class orientation of the integration movement, and because of its subconscious racism, and because of its non-violent approach, it has never been able to involve the black proletariat,' says Stokely Carmichael, in a recent lecture on Black Power.[48]

According to Carmichael and Hamilton,[49] 'The goal of black self-determination and black self-identity—Black Power—is full participation in the decision-making processes affecting the lives of black people'. They maintain that existing liberal organisations, both black and white, compromise this goal.

The passivity and dependency of subordinate groups has been fostered by a variety of factors. The bureaucratic implementation of liberal policies has meant that already powerless members of subordinate groups are confronted by a monolithic structure of associated administrative bodies with unified interests. And, as Silberman points out,[50] the whole history and nature of American social welfare has been one of social workers doing things for, by, to and because of, but never *with* their clients.

Indeed, one of the characteristics of bureaucratic organisation is that officials tend to develop interests of their own, including the perpetuation of the organisation's existence. By their focus on individual 'maladjustment' officials avoid dealing with the basic structural preconditions of problems and thus continue to produce the 'clients' who are the *raison d'être* of their welfare organisation. A frequent liberal rationalisation for the non-participation of the 'clientèle' is that there are barriers to communication. Better communication, however, would only reveal the previously latent conflicts. One cannot assume that a general consensus already exists which improved communication would make manifest. The liberals' 'community consensus' may not exist if the clientèle are admitted as being part of the community.

The changes brought about by administrative bodies or legal measures may be even less significant than even the liberals hope for. The Liberal Samuel Lubell has unwittingly made the point for us:[51] 'Individuals may continue to fear, hate or shun the Negro, but that should be their own private affair and not be enforced or institutionalised by law. A barber's wife in Greenboro expressed the distinction to be drawn when she said, "I don't believe in intermarriage but I can teach my children to avoid that. We don't have to keep abusing the coloured people to avoid that."' In Weberian terms, discrimination may remain institutionalised by virtue of convention instead of law.[52]

Sociological orientations for practice[53]

To prescribe or devise specific educational techniques would be both sociologically elliptical and space-consuming. Therefore, we shall limit our comments to (a) recommending a few immediate, short-term measures for redressing some of the present inadequacies and (b) suggesting some sociological foundations upon which a more 'universalistic' practice may be built.

(a) First, from a general point of view, knowledge regarding how educational processes affect large categories of children must be disseminated; theoretically at least, the mass media contain much potential in this area. Existing knowledge on educational disadvantage simply never reaches subordinate group members. However, in approaching the mass media, one obviously comes up against barriers of ideology, as well as financial and other vested interests. Mass media in nations where the ideology of democratic equality of opportunity is supported at the institutional level have a political vested interest in ignoring educational equality. There is a need for the creation of greater consciousness among subordinate group members of their own collective position, in order to intensify critical pressure upon the establishment. On the other hand the media for fostering such consciousness reflect the interests and perspectives of the establishment themselves. From a practical point of view, one can only say that the dilemma and fate of the education of subordinate groups is but one aspect of a wider power struggle. This means that our suggested orientations for practice within education will have little effect unless wider structural reorientations, which our suggestions imply, are effected. Related to the role of the mass media is the gap between educational theory and practice, between researchers and teachers.[54] Researchers in education (especially sociologists) have for some time been aware of certain aspects of the dominant group orientation of formal education, but most teachers have been unable to avail themselves of the full significance of these findings.

As short-term measures, one might suggest such things as staff-student critical seminars (with students in a numerical majority, as they are in the classroom) on improving the education of both parties, plus compulsory[55] and subsidised refresher courses held in colleges and universities at regular intervals for practising teachers. These courses would be explicitly geared to apprising teachers of the dominant group orientation of formal education, how this orientation comes about, and to the presentation of research on how teachers inculcate this orientation. More extensive libraries for teachers should be made available in each school, with budget provision for the ongoing addition of relevant research reports, manuals, and other volumes.

Moreover, parent-teacher associations and other links with parents might be extended, but on the parents' terms, not the teachers'. This is also of crucial importance in achieving a more permanent solution, as we will see below. Parent-teacher associations have usually been heavily oriented (in terms of key personnel, etc.) to the teachers, and their views, perspectives and plans. PTAs in the past have all too easily been the mere mouthpiece of the local 'teaching establishment';[56] they have been perceived as such by minority group members, and have done little to elicit genuine feedback from a representative cross-section of the parents. It is also notable that most PTAs have excluded the one group who can provide true experiential links between parents and teachers—the students themselves. Much softening of long-hardened bureaucratic and procedural arteries seems called for, as well as a very substantial redistribution of power and the authority to make decisions.

(b) However, all such recommendations are of a short-term, makeshift character. To begin truly to redress the problem of dominant-group bias in formal education, one must embark upon fundamental structural reorganisation while possibly using the above measures and principles as an initial lever. In a recent paper Bernstein[57] has provided some insights into possible means of making such changes fully effective. He advocates basic social reforms to encourage ways in which subordinate group parents can relate their spheres of competence to the child's educational experiences. This means orienting these experiences to the local subcultural community, not only in order to render formal education consistent with and relevant to the child's total life-situation, but also so that parents, through their competences, can become more fully involved in educating their children.

For teachers, not only does this involve accepting the experiences of the local community members as valid and worthwhile, but above all, it means that teachers should *know* the culture and social structure of their communities, and should be involved in them in ways other than simply performing their present job within the school. Teachers must cease to view the local community simply as the source of all educational deficits, and seek to accept and relate to the skill orders, moral symbols, cultural meanings and sensitivities of the local community. In the past, only lip-service has been paid to this principle, partly because to go beyond lip-service involves not only basic changes in the organisation of the school and its relation to the local setting, but also assumes fundamental changes in teachers' professional commitments and ideology.

Fantini[58] puts the question this way: 'How can an educational process be developed that can deal effectively with diversity?' An important step is the recognition that children are motivated within their own experiental framework as conditioned by their immediate social context as a whole. In relation to IQ testing, Havighurst[59] has claimed that

> middle-class and lower-class children bring to the intelligence-test situation widely disparate cultural experiences by virtue of their social class experience, and that middle-class children get more out of themselves in the ordinary school test situation than do lower-class children. An intelligence test which is to get at the 'real' problem-

solving ability of children must draw its problems entirely from experiences which are common to all or nearly all the children to be tested; at the same time, such a test must be given under conditions which motivate lower-class children to do their best and which teach them to expect that they will be rewarded for doing their best.

It may very well be that such 'culture-fair' IQ tests are an impossibility and that any IQ test is bound to compare groups in terms of a set of standards not equally espoused by all groups. The orientation of IQ tests towards *individual* performance may well in itself imply a positive valuation of individualism which some groups clearly espouse more than others.

The fundamental reorientation of the structure of the school (both internally and in relation to its wider social context), whilst involving basic changes, is not impossible. We shall deal first with the teacher-pupil relationship. According to Bernstein,[60] most working-class children do possess in their *passive* vocabulary the vocabulary used by middle-class children. The use of what Bernstein calls a 'restricted (linguistic) code' does not mean that most working-class children do not use or implicitly grasp the basic linguistic rule system as such. Nor, for that matter, does anything in the structure of dialects prevent children from learning to use universalistic meanings (i.e. meanings which are relatively freed from implicit reference to the specific context referred to).

However, the existence of a restricted code does mean that, owing to differences in working-class as opposed to middle-class values and socialisation experiences, the social conditions under which a working-class child will linguistically realise universalistic meanings will differ from those presently expected by a middle-class teacher. Moreover the nature of the context referred to also helps dictate whether the working-class child will linguistically realise relatively universalistic and elaborated meanings, compared to his realisation of more particularistic, more context-bound meanings in other contexts.[61]

Bernstein and Henderson's research on induction of children into the moral (person) orders and skill (object) orders helps specify the conditions and contexts in which children of varying class background will orient themselves to the elaborated explication of meanings.[62] Teachers must make the effort to grasp these contexts, and to establish their specific manifestations in their community, using data related to the specific community setting in which the teacher is working; Bernstein's researches provide an invaluable framework for interpreting such data.

This is where the parents come in, in all sorts of ways. They can teach the teacher many things about their children and their experiences. Once the teacher appreciates the relevance of such knowledge, he can then begin to use it—hopefully, by more adequately relating his teaching to the child's experiences—to build upon the child's tacit understanding of the linguistic rule system in order that the child learns to realise orders of relevance and relation, universalistic meanings, and public modes of thought in *new* conditions and contexts. The task of 'context-creation' does not in itself make working-class children into middle-class children. Any teaching relationship, formal or informal, uses techniques of context-creation. It is simply that teachers must create teaching contexts which are relevant to the experiences of working-class children. This is not 'compensatory education'; it is simply 'education'. Working-class children need not be segregated temporally or spatially for this to be achieved.

But it does require basic changes in the existing school setting, since at present the conditions and contexts used as starting-points for the educative process are far more consonant with the socialisation and out-of-school experiences of middle-class children and are therefore less effective in triggering working-class children's imaginations and capacities. To counteract this bias requires the fullest appreciation of varying social backgrounds and contexts, and their relation to the child's experiences. It involves the teacher learning to build experiental bridges on the basis of this appreciation. As Bernstein says: 'We should start knowing that the social experience the child already possesses is valid and significant, and this social experience should be reflected back to him as valid and significant. It can only be reflected back to him if it is part of the texture of learning experience we create'.[63]

Bernstein also makes the point that such 'context-creation', if it is to be effective, cannot be of the 'piecemeal' kind, but must be a continuous, consistent and systematic process. As research has shown, any possible advantage gained in a special pre-school compensatory education programme for the three-to-five age range will almost certainly be lost if the educational contexts of the child after age five show no consonance with his previous experiences. Bernstein implies that the primary stage of education should be seen as an irreducible unit based on systematic, co-ordinated sequencing of learning. From this point of view, the traditional administrative infant-junior division in Britain, and the growing middle-school division in the USA not only reflect the piecemeal bureaucratic approach to social problem-solving but actually work against the aims of educators who show concern for children from subordinate groups.

To dissolve the present administrative divisions requires a basic restructuring, not only of the present school system but also of teacher education which at present is based upon the tacit assumption that these administrative divisions are clearly recognisable and valid in terms of child development and educational methods. A reorientation would, in fact, necessarily force those teachers who consider themselves to be experts on (for example) 'the primary stage' to consider the educative process in a wider and, from an educational point of view, more fruitful developmental context. Redistribution of power, in a direction favouring the parents and students, would also serve to guide teachers into such a reorientation.

In a broad sociological frame of reference, then, it is crucial that both research and action recognise that subordinate group members live, function, and are motivated within the experiential framework which is appropriate to their immediate social context. This, of course, will often include exposure to the stigma of discrimination as well as other components of subordinate-group status.[64]

We contend that failure to take this diversity of life experiences and values into account, is in all probability a major factor underlying the failure of many antipoverty and other welfare programmes (including those of compensatory education), in spite of rapidly increasing expenditure on these programmes during the middle 1960s.

Notes

1 The authors wish to thank Mr E. C. Cuff for his assistance in the proof-reading of an early draft of this paper, and the Bernard van Leer Foundation of Holland and the New World Foundation of New York for their financial assistance.
2 See, for example, the reader edited by A. H. Halsey, J. Floud, and C. A. Anderson, *Education, Economy and Society*, London and New York, 1961 for some of the material which established this empirical generalisation.

3 See E. W. Gordon, 'Programs of compensatory education', in M. Deutsch *et al.*, *Social Class, Race and Psychological Development*, New York, 1968; H. L. Miller, *Education for the Disadvantaged*, New York, 1967; A. H. Passow, *Education in Depressed Areas*, New York, 1963; H. Rees, *Deprivation and Compensatory Education*, New York, 1968.

4 For an outline of the data cast in terms of these alleged deficits, see the social psychologist E. E. Pettigrew: *A Profile of the Negro American*, Princeton, 1964, chapter 5. Pettigrew also makes reference to compensatory programmes in this chapter (see pp. 125–6).

5 For a more cautious assessment of this widespread supposition, see C. A. Anderson, 'A sceptical note on education and mobility' in A. H. Halsey, J. Floud and C. A. Anderson, *op. cit.*; and S. M. Lipset and R. Bendix, *Social Mobility in Industrial Societies*, Univ. of California Press, 1959, chap. VII.

6 Here we are really referring to the modern form of the liberal ideology, which, as will be seen, assumes certain relationships to the state and the powerful bureaucracies. Nineteenth-century liberalism tended, relatively speaking, to be more anti-bureaucratic, anti-clerical and anti-elitist than its modern counterpart. In this section we stress the basic components of modern liberalism in ideal-type form.

7 Of course, neither liberals in the general sense nor 'compensatory educationists' concentrate solely upon a specific group (e.g. Negroes) as opposed to other 'underprivileged' groups. We cite the case of 'underprivileged Negroes' as one of many examples from groups of low socio-economic status upon which a political position may be assumed.

8 S. Lubell, *White and Black: Test of a Nation*, New York, 1964, pp. 190–1.

9 K. Mannheim, *Ideology and Utopia*, London, Routledge & Kegan Paul, 1960.

10 This administrative bias is by no means to be simply equated with governmental intervention. It also extends to 'liberal' policies fostered by private enterprise, such as the Ford Foundation programmes. 'The Ford Foundation,' says C. E. Silberman, 'which is sponsoring large scale "gray area" programmes in five cities, plus a state-wide project in North Carolina, has bet millions on a grandiose fusion of paternalism and bureaucracy'; see his *Crisis in Black and White*, New York, 1964, pp. 351–6.

11 Among those who contributed to this was M. Harrington, through his book *The Other America*, New York, 1962.

12 See J. B. Conant, *Slums and Suburbs: A Commentary on Schools in Metropolitan Areas*, New York, 1961, p. 10. In relation to liberal policies of large-scale corporate bureaucracies in the private sector, see R. A. Cloward and F. Fox Piven's article 'Corporate imperialism for the poor', *Nation*, 16 October 1967, pp. 365–7. Cloward and Piven attribute the efforts of large-scale department stores and insurance companies in this respect to their vested interests in establishing social order, so as to reduce huge damage to their property in ghetto riots. See also A. Sinfield, 'Poverty rediscovered', *Race*, 1968, pp. 202–9, on the 'special areas' approach.

13 See P. Meranto, *The Politics of Federal Aid to Education*, New York, 1967, p. 36.

14 Our insertion. For an account of how similar concerns for social order and

discipline pervaded the movement towards providing universal secondary education in England, see D. V. Glass, 'Education and social change in modern England', in Halsey, Floud and Anderson, *op. cit.*, pp. 394–5.

15 P. Meranto, *op. cit.*, p. 41.

16 M. D. Fantini, in his article 'Beyond cultural deprivation and compensatory education', *Psychiatry and Social Science Review*, 13, 1969, pp. 6–13, testifies to the prevalence of these 'adjustment criteria' in the schools (pp. 6–8), but since he, unlike the present authors, is not explicitly concerned with an ideology analysis, he does not note the broad ideological roots of such an assumption. So he does not note the prevalence of its application to structural situations outside formal education.

17 J. Horton, 'Order and conflict theories of social problems as competing ideologies', *American Journal of Sociology*, May 1966, pp. 701–13. See also C. Wright Mills, 'The professional ideology of social pathologists', *American Journal of Sociology*, 49, 1942, pp. 165–80.

18 Martin Luther King, Jr., 'The meaning of non-violence', *Dialogue*, 1 (2), 1968, pp. 3–4.

19 S. Lubell, *op. cit.*, p. 190.

20 See A. Sinfield, *op. cit.*, for a critique of the special areas approach, and see B. Bernstein and D. Young, 'Social class differences in conceptions of the uses of toys', *Sociology*, 1, 1967, pp. 131–40, and B. Bernstein and D. Henderson, 'Social class differences in the relevance of language to socialization', *Sociology*, 3, 1969, pp. 1–20, among many other contributions testifying to the middle-class bias of the formal educational system, such as H. S. Becker, 'Social class variations in the teacher-pupil relationship', *Journal of Educational Sociology*, 25, 1952, pp. 451–65; A. V. Cicourel and J. I. Kitsuse, *The Educational Decision-Makers*, Indianapolis, 1963.

21 See the paradigm presented by J. Horton, *op. cit.*, p. 706, and his comments on pp. 705, 709.

22 See K. Mannheim, *op. cit.*, p. 199.

23 Tape-recording of B. Rustin. 'The Negro revolution', Center for the Study of Democratic Institutions.

24 See P. Goodman's essay on vocational guidance in *Utopian Essays and Practical Proposals*, New York, 1962, for a critical attack upon social-work policies based on such assumptions.

25 That non-middle-class cultures exist and are widespread in American society is well documented by such studies as Oscar Lewis's *La Villa*, New York, 1966, and 'The culture of poverty', *Scientific American*, 215, Oct. 1966, and B. Jackson, *Working Class Community*, London, Routledge & Kegan Paul, 1968.

26 See C. Wright Mills, 'Situated actions and vocabularies of motive', *American Sociological Review*, V, 1940, pp. 901–13; and 'The professional ideology of social pathologists', *op. cit.*

27 See K. Eells, A Davis, *et al.*, *Intelligence and Cultural Differences*, University of Chicago Press, 1951, pp. 5 and 26, and O. Klineberg, *Race and Psychology*, Paris, UNESCO, 1958.

28 See K. Eells, *et al.*, *ibid.*, chapter V.

29 See F. Goodenough and D. B. Harris, 'Studies in the psychology of children's drawings', *Psychological Bulletin*, Sept. 1950.

30 See K. Eells, *et al.*, *op. cit.*, p. 26, and C. E. Silberman, *op. cit.*, pp. 267–8, for a very similar statement.

31 See H. S. Becker, *op. cit.*, for validation of this point (our footnote).

32 See B. Bernstein and D. Henderson, *op. cit.*

33 Pettigrew, *op. cit.*, in his chapter on Negro American intelligence plays down the questioning bias in IQ tests. Although paying lipservice to the 'class linked' nature of IQ tests, Pettigrew treats the tests as being *to all intents and purposes* valid indicators of intelligence. M. D. Fantini also implicitly accepts IQ tests as valid measures of intellectual ability and development (*op. cit.*, p. 8).

34 See K. Eells, *et al.*, *op. cit.*, pp. 285–6.

35 See O. Klineberg, *op. cit.*, p. 12.

36 Liberals, in their ideologies and policies, often ignore factors relating to IQ tests that traditional conservatives stress – e.g. arguments for the genetic basis of IQ test performance. These contradict the liberals' heavy emphasis on 'environmentalism', which is the assumption underlying most compensatory education programmes. On the alleged genetic basis of IQ test performance and possible implications for educational technique, see A. Jensen, 'How much can we boost IQ and scholastic achievement?' *Harvard Educational Review*, 39, 1969, pp. 1–123.

37 Fantini's article, *op. cit.*, is a good example of this myopia. He speaks of a 'reformed educational system'.

38 See B. Rustin, *op. cit.*, and R. K. Merton, 'The machine, the worker and the engineer' in R. K. Merton, *op. cit.*, on how the 'technological revolution' is often used as a weapon by employers against the demands of workers.

39 See R. K. Merton's essay 'Social structure and anomie' in Merton, *op. cit.*, and also L. Killian and C. Grigg, *Racial Crisis in America*, New York, p. 114, for a similar theme regarding segregation.

40 See R. K. Merton's essay 'The self-fulfilling prophecy' in Merton, *op. cit.* Fundamentally conservative policies, in the past, have resolved this contradiction by educating subordinate groups to dominant group values, especially values recognising the legitimacy of the existing overall social order and the legitimacy of the subordinate groups' 'special', i.e. separate, lowly position in that social order. See for example, J. Dollard, *Castè and Class in a Southern Town*, New York, 1949.

41 As Silberman (*op. cit.*, p. 316) says, 'The Negroes' failure to "acculturate" is due only partly to ignorance or indifference; they do not acculturate because they regard doing the things implied by that term as treason to their race – as "going along with Mr. Charlie's program".'

42 Willard Waller, in his article 'Social problems and the mores', *American Sociological Review*, 1, 1936, pp. 922–33, brings out the contradictions in such 'liberal-humanitarian' approaches to social problem-solving. Liberal-humanitarians define certain problems in terms of their humanitarian mores (sense of justice, etc.). But Waller says that really to solve social problems a change in the more fundamental 'organisational' mores would have to be effected – that is a change in the values (e.g., the reverence for private property) which are the foundation of the American social order. Humanitarians, in spite of their adherence to humanitarian mores, balk at such basic change; they want the organisational mores to be left intact, even if this means not solving the problems which they seem so concerned

about from the perspective of their humanitarian mores. See G. Myrdal, *An American Dilemma*, New York, 1962, on how such value conflicts affect the social situation.

43 L. Killian and C. Grigg, *op. cit.*, p. 133.
44 B. Rustin, *op. cit.*
45 See J. Horton, *op. cit.*, p. 712.
46 See J. Cohen and W. Murphy *'Burn, Baby, Burn': The Los Angeles Race Riots, August 1965*, London, 1967, for a similar argument (our note).
47 See S. Carmichael and C. V. Hamilton, *'Black Power': The Politics of Liberation in America*, New York, 1967, p. 61.
48 Carmichael's lecture is transcribed in D. Cooper, *The Dialectics of Liberation*, Pelican, 1968, pp. 150–74 (quotation from p. 162).
49 S. Carmichael and C. V. Hamilton, *op. cit.*, p. 47.
50 See C. E. Silberman, *op. cit.*, p. 313.
51 See S. Lubell, *op. cit.*, p. 191.
52 We are indebted to Mr. M. A. Atkinson for this point.
53 For an outline (though lacking in rigour) which at some point parallels our proposals, see Fantini, *op. cit.*, p. 13.
54 It has often been noted that the (hopefully) research-based principles which are taught to student teachers never come to be used by the practising teacher, nor are they by any means always used even by the education lecturer. B. Bernstein, in his paper 'A critique of the concept of compensatory education' (reprinted in full in A. Cashdan and E. Grugeon (eds), *Language in Education* (The Open University E 262 Reader) and in part in this volume, p. 79), has said that the simple principle 'Work with What the Child Can Offer' has never been fully implemented in practice.
55 Or, if one shies from compulsory courses, one might compromise to the point of providing strong incentives for teachers to attend such courses – e.g. gearing graduation from such courses to salary increments, or paying above average salary for course attendance.
56 Those parents who did participate with any kind of influence were usually middle class. Fantini, *op. cit.*, points out the 'public relations' role of P T A S as well.
57 Bernstein, 'A critique . . .', *op. cit.*
58 M. Fantini, *op. cit.*
59 See K. Eells, *et al.*, *op. cit.*, p. 21.
60 Bernstein, 'A critique . . .', *op. cit.*
61 Bernstein and Henderson, *op. cit.*
62 *Ibid.*
63 Bernstein, 'A critique . . .', *op. cit.*
64 The stress on the participants' own terms, the terms of their own values and life-experiences, rather than those of the dominant groups are, in part, what differentiates the 'left-wing' ideological stance from liberal stances stressing 'maximum feasible participation'. If one stays within the dominant group notions in liberal policies espoused by community agencies and administrations, maximum 'feasible' participation is, in fact, very low indeed, as Silberman points out (*op. cit.*, chapter X).

1.4 Educational priority areas

132 In a neighbourhood where the jobs people do and the status they hold owe little to their education it is natural for children as they grow older to regard school as a brief prelude to work rather than an avenue to future opportunities. Some of these neighbourhoods have for generations been starved of new schools, new houses and new investment of every kind. Everyone knows this; but for year after year priority had been given to the new towns and new suburbs, because if new schools do not keep pace with the new houses some children will be unable to go to school at all. The continually rising proportion of children staying on at school beyond the minimum age has led some authorities to build secondary schools and postpone the rebuilding of older primary schools. Not surprisingly, many teachers are unwilling to work in a neighbourhood where the schools are old, where housing of the sort they want is unobtainable, and where education does not attain the standards they expect for their own children. From some neighbourhoods, urban and rural, there has been a continuing outflow of the more successful young people. The loss of their enterprise and skill makes things worse for those left behind. Thus the vicious circle may turn from generation to generation and the schools play a central part in the process, both causing and suffering cumulative deprivation.

133 We have ourselves seen schools caught in such vicious circles and read accounts of many more. They are quite untypical of schools in the rest of the country. We noted the grim approaches; incessant traffic noise in narrow streets; parked vehicles hemming in the pavement; rubbish dumps on waste land nearby; the absence of green playing spaces on or near the school sites; tiny playgrounds; gaunt looking buildings; often poor

Source: *Children and their Primary Schools* (The Plowden Report), vol. 1, HMSO (1967), paras 132–6, 138, 141, 143–54, 174–7.

decorative conditions inside; narrow passages; dark rooms; un-heated and cramped cloakrooms; unroofed outside lavatories; tiny staff rooms; inadequate storage space with consequent restriction on teaching materials and therefore methods; inadequate space for movement and PE; meals in classrooms; art on desks; music only to the discomfort of others in an echoing building; non-soundproof partitions between classes; lack of smaller rooms for group work; lack of spare room for tuition of small groups; in-sufficient display space; attractive books kept unseen in cupboards for lack of space to lay them out; no privacy for parents waiting to see the head; sometimes the head and his secretary sharing the same room; and, sometimes all around, the ingrained grime of genera-tions.

134 We heard from local education authorities of growing difficulty in replacing heads with successors of similar calibre. It is becoming particularly hard to find good heads of infant or deputy heads of junior schools. We are not surprised to hear of the rapid turnover of staff, of vacancies sometimes unfilled or filled with a succession of temporary and supply teachers of one kind or another. Probationary teachers are trained by heads to meet the needs of their schools but then pass on to others where strains are not so great. Many teachers able to do a decent job in an ordinary school are defeated by these conditions. Some become dispirited by long journeys to decaying buildings to see each morning children among whom some seem to have learned only how not to learn. Heads rely on the faithful, devoted and hard working regulars. There may be one or two in any school, or they may be as many as half the staff, who have so much to do in keeping the school running that they are sometimes too tired even to enjoy their own holidays.

135 We saw admission registers whose pages of new names with so many rapid crossings out told their own story of a migratory population. In one school 111 out of 150 pupils were recent new-comers. We heard heads explain as they looked down the lines, that many of those who had gone were good pupils, while a high proportion of those who had been long in the school came from crowded, down-at-heel homes.

The educational needs of deprived areas

136 What these deprived areas need most are perfectly nor-

mal, good primary schools alive with experience from which children of all kinds can benefit. What we say elsewhere about primary school work generally applies equally to these difficult areas. The best schools already there show that it is absurd to say, as one used to hear, 'It may be all very well in a nice suburb, but it won't work here'. But, of course, there are special and additional demands on teachers who work in deprived areas with deprived children. They meet special challenges. Teachers must be constantly aware that ideas, values and relationships within the school may conflict with those of the home, and that the world assumed by teachers and school books may be unreal to the children . . .

Hope for the future

138 In our cities there are whole districts which have been scarcely touched by the advances made in more fortunate places. Yet such conditions have been overcome and striking progress has been achieved where sufficiently determined and comprehensive attack has been made on the problem. In the most deprived areas, one of HM Inspectors reported, 'Some heads approach magnificence, but they cannot do everything . . . The demands on them as welfare agents are never ending.' Many children with parents in the least skilled jobs do outstandingly well in school. The educational aspirations of parents and the support and encouragement given to children in some of the poorest neighbourhoods are impressive. Over half of the unskilled workers in our National Survey want their children to be given homework to do after school hours; over half want their children to stay at school beyond the minimum leaving age. One third of them hoped their children would go to a grammar school or one with similar opportunities. The educational aspirations of unskilled workers for their children have risen year by year. It has been stressed[1] to us that the range of ability in all social classes is so wide that there is a great reservoir of unrealised potential in families dependent on the least skilled and lowest paid work. A larger part of the housing programme than ever before is to be devoted to rebuilding and renewing obsolete and decaying neighbourhoods. The opportunity must be seized to rebuild the schools as well as the houses, and to see that both schools and houses serve families from every social class . . .

Educational assumptions and policies

141 During the second world war there was a considerable improvement in the living conditions which bear most directly upon children in deprived groups and areas. In spite of this there has not been any appreciable narrowing of the gap between the least well off and the rest of the population. This is most obvious among children, particularly those in large families. 'It is . . . clear that, on average, the larger families in all classes, and also those containing adolescents and children, constitute the most vulnerable groups nutritionally.'[2,3] Signs of rickets have recently been reported again from the slums of Glasgow; mortality among children during the first year of life has fallen sharply since 1950, but the difference between social classes remains great.[4] Much the same goes for stillbirth rates which, in different social classes 'despite a dramatic wartime fall, were as far apart in 1950 as in 1939'. Meanwhile 'class differentials in perinatal mortality are as resistant to change as those of infant mortality. The results of the (Perinatal Mortality) Survey suggest, indeed, that the gap may be increasing rather than narrowing.'[5] The Milner Holland Committee's study of housing conditions in London covered a period in which this country probably achieved a faster rate of economic growth than it has ever experienced before, and an area in which conditions are generally better and improving faster than elsewhere. But it showed that progress has been most rapid in those parts of the town where conditions were already best. In less fortunate neighbourhoods there has been less improvement and in some respects an appreciable deterioration. Families with low incomes and several young children were among those who suffered most.[6]

143 . . . Our educational system, originally moulded by the impress of Victorian economic and social requirements, may not yet have been fully adapted to present needs. In the deprived areas with which this chapter is concerned too many children leave school as soon as they are allowed to with no desire to carry their education further and without the knowledge to fit them for a job more intellectually demanding than their father's or their grandfather's. Yet they face a future in which they must expect during their working life to have to change their job, to learn new skills, to adapt themselves to new economic conditions and to form new human relationships. They will suffer, and so will the

economy; both needlessly. It should not be assumed that even the ablest children can surmount every handicap. They may suffer as much as any from adverse conditions.

144 If the schools are to play their part in resolving and forestalling these problems much of the action required must be taken at the secondary and higher stages of the system. But this action cannot be fully effective if it does not touch the primary schools. Recent research has shown how early in the lives of children the selective processes begin to operate.[7] There are primary schools from which scarcely any children ever take a secondary school course which leads them to 'O' level in GCE. Children of good potential ability enter them, but the doors to educational opportunity have already closed against them when their schooling has scarcely begun. Reforming zeal and expenditure directed to later stages of education will be wasted unless early handicaps can be reduced.

145 The schools unaided cannot provide all the opportunities their pupils deserve, or create the labour force this country needs. Industry, and the authorities responsible for housing, planning, employment and other services must also play their part. But, from the earliest stages of education, the schools enlarge or restrict the contribution their pupils can make to the life of the nation. Money spent on education is an investment which helps to determine the scope for future economic and social development.

146 Our argument thus far can be briefly summarised. As things are at the moment there is no reason why the educational handicaps of the most deprived children should disappear. Although standards will rise, inequalities will persist and the potential of many children will never be realised. The range of achievement amongst English children is wide, and the standards attained by the most and the least successful begin to diverge very early. Steps should be taken to improve the educational chances and the attainments of the least well placed, and to bring them up to the levels that prevail generally. This will call for a new distribution of educational resources.

The distribution of resources

147 The principle that certain local authorities (but not districts within local authorities) should receive special help from the

rest of the community is already recognised. At the national level the government takes needs into account when distributing grants to local authorities for educational and other purposes. The basic grant consists of so much per head of population plus so much for each child under 15 years of age. The supplementary grants allow for:

the number of children under five,
the number of people over 65,
school children in excess of a prescribed proportion,
density,
sparsity,
declining population, and
Metropolitan Areas.

There is also a formula that increases the grant paid to authorities with lower rateable values and reduces it for wealthier ones. The same principle of district priorities applies to educational building programmes. The needs of district priorities applies to educational building programmes. The needs of districts with a growing population come first; the next buildings to be sanctioned must be for the purpose of making good the deficiencies of existing schools. This principle can also be seen at work in the distribution of teachers. Local education authorities with an exceptionally high proportion of immigrant children may apply for an addition to their quota of teachers.

148 Redistribution of resources within local authority areas has been less marked. 'Equality' has an appealing ring, 'discrimination' has not. It is simpler and easier, for example, to defend staff–pupil ratios that are roughly the same in each school than to explain why they should be better in some and to decide which are to be the favoured. Even so, more and more local authorities do discriminate. They look with a more generous eye on schools whose 'social need' is greatest, as reckoned by the free dinner list, by the proportion of children who do not speak English at home, or (which may be an even better guide) by the opinion of experienced teachers and administrators. These schools may be allowed an extra teacher or more non-teaching help, or a slightly bigger ration of 'consumable stocks'.

149 These are no more than a tentative beginning. The formulae for allocating grants are designed to equalise the financial resources of poorer and wealthier authorities. But equality is not

enough. The formulae do not distinguish between the districts within authorities' areas in which children and schools are most severely handicapped. These districts need more spending on them, and government and local authorities between them must provide the funds. Permission is required before the money can be spent on what is most needed—additional teachers and better buildings. The authority's quota must be raised before extra teachers can be engaged, and additions to the building programme must be sanctioned by the Department of Education. Even if this happens the battle is not over. Some authorities whose need for teachers is great find it impossible to recruit for deprived schools the teachers to whom they are entitled. The vicious circle continues.

150 A study of the educational expenditure of 83 county boroughs has been made for us by Mr B. P. Davies.[8] He compared the way money was spent with the evidence about the needs of each borough. He found no link between the amount spent on primary schools and their pupils and the social character of the area they served. In general, deprived areas were neither more nor less likely than others to get a bigger share of the total expenditure. A large proportion of expenditure was devoted to the salaries of teachers, whose distribution is subject to quota rules, and to the provision of those essential services which give little scope for variation. Other services, on which an education authority has great scope for independent decision, often tended to have more spent on them in those boroughs where the needs appeared to be less urgent. There are signs of this in the expenditure on nursery schools, and (less clearly) on child guidance. The same applied to schools meals where parental preferences exert an influence. More striking, perhaps, was the persistence of these patterns. The boroughs in which expenditure was generally low were much the same in 1960–61 as they were in 1950–51.

Educational priority areas

151 The many teachers who do so well in face of adversity cannot manage without cost to themselves. They carry the burdens of parents, probation officers and welfare officers on top of their classroom duties. It is time the nation came to their aid. The principle, already accepted, that special need calls for special help, should be given a new cutting edge. We ask for

'positive discrimination' in favour of such schools and the children in them, going well beyond an attempt to equalise resources. Schools in deprived areas should be given priority in many respects. The first step must be to raise the schools with low standards to the national average; the second, quite deliberately to make them better. The justification is that the homes and neighbourhoods from which many of their children come provide little support and stimulus for learning. The schools must supply a compensating environment. The attempts so far made within the educational system to do this have not been sufficiently generous or sustained, because the handicaps imposed by the environment have not been explicitly and sufficiently allowed for. They should be.

152 The proposition that good schools should make up for a poor environment is far from new. It derives from the notion that there should be equality of opportunity for all, but recognises that children in some districts will only get the same opportunity as those who live elsewhere if they have unequally generous treatment. It was accepted before the first world war that some children could not be effectively taught until they had been properly fed. Hence free meals were provided. Today their need is for enriched intellectual nourishment. Planned and positive discrimination in favour of deprived areas could bring about an advance in the education of children in the 1970s as great as the advance in their nutrition to which school meals and milk contributed so much.

153 Every authority where deprivation is found should be asked to adopt 'positive discrimination' within its own area, and to report from time to time on the progress made. Some authorities contain schools or even one school of this kind where deprivation is so serious that they need special help. Most of these schools and areas are already well known to teachers, administrators, local Inspectors and HM Inspectors. Local knowledge will not be sufficient to justify decisions which are bound on occasion to be controversial. Objective criteria for the selection of 'educational priority schools and areas' will be needed to identify those schools which need special help and to determine how much assistance should be given by the government. Our National Survey showed the prime importance of parental attitudes, and it might be thought that a measure of these attitudes could be devised. But the data for the selection of priority schools and areas must be readily available, without additional surveys, and in any event

the validity of answers given by parents with the education of their children at stake might fairly be questioned. The criteria required must identify those places where educational handicaps are reinforced by social handicaps. Some of the main criteria which could be used in an assessment of deprivation are given below. They are not placed in order of importance, nor is any formula suggested by which they should be combined. They may require further study. The criteria are:

(a) *Occupation.* The National Census can report on occupations within quite small areas, and, for particular schools, the data can be supplemented without too much difficulty. The analyses would show the proportions of unskilled and semi-skilled manual workers.

(b) *Size of families.* The larger the family, the more likely are the children to be in poverty. Wages are no larger for a married man with young children than they are for a single man with none. Family size is still associated with social class, and men with four or more children tend to be amongst the lowest wage earners. Family size also correlates with the results of intelligence tests— the larger the family, the lower the scores of the children. The children are liable to suffer from a double handicap, both genetic and environmental—the latter because, it is suggested, they have less encouragement and stimulus from parents who have more children amongst whom to divide their attention. Those earning the lowest wages often make up their incomes by working longer hours. Often, too, their wives have less time and energy to devote to their children. Family size likewise correlates with nutrition, with physical growth and with overcrowding, and is therefore an apt indicator (when allowance is made for the age structure of the local population, and particularly the number of mothers of child bearing age) of the poor home conditions for which schools should compensate. The National Census, supplemented by the schools censuses made by the education authorities, would provide the information required.

(c) *Supplements in cash or kind from the state* are of various kinds. Where the parents are needy, children are allowed school meals free. The proportions so benefiting vary greatly from school to school, and afford a reasonably good guide to relative need. The procedures laid down are designed to give free meals according to scales similar to those used by the Ministry of Social Security. Another criterion of the same type is the number of families depending on National Assistance, or its future equivalent, in a particular locality. The weakness of these criteria taken by themselves is that some people do not know their rights or are unwilling to seek them.

(d) *Overcrowding and sharing of houses* should certainly be included amongst the criteria. It will identify families in cramped accommodation in central and run-down areas of our cities. It is a less sure guide than some others because it may miss the educational needs of some housing estates and other areas which can also be severe.

(e) *Poor attendance and truancy* are a pointer to home conditions, and to what Burt long ago singled out as a determinant of school progress, the 'efficiency of the mother'. Truancy is also related to delinquency. The National Survey showed that four per cent of the children in the sample were absent, on their teachers' assessment, for unsatisfactory reasons.

(f) *Proportions of retarded, disturbed or handicapped pupils* in ordinary schools. These vary from authority to authority according to the special schools available and the policies governing their use. But, everywhere the proportions tend to be highest in deprived districts. It is accepted that special schools need additional staff, and the same advantages should be extended to normal schools with many pupils of a similar kind.

(g) *Incomplete families* where one or other of the parents is dead, or not living at home for whatever reason, are often unable to provide a satisfactory upbringing for their children without special help.

(h) *Children unable to speak English* need much extra attention if they are to find their feet in England. This is already recognised in arranging teachers' quotas, but should also be used as a general criterion.

154 All authorities would be asked to consider which of their schools should qualify, to rank them according to criteria such as those we have listed, and to submit supporting data. Advice would also be available from HM Inspectors of Schools. In this way the Department of Education and Science would have full information both about the social and the educational needs of the schools and areas. Many of the criteria would be closely correlated. With experience the data required could be simplified so as to ease administration; but meanwhile, a wide variety of criteria should be employed. The schools near the bottom of the resulting rankings would be entitled to priority. We envisage a formal

procedure enabling the Secretary of State for Education and Science to designate particular schools or groups of schools as priority schools or areas. Those so designated would qualify for the favourable treatment described later in this chapter. Local education authorities would submit regular reports on these schools to the Secretary of State for the purpose of determining what progress was being made, how long their designation should continue, which aspects of the programme were proving most effective, and what further steps should be taken.

Recommendations

174 (i) As a matter of national policy, 'positive discrimination' should favour schools in neighbourhoods where children are most severely handicapped by home conditions. The programme should be phased to make schools in the most deprived areas as good as the best in the country. For this, it may be necessary that their greater claim on resources should be maintained.

(ii) A start should be made as soon as possible by giving priority to the most severely deprived pupils, starting with 2 per cent of the pupils and building up to 10 per cent over five years. The purpose of the short term programme would be partly to discover which measures best compensate for educational deprivation. In the longer term, the programme may be expanded to cover a larger proportion of the population.

(iii) Every local education authority having schools in which children's educational handicaps are reinforced by social deprivation should be asked to adopt the measures suggested below and to report from time to time on the progress made. Local authorities should be encouraged to select schools within their areas for special attention even though they are not eligible for extra help from national resources.

(iv) A wide variety of criteria should be employed initially. Experience will show which of these criteria are most useful.

(v) Authorities should be asked to say which of their schools should receive extra help from national resources. The Department of Education should formally designate those schools and areas in most need as educational priority areas. Priority areas and the progress made in them should be reappraised regularly by local education authorities and the Department of Education and Science.

(vi) Authorities and the Department of Education and Science should ensure that the needs of other educationally deprived groups, such as gypsies, which will not be picked out by the general criteria laid down, are not overlooked.

Steps to be taken: 1968 to 1972

175 (i) Measures should be taken to improve the ratio of teachers to children in educational priority areas to a point at which no class in these areas exceeds 30. Additions to salary amounting in total to £120 for every teacher in the priority areas should be paid. It should be open to authorities to award increases according to any plan approved by the Department of Education and Science as being likely to improve education in these areas.

(ii) Teachers' aides should be provided in the priority schools at a ratio of one to every two infant and junior classes.

(iii) In building programmes, priority should be given to these areas for the replacement or improvement of schools with old or out of date premises. The element of the total school building programme reserved for minor works should be increased specifically for their benefit. Approximately £5,000 should be allocated for minor works in each school.

(iv) Extra books and equipment should be given for schools in priority areas.

(v) The expansion of nursery education should begin in the priority areas.

176 (i) The Department of Education and Science should modify its quota arrangements so that they take into account the varying resources of immobile teachers available in each area. Authorities with large numbers of qualified married women willing to teach but unable to work in other areas should gradually be persuaded to employ all of them before drawing on mobile teachers who might be available for priority areas.

(ii) Colleges of education should, wherever possible, establish a continuing link with priority schools. Students should do part of their teaching practice in these schools.

(iii) Teachers' centres should be set up for in-service training. They might run longer courses with the co-operation of local colleges of education. Such courses might be recognised for salary purposes.

(iv) The development of social work in conjunction with schools should begin in priority areas and be more heavily concentrated there subsequently.

(v) Community schools should be tried out first in priority areas.

177 (i) Sustained efforts should be made to diversify the social composition of the districts where priority schools are so that teachers and others who make an essential contribution to the life and public services of the neighbourhood are not excluded from them. Co-ordinated action will be necessary on the part of authorities responsible for employment, industrial training, housing and town planning if educational deprivation is to be rapidly reduced.

(ii) Research should be started to discover which of the developments in educational priority areas have the most constructive effects, so as to assist in planning the longer term programme to follow.

(iii) Exchequer grants to local authorities with educational priority areas should be increased and the necessary changes in the grant making system made.

References

1 Professor S. Wiseman. Oral evidence to Council.
2 National Food Survey, 1963.
3 R. Lambert, *Nutrition in Britain 1950–1960*, Codicote Press, 1964.
4 G. C. Arneil and J. C, Crosbie, 'Infantile rickets returns to Glasgow', *Lancet* (1963), ii, 423. Quoted in T. Arie, 'Class and disease', *New Society*, 27 January 1966.
5 R. Illsley and J. C. Kincaid, 'Social correlation of perinatal mortality', p. 271 in N. R. Butler, and D. G. Bonham, *Perinatal Mortality*, Livingstone, 1963.
6 Milner Holland Report. *Report of the Committee on Housing in Greater London*, Cmnd 2605, 1965.
7 For example, J. W. B. Douglas, *Home and School*, MacGibbon & Kee, 1964. The same data form the bases of arguments in the Robbins Report, vol. II.
8 B. Davies, 'Relative inequality and interrelationships between standards of provision of primary, secondary and other forms of education and socio-economic factors affecting education performance' (to be published).

1·5   Education cannot compensate for society[1]

Basil Bernstein

Since the late 1950s there has been a steady outpouring of papers and books in the United States which are concerned with the education of children of low social class whose *material* circumstances are inadequate, or with the education of black children of low social class whose *material* circumstances are chronically inadequate. A vast research and educational bureaucracy developed in the United States, which was financed by funds obtained from federal, state or private foundations. New educational categories were developed—'the culturally deprived', 'the linguistically deprived', 'the socially disadvantaged'; and the notion of 'compensatory education' was introduced as a means of changing the status of the children in these categories.

Compensatory education emerged in the form of massive pre-school programmes like Project Headstart (see Ruth Adam, *New Society*, 30 October 1969), large-scale research programmes such as those of Deutsch in the early 1960s and a plethora of small-scale 'intervention' or 'enrichment' programmes for pre-school children or children in the first years of compulsory education. Very few sociologists were involved in these studies, because education was a low-status area. On the whole they were carried out by psychologists.

The focus of these studies was on the child in the family and on the local classroom relationship between teacher and child. In the last two years one can detect a change in this focus. As a result of the movements towards integration and the opposed movement towards segregation (the latter a response to the wishes of the various Black Power groups), more studies are being made in the United States of the *school*. Robert Rosenthal's classic study, *Pygmalion in the Classroom*, drew attention to the critical importance of the teacher's expectations of the child.

Source: *New Society*, 26 February 1970, 344–7.

In this country we have been aware of the educational problem since the writings of Sir Cyril Burt before the war. His book, *The Backward Child*, is probably still the best study we have. After the war, a series of sociological surveys and public inquiries into education brought this educational problem into the arena of national debate, and so of social policy. Now in Wales there is a large research unit, financed by the Schools Council, concerned with compensatory education. Important research of a different kind is taking place in the University of Birmingham into the problems of the education of Commonwealth children. The Social Science Research Council and the Department of Education and Science have given £175,000, in part for the development of special pre-school programmes concerned to introduce children to compensatory education. There is also the whole educational priority area programme (described by Anne Corbett in 'Are educational priority areas working?' *New Society*, 13 November 1969).

One university department of education offers an advanced diploma in compensatory education. Colleges of education also offer special courses under the same title. So it might be worth a few lines to consider the assumptions underlying this work and the concepts which describe it, particularly as my own writings have sometimes been used (and more often abused) to highlight aspects of the general problems and dilemmas.

To begin with, I find the term, 'compensatory education', a curious one for a number of reasons. I do not understand how we can talk about offering compensatory education to children who in the first place have not, as yet, been offered an adequate education environment. The Newsom Report on secondary modern schools showed that 79 per cent of all secondary modern schools in slum and problem areas were materially grossly inadequate, and that the holding power of these schools over the teachers was horrifyingly low. The same report also showed very clearly the depression in the reading scores of these children, compared with the reading scores of children who were at school in areas which were neither problem nor slum. This does not conflict with the finding that, on average, for the country as a whole, there has been an improvement in children's reading ability. The Plowden Report on the primary schools was rather more coy about all the above points, but we have little reason to believe that the situation is very much better for primary schools in similar areas.

Thus we offer a large number of children, both at the primary and secondary levels, materially inadequate schools and a higher turnover of teaching staff; and we further expect a small group of dedicated teachers to cope. The strain on these teachers inevitably produces fatigue and illness and it is not uncommon to find, in any week, teachers having to deal with doubled-up classes of 80 children. And we wonder why the children display very early in their educational life a range of learning difficulties.

At the same time, the organization of schools creates delicate overt and covert streaming arrangements which neatly lower the expectations and motivations of both teachers and taught. A vicious spiral is set up, with an all too determinate outcome. It would seem, then, that we have failed to provide, on the scale required, an *initial* satisfactory educational environment.

The concept, 'compensatory education', serves to direct attention away from the internal organization and the educational context of the school, and focus our attention on the families and children. 'Compensatory education' implies that something is lacking in the family, and so in the child. As a result, the children are unable to benefit from schools.

It follows, then, that the school has to 'compensate' for the something which is missing in the family, and the children are looked at as deficit systems. If only the parents were interested in the goodies we offer, if only they were like middle-class parents, then we could do our job. Once the problem is seen even implicitly in this way, then it becomes appropriate to coin the terms 'cultural deprivation', 'linguistic deprivation', and so on. And then these labels do their own sad work.

If children are labelled 'culturally deprived', then it follows that the parents are inadequate; the spontaneous realizations of their culture, its images and symbolic representations are of reduced value and significance. Teachers will have lower expectations of the children, which the children will undoubtedly fulfil. All that informs the child, that gives meaning and purpose to him outside of the school, ceases to be valid or accorded significance and opportunity for enhancement within the school. He has to orient towards a different structure of meaning, whether it is in the form of reading books (*Janet and John*), in the form of language use and dialect, or in the patterns of social relationships.

Alternatively the meaning structure of the school is explained to the parents and imposed on, rather than integrated within, the form and content of their world. A wedge is progressively driven between the child as a member of a family and community, and the child as a member of a school. Either way the child is expected, and his parents as well, to drop their social identity, their way of life and its symbolic representations, at the school gate. For, by definition, their culture is deprived, and the parents are inadequate in both the moral and the skill orders they transmit.

I do not mean by this that in these circumstances no satisfactory home-school relations can take place or do take place: I mean rather that the best thing is for the parents to be brought *within* the educational experience of the schoolchild by doing what they can do, and this with confidence. There are many ways in which parents can help the child in this learning, which are within the parents' spheres of competence. If this happens, then the parents can feel adequate and confident both in relation to the child and the school. This may mean that the contents of the learning in school should be drawn much more from the child's experience in his family and community.

So far I have criticized the use of the concept of 'compensatory education' because it distracts attention from the deficiencies in the school itself and focuses upon deficiencies within the community, family and child. We can add to these criticisms a third.

This concept points to the overwhelming significance of the early years of the child's life in the shaping of his later development. Clearly there is much evidence to support this view and to support its implication that we should create an extensive nursery-school system. However, it would be foolhardy indeed to write off the post-seven-years-of-age educational experience as having little influence.

Minimally, what is required *initially* is to consider the whole age period up to the conclusion of the primary stages as a unity. This would require considering our approach, at any *one* age, in the context of the whole of the primary stage. This implies a systematic, rather than a piecemeal, approach. I am arguing here for taking as the unit, not a particular period in the life of the child—for example, three to five years, or five to seven years—but taking as the unit a stage of education: the primary stage. We should see all we do in terms of the sequencing of learning, the development of sensitivities within the context of the primary stage. In order to accomplish this, the present social and educational division between infant and junior stages must be weakened, as well as the insulation between primary and secondary stages. Otherwise gains at any one age, for the child, may well be vitiated by losses at a later age.

We should stop thinking in terms of 'compensatory education' but consider, instead, most seriously and systematically the conditions and contexts of the educational environment.

The very form our research takes tends to confirm the beliefs underlying the organization, transmission and evaluation of knowledge by the school. Research proceeds by assessing the criteria of attainment that schools hold, and then measures the competence of different social groups in reaching these criteria. We take one group of children, whom we know beforehand possess attributes favourable to school achievement; and a second group of children, whom we know beforehand lack these attributes. Then we evaluate one group in terms of what it *lacks* when compared with another. In this way research, unwittingly, underscores the notion of *deficit* and confirms the status quo of a given organization, transmission and, in particular, evaluation of knowledge. Research very rarely challenges or exposes the social assumptions underlying what counts as valid knowledge, or what counts as a valid realization of that knowledge. There are exceptions in the area of curriculum development; but, even here, the work often has no built-in attempt to evaluate the changes. This holds particularly for educational priority area 'feasibility' projects. . . .

Much of the context of our schools is unwittingly drawn from aspects of the symbolic world of the middle class, and so when the child steps into school he is stepping into a symbolic system which does not provide for him a linkage with his life outside.

It is an accepted educational principle that we should work with what the child can offer; why don't we practise it? The introduction of the child to the universalistic meanings of public forms of thought is not 'compensatory education'; *it is education*. It is not making children middle class; how it is done, through the implicit values underlying the form and content of the educational environment, might.

We need to distinguish between the principles and operations that teachers transmit and develop in the children, and the contexts they create in order to do this. We should start knowing that the social experience the child already possesses is valid and significant, and that this social experience should be reflected back to him as being valid and significant. It can only be reflected back to him if it is part of the texture of the learning experience we create.

If we spent as much time thinking through the implications of this as we do thinking about the implications of Piaget's development sequences, then it would be possible for schools to become exciting and challenging environments for parents, the children themselves and teachers.

We need to examine the social assumptions underlying the organization, distribution and evaluation of knowledge, for there is not one, and only one, answer. The power relationships created outside the school penetrate the organization, distribution and evaluation of knowledge through the social context. The definition of 'educability' is itself, at any one time, an attenuated consequence of these power relationships.

We must consider Robert Lynd's question: 'knowledge for what?' And the answer cannot be given only in terms of whether six-year-old children should be able to read, count and write. We do not know what a child is capable of, as we have as yet no theory which enables us to create sets of optimal learning environments; and even if such a theory existed, it is most unlikely that resources would be available to make it substantive on the scale required. It may well be that one of the tests of an educational system is that its outcomes are relatively unpredictable.

Note

1 This article is a more spelled-out version of one which forms a chapter in *Education for Democracy*, ed. David Rubinstein and Colin Stoneman, Penguin Education Special (1970), 110–21.

1.6 Political ends and educational means

A. H. Halsey

To find a strategy for educational roads to equality! That has been a central theme of educational discussion from the beginning of the twentieth century. It has produced a prolific sociology of education over the last generation in which the centrality of educational systems to the structure and the functioning of industrial societies has become a commonplace. In the 1950s education in these societies was seen as having a crucial role for economic growth and change. More recently the emphasis has shifted to the part played by formal educational organisations in defining what is and what is not knowledge, and as selective agencies allocating individuals to social positions, moulding their social personalities and their definitions of the world around them. But the underlying question is whether, and if so under what circumstances, education can change society.

The answer, whatever its form, has been controversial in two apparently different ways. Debate has turned on the *desirability* of using educational means for political ends. But also, and much more fruitfully, it has turned on the feasibility of different educational means towards agreed ends. Thus 'keeping education out of politics' can be a crude evasion of the incontrovertible fact that, in a modern or a modernising society, educational arrangements are an important determinant of the life and livelihood of individuals: education is a social distributor of life chances. In its more subtle forms, however, this political or moral stance may be a protest against narrow definitions of the social consequences of educational reform. As such it belongs neither to the political right nor to the political left. It is of course associated with such writers as T. S. Eliot,[1] Professor Bantock[2] and the authors of the Black Papers,[3] but there are equally important radical criticisms of narrowness in the sociological imagination; for example reform in

Source: *Educational Priority*, ed. A. H. Halsey, HMSO (1972), vol. 1, 3–12.

the direction of meritocracy may fail to take account of those ramified consequences which Professor Bernstein has referred to as 'the individualisation of failure' and there is a good deal of current writing from an interactionist or phenomenological point of view which insists on the importance of education as structuring reality for those exposed to it in broader terms than that associated with a definition of schooling as the agency through which individuals are allocated to the labour force.

The problem of the entanglement of analysis with value assumptions is intrinsic to sociological study. To get it straight we must first distinguish the 'scientific' from the 'value' problem: to ask separately what is possible and thereby, with the issues and alternatives sharply defined, to decide on preferences and priorities. In this way the challenge to social science becomes clear and the task for the sociologist is, literally, to inform the political debate. Of course the distinction between sociology and politics is much less easy than a naive positivism would presuppose. It is necessary at every step to try to make explicit what are the implicit assumptions of political aims and the value premises of sociological analysis. There is no final or ready-made procedure for either of these tasks. We have only imperfect aids beyond the injunction to constant vigilance.

One aid of particular relevance to our problem in this book can be taken from John Goldthorpe's discussion of futurology.[4] Goldthorpe distinguishes between futurology as *prediction* and futurology as *design*. Conventional futurology is essentially extrapolation to the future of trends from the recent past. It therefore tends to carry with it the value assumptions of the status quo and is in that sense conservative. That is why the book covers of this literature (*U.S.A. 2000*) are, as Raymond Aron has remarked, so much more exciting than the pages. The future is only the present, usually writ slightly larger. Futurology as *design* is quite another matter, and not only because it is inherently more radical in its political possibilities. It is scientifically much more challenging in that it directly requires the social scientist to state clearly what he knows or does not know about the possibility of moving from the present state to a postulated, presumably desired, future state.

Political aims and programmes in general and the aim of educational equality in particular, together with the various programmes for its attainment, lend themselves fairly readily to translation into futurology as design. The translation can be used to define the critical and constructive role of the social scientist, in this case with relation to the problems of educational reform through political and administrative action. And action-research, as we understand it, is an experimental or quasi-experimental version of futurology as design. Ends are stated together with means to their achievement. In this case the ends are greater social equality of educational opportunity and attainment and the means are Plowden's positive discrimination for educational priority areas. Ends and means are modified and explicated in a programme of action and the relation between them is analysed by research monitoring of the action programme.

A second and related aid to understanding the social science task is the Popperian distinction between holistic and piecemeal reform. The general arguments against holism cannot be rehearsed here. What is relevant however is not a debate over the dichotomy but over the appropriate scale of the piecemeal. It is not so much a question of whether education can change society: it is a question of the level of ambitiousness of social engineering which may be required to change an undesired state of affairs. The Plowden analysis of low educational standards in EPAs points to causes outside the school in the neighbourhood structure of life and therefore calls for a widely based programme of social reform alongside positive discrimination in education. Within this framework Plowden postulates that 'what these deprived areas need most are perfectly normal, good primary schools.' There is in other words a belief here in educational cures for educational evils. Some of the early American compensatory education programmes seem to have gone much further and approached the belief that poverty can be completely abolished through educational reform. Others take an opposing and more radical view of the changes necessary to ameliorate either poverty in general or educational poverty in particular. K. Coates and R. Silburn have expressed this view in a recent comment on the Plowden ideas.[5]

> the schools themselves could become, to a degree, centres of social regeneration: growth points of a new social consciousness among the poor, which might at last bring poverty under attack from its sufferers no less than from the all-too-small battalions of liberal welfare workers and social administrators.

Obviously many of these are sensible aims. Yet it is important at the same time to state baldly what these aims could *not* achieve. Education, in itself, will not solve the problem of poverty. The social structure that generates poverty generates its own shabby education system to serve it; and while it is useful to attack the symptom, the disease itself will continually find new manifestations if it is not understood and remedied. The solution to poverty involves, of course, the redistribution of effective social power. Self-confidence, no less than material welfare, is a crucial lack of the poor, and both can only be won by effective joint action. More contentiously, it seems to us that educational provision alone cannot solve even the problem of educational poverty, if only because in this sphere there are *no* purely educational problems.

Our own view in undertaking the EPA action-research was cautiously open-minded on the capacity of the educational system to reform itself, dubious about an educational approach to the abolition of poverty, but at least as optimistic as Plowden about the primary school and pre-schooling as points of entry for action-research aimed at inducing changes in the relation between school and community.

In principle action-research can approach the holistic end of the continuum. In practice it usually operates at the other extreme though often with implicit holistic expectations of the kind reflected in the early euphoria and rhetoric of the American Headstart programme. Perhaps it is mainly the confused contradiction between astronomical ends and minuscule means that underlies the asperity of such criticisms as Bernstein's 'education cannot compensate for society'. We have to know what is sociologically and politically possible. In part the answer to both questions turns on the willingness and power of a society to define education imperiously in relation to the other social organisations which carry educative or culturally transmitting functions, especially the family but also classes, neighbourhoods, ethnic groups and local communities. This depends again in part on economic and technical means. Obviously the feasibility of education as the dominant means to a particular social design is eased by wealth and growth, but the crucial factor here is political—the political structure and the will of political leadership.

Perhaps the importance of the economic and technical base for educational development is exaggerated. There are conspicuous variations in the level of educational development between countries of similar income and wealth per capita. And the remarkably durable success of classical China in using her educational system to create and maintain a ruling administrative class of mandarins was, it should be remembered, the invention of a pre-industrial society. Perhaps also the serviceability of education as an agent of social selection and distribution is exaggerated until one examines the evidence: for example it was shown in the Robbins Report that two-thirds of *middle-class* children with IQs of 130+ who were born in 1940–41 did not go on to a university education. Nevertheless it still remains a crucial question as to how seriously a society determines to realise the values in which the use of the educational system as a means is involved. That is the crux of the problem of educational inequality and the ultimate determinant of whether or not Plowden's positive discrimination will bring about its intended effects.

What, then, are the sought ends in the politics of education in modern Britain? The dominant slogans are combinations of efficiency and equality. Efficiency for modernity. Equality for efficiency and justice. But both the meaning of these combined ends and the means postulated as adequate to their attainment remain dubious and confused. Thus the combination of equality of educational opportunity with the goal of national efficiency has led to policies designed to create and maintain a meritocracy—a principle which by no means commands universal acceptance.

However the essential fact of twentieth-century educational history is that egalitarian policies have failed. This must be the starting point for understanding the significance of our studies and to reach it we must review past principles and policies. There appears to us to have been a developing theoretical and practical debate in three stages about the way education can be used as a means towards the political and social end of equality.

In the first phase, from the beginning of the century to the end of the 1950s, the definition of policy was liberal—equality of opportunity. It meant equality of access to the more advanced stages of education for all children irrespective of their sex or social origin in classes, religious and ethnic groups or regions. It therefore expressed itself in such measures as building the scholarship ladder, abolishing grammar school fees, doing away with a system of separate secondary education for the minority and elementary education for the majority and substituting a system of common schooling with secondary schools 'end-on' to primary schools. In the later years of this phase it also meant expansion of higher education.

The logical end of the first phase, when equality of opportunity is combined with national efficiency, is meritocracy. In its most advanced educational expression this essentially liberal principle is to be found in the Preface to the Newsom Report written by the then Minister for Education, Sir Edward (later Lord) Boyle: 'The essential point is that all children should have an equal opportunity of acquiring intelligence, and of developing their talents and abilities to the full.' But the inexactitudes of psychometrics, the capriciousness of late developers, the survival of the private market in education along with the continuous renewal of non-educational avenues to higher social positions—all these factors together have prevented the emergence of an educationally based meritocracy.

The liberal notion of equality of opportunity dominated discussion at least until the 1950s. But it was never unchallenged by those who wrote in the tradition of R. H. Tawney and it was effectively lampooned in Michael Young's *Rise of the Meritocracy*. Writers like Tawney and Raymond Williams[6] always sought for an educational system which would be egalitarian in the much broader sense of providing a common culture irrespective of the more or less inescapable function of selection for different occupational destinies. There is a broad distinction of political and social aims here which, in the end, come to the most fundamental issue of the purposes of education in an urban industrial society and about which judgements are explicitly or implicitly made in any action-research programme of the type we have undertaken. One way of putting the distinction is that the liberal goal of efficient equality of opportunity is too restrictive: we have also to consider liberty and fraternity. Properly conceived the community school, an idea which we discuss in detail below, reflects the attribution of value to these other two great abstractions of the modern trilogy of political aims.

All this is to say nothing about the problem of feasibility of either narrowly or broadly conceived egalitarian aims. Tawney took it for granted that the processes of parliamentary democracy, serviced by the British type of civil administration, would be adequate as means to these ends. There is less confidence now and much more questioning as to what it might mean politically to achieve what Coates and Silburn have referred to as 'the redistribution of effective social power'. Questioning of this kind comes from many sources, but not least from recognition of the failures of past policies directed towards a greater equality of educational opportunity.

The essential judgement must be that the 'liberal' policies failed even in their own terms. For example, when, in a large number of the richer countries during the 1950s, a considerable expansion of educational facilities was envisaged, it was more or less assumed that, by making more facilities available, there would be a marked change in the social composition of student bodies and in the flow of people from the less favoured classes into the secondary schools and higher educational institutions. This has certainly not happened to the degree expected. While expansion of education was accompanied by some increase in both the absolute numbers and the proportions from poor families who reached the higher levels and the more prestigious types of education, nevertheless progress towards greater equality of educational opportunity as traditionally defined has been disappointing. It is now plain that the problem is more difficult than had been supposed and needs, in fact, to be posed in new terms.[7]

Too much has been claimed for the power of educational systems as instruments for the wholesale reform of societies which are characteristically hierarchical in their distribution of chances in life as between races, classes, the sexes and as between metro-politan/suburban and provincial/rural populations. The typical history of educational expansion in the 1950s and 1960s can be represented by a graph of inequality of attainment between the above-mentioned social categories which has shifted markedly upwards without changing its slope. In other words, relative chances did not alter materially despite expansion. No doubt, the higher norms of educational attainment contributed something towards raising the quality of life in urban industrial society—that, at least, is the faith of the educationist. But in terms of relative chances of income, status and welfare at birth, the impact of the educational system on the life of children remained heavily determined by their family and class origins. From the same point of view, what appears to have happened was a general adjust-ment of the occupational structure such that entry to it was in process of continuous upward redefinition in terms of educational qualifications. The traditional social pattern of selection remained remarkably stable. The school is only one influence among others, and, in relation to the phenomenon of social stratification, probably a fairly minor one. Attitudes towards schooling, and actual performance in school, reflect children's general social milieu and family background, and, probably most important of all, the expectations, built in by constraining custom, of his teachers. School reform [helps but the improvement of teacher/ pupil ratios, the building of new schools and even the provision of a wider variety of curricula have at best a limited effect as counterweights.

Moreover there has been a tendency to treat education as the waste paper basket of social policy—a repository for dealing with social problems where solutions are uncertain or where there is disinclination to wrestle with them seriously. Such problems are prone to be dubbed 'educational' and turned over to the schools to solve. But it was now increasingly plain that the schools cannot accomplish important social reforms such as the democratisation of opportunity unless social reforms accompany the educational effort. And it also became more evident that the schools are hampered in achieving even their more traditional and strictly 'educational' purposes when, in societies changing rapidly in their technologies and in the aspirations of their populations, a comparable effort to make the required change in social structures and political organisation is lacking.

In summary, it may be said that liberal policies failed basically on an inadequate theory of learning. They failed to notice that the major determinants of educational attainment were not schoolmasters but social situations, not curriculum but motivation, not formal access to the school but support in the family and the community.

So the second phase began with its new emphasis on a theory of non-educational determination of education. In consequence of the experience of the first phase in trying to bring about greater equality of educational opportunity, there had to be a change in the meaning assigned to the phase. Its earlier meaning was equality of access to education: in the second phase its meaning gradually became equality of achievement. In this new interpretation a society affords equality of educational opportunity if the proportion of people from different social, economic or ethnic categories at all levels and in all types of education are more or less the same as the proportion of these people in the population at large. In other words the goal should not be the liberal one of equality of access but equality of outcome for the median member of each identifiable non-educationally defined group, i.e. the *average* woman or Negro or proletarian or rural dweller should have the same level of educational attainment as the average male, white, white-collar, suburbanite. If not there has been injustice.

This important social-cum-educational principle, with its radical implications for both social and educational policies, was graphically illustrated in the findings of the American Coleman Report[8] where educational attainments were compared as between Northerners and Southerners of white and non-white race. Figure 1 shows that schooling between ages 6 and 18 (grades 1–12, in American schools) is associated with a divergence of the mean attainment of four categories of children who are not directly defined in educational terms.[9] The radical goal of educational equality of opportunity would, if realised, produce converging as opposed to diverging lines.

The Plowden Report belongs to this phase in the development of our understanding of the egalitarian issues in education and relates them to the social setting of the school.

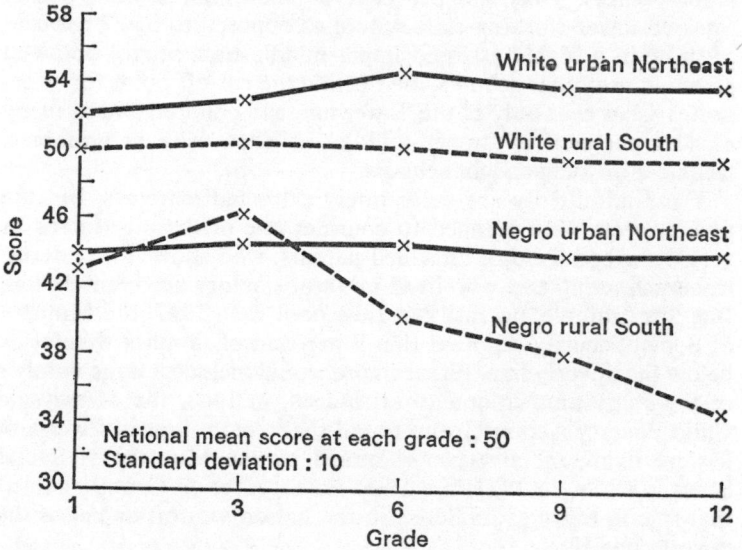

Figure 1 Patterns of achievement in verbal skills at various grade levels by race and region.

With Plowden the close relationship of social deprivation, in neighbourhood and home, and educational attainment was well founded in research. Equally valid is the corollary that, if social conditions and parental interest could be improved, achievement might be expected to rise. One or two examples must suffice. J. W. B. Douglas in 1964 set the attainment scores of a large sample of upper primary children against a number of social factors.[10] From this survey certain extreme cases might be extrapolated. At eleven years of age and with 50 as the average mark, lower manual working-class children in unsatisfactory housing were scoring on average 46·66 as against the 56·91 of upper-middle-class children in satisfactory accommodation; as between the same groups divided by low and high levels of parental interest the scores were 46·32 and 59·26; polarised by 'very disturbed' and 'undisturbed' assessments, the two groups averaged 44·49 and 57·53; while the seventh child of the lower bracket of parents obtained 42·19 over against the 59·87 of the first child in the higher social category. Eleven per cent of the lower manual group and 54·3 per cent of the upper middle group obtained grammar-school places. Only 4·8 per cent of the children in a poorly assessed lower-working-class school as opposed to 53·22 per cent of those in a highly assessed upper-middle-class school obtained places in grammar schools. Just below the cut-off point for selection, 1·4 per cent only of the 'lower manual' children and as many as 42·9 per cent of 'upper middle' children were in grammar, technical or independent schools.

These admittedly are deliberately extracted extremes, but the EPA projects were planned to consider one of these extremes. A very disturbed child of unskilled parents, who showed no interest in his schooling and who lived in unsatisfactory accommodation, was, for example, no rarity in Liverpool 7. In 1967, the Ministry of Social Security reported that 7 per cent of families were at or below the poverty line. Either figure would include a large number of the study area's population; indeed, in 1968, the Merseyside Child Poverty Action Group found that one in three in Liverpool 8 were living in poverty as defined by the Ministry of Social Security while, in 1971, the Child Poverty Action Group claimed that one in every six children in the nation was on or below the poverty line.[11]

Professor Wiseman argued convincingly that '"home" variables have, pro rata, twice the weight of "neighbourhood" and "school" variables put together' when correlated with educational attainment.[12] His research indicated that it was parental attitudes rather than social levels which were more important in the home. Again, the National Child Development Study showed that parents in the highest occupational grouping were much readier to initiate school contacts than those in the lowest grouping, and there was a similar social gap in terms of adjustment to school.[13] A recent examination of truancy suggests that gross absenteeism is solidly linked with unsatisfactory home life and uninterested parents.[14]

We are not here, it must be added, embracing the view that the pre-Plowden literature had overemphasised the part played by class in determining educational performance. On the contrary we agree with the sociological critique of the Plowden Report by B. Bernstein and B. Davies, in which they expressed the view that, by its concentration on child centredness, Plowden had underestimated class distinctions.[15] As these writers argue, 'evidence suggests a strong relationship between social class and the extent of the mother's preparation of her child for school' and that 'one would wish to guard against an argument that avoided including attitudes as a dimension of class differences.'

At all events, in reading the Plowden Report, one could hardly escape the view that equality of opportunity was, without equality of conditions, a sham. Home circumstances were obviously critical and these in turn were adversely affected by class and neighbourhood patterns. The school, where, after all, the children spent only five hours of the day, seemed comparatively powerless to alter matters radically of its own volition. Assuredly, a decision to consider the EPA school in its communal setting was a wise one, and the Plowden Committee had been well advised to recommend that community schools should be developed in all areas but especially in EPAs.

Our own definition of the problem in 1968 was consonant with the debate up to this point and was in accord with the Plowden approach accepting that positive discrimination held out the hope of further steps towards the new definition of equality of opportunity.

But in the early months of our work we began to realise that there were unsolved issues behind the equality debate even in its advanced formulation and especially when applied to the children of the educational priority areas. The debate could be taken beyond equality of educational opportunity to a third phase which involves reappraisal of the functions of education in contemporary society. Education for what? The debate over equality as we have summarised it—a movement from preoccupation with equality of access towards concern with equality of outcomes as between social groups—is essentially a discussion about education for whom and to do what. In planning our intervention in schools we were forced sooner or later to consider both questions and in doing so to question whether an EPA programme is anything more than a new formula for fair competition in the educational selection race.

What assumptions could or should be made about the world into which our EPA children would enter after school? Were we concerned simply to introduce a greater measure of justice into an educational system which traditionally selected the minority for higher education and upward social mobility out of the EPA district, leaving the majority to be taught, mainly by a huge hidden curriculum, a sense of their own relative incompetence and impotence—a modern, humane and even relatively enjoyed form of gentling the masses? Or could we assume a wide programme of social reform which would democratise local power structures and diversify local occupational opportunities so that society would look to its schools for a supply of young people educated for political and social responsibility and linked to their communities not by failure in the competition but by rich opportunities for work and life? Even short of the assumption of extra-educational reform how far should we concentrate on making recognition easier for the able minority and how far on the majority who are destined to live their lives in the EPA? And if the latter did this not mean posing an alternative curriculum realistically related to the EPA environment and designed to equip the rising generation with the knowledge and skills to cope with, give power over and in the end to transform the conditions of their local community?

It was, and is, commonly felt that a discriminatory boost was needed in the backward areas to bring education up to scratch so that, for instance, the thousands leaving school at fifteen who had the potential to benefit from advanced schooling might stay on. The Plowden Report argued this respectable and widely held thesis with admirable spirit. It detailed a programme of 'positive discrimination' and 'a new distribution of educational resources', through priority building and minor works, improved staffing and auxiliary help, supplemented salaries and so on. This was designed to cater for 'a great reservoir of unrealised potential', for 'what these deprived areas need most are perfectly normal good primary schools'. Twice over Plowden decreed that the EPA schools should be as good as the best in the land.[16]

Because the national system of education was seen not to operate efficiently in its uniform application across the country, it was accepted that a differential application would help close, to quote Plowden again, 'the gap between the educational opportunities of the most and least fortunate children . . . for economic and social reasons alike'. But, logically, an alternative existed. It was worth considering that what was wrong was a uniform system, and that differing areas required differing educational formats.

This viewpoint, Eric Midwinter insisted in our early conferences, does no disservice to the pioneers who campaigned for parity of opportunity. They doubtless imagined that equality of opportunity would beget conditions in which forthcoming generations would automatically start at par. This has not, unhappily, transpired. Those working in a deprived area are typically sympathetic to the egalitarian tradition and find the alarums and the postures of the anti-egalitarian commentators laughable.[17] They shout before they are hurt. One might recall the words of R. H. Tawney: of the nation's children, he wrote 'if, instead of rejuvenating the world, they grind corn for the Philistines and doff bobbins for the mill-owners, the responsibility is ours into whose hands the prodigality of nature pours life itself'.[18] Eventually an EPA community must stand on its own feet like any other and rejuvenate its world, and that is a dogma which might hold good on both political wings.

References

1 See *Notes Towards a Definition of Culture*.
2 *Education and Values*, Faber, 1965, especially chapter 7.
3 C. B. Cox and A. E. Dyson (eds), *Fight for Education*; T. E. B. Howarth, *Culture, Anarchy and the Public Schools*, Critical Quarterly Society, 1969.
4 J. Goldthorpe, 'Theories of industrial society: Reflections on the recrudescence of historicism and the future of futurology', *European Journal of Sociology*, vol. 12, 1972, pp. 263–88.
5 'Education in poverty' in David Rubinstein and Colin Stoneman (eds), *Education for Democracy*, Penguin Education Special, 1970.
6 See, for example, Raymond Williams, *Culture and Society*, Penguin, 1966; *The Long Revolution*, Penguin, 1965.

7 Cf. Charles Frankel's and A. H. Halsey's Introduction to *Educational Policies for the 1970s*, OECD, 1971, pp. 14ff.

8 James S. Coleman *et al.*, *Equality of Educational Opportunity*, US Government Printing Office, Washington D.C., 1966.

9 We found some evidence of similar patterns in our EPA schools (*Educational Priority*, vol. 1, chapter 5).

10 J. W. B. Douglas, *The Home and the School*, MacGibbon & Kee, 1964.

11 R. Boyson (ed.), *Down with the Poor*, CPAG, 1971.

12 S. Wiseman, 'The Manchester survey', App. IX, *Plowden Report*, ii.

13 1st Report of the National Child Development Study (1958 Cohort), April 1966, App. X, *Plowden Report*, ii, *Research and Surveys*, 1967.

14 M. J. Tyerman, *Truancy*, University of London Press, 1968.

15 B. Bernstein and B. Davies, 'Some sociological comments on Plowden', in R. S. Peters (ed.), *Perspectives on Plowden*, Routledge & Kegan Paul, 1969, pp. 58–77.

16 Plowden, *op. cit.*, ch. 5, especially paras 136–52 and 158–73.

17 For instance, C. B. Cox and A. E. Dyson (eds.), *op. cit.*

18 R. H. Tawney, *The Acquisitive Society*, Bell, 1921, republished 1961 (Fontana), p. 81.

Introduction to Section 2

The distribution of education resources

Who gets what in education and where they have to live to get it is a neglected topic of educational and political enquiry. And yet it is clear that there are variations, often wide, in resources allocated to education in different regions of the country and between different authorities, and that this affects the educational achievement of the children in schools.

Education is the largest of the services administered by local government and is therefore subject to party political conflict at its sharpest.

In a general study of local authority services, Boaden (2.1) found that the total level of education spending correlated most highly with 'need' (in terms of the school-age population) and with council 'disposition' (in terms of party politics), Labour councils spending more whatever the context of need. Boaden suggests that since state school provision extends across class boundaries, the social class composition of an authority is more important in determining the *direction* of spending (for example, the decision to go comprehensive) than the overall *level* of spending.

The article by Reddin (2.2) provides a simple example of variation in resource distribution. Educational maintenance allowances are intended to help children from poor families stay on at school. However, the award system works in such a way that not only are the 'working poor' unlikely to qualify, but also the disparities in how much, and to whom money is given, suggest that LEA policy is at least as important a deciding factor as the resources available.

Despite Boaden's claim (2.1) that resources have 'little independent effect on the level of educational spending', the fact remains that LEAs do not possess equality of wealth in relation to need. Taylor (2.3) describes the vicious circle in the North between deteriorating economy, inadequate educational resources, and low educational attainment, and argues that redistribution of central government aid is fundamental to the achievement of equality of educational opportunity.

Byrne and Williamson (2.4) demonstrate a positive relationship between LEA policy and educational attainment in a case study of eleven urban LEAs in the North-east. Their evidence indicates that two policy models may be appropriate, viz. the elite-orientated or the egalitarian authority model, and that (cf. Boaden 2.1) the social class composition of an LEA determines the type of policy that is pursued.

2.1 Local authorities and education

Noel Boaden

Among the many services provided by local authorities, education is perhaps the most important. Certainly in terms of resources devoted to the service it is outstanding, both in terms of capital and revenue account. This financial significance shows no sign of diminishing, and the recent trend has been towards an increase. The increasing expectations of parents for their children, and of educationists and politicians generally, seem likely to maintain this growth into the future as well, though other pressures are very apparent. This is not different in principle from the position in other services but is more significant in an area where the level of expenditure is already somewhat disproportionately high. The significance of education, however, goes far beyond its financial implications. The full utilisation of our individual talent and the collective development of many aspects of our national life depend in large measure on the quantity and quality of the education provided by local authorities. It is this fact which lies at the core of pressures to centralise and create uniform standards and which has given rise to the numerous reforming reports on the educational system. That many of the recommendations in such reports are not implemented reflects in part the existing financial pressures and the cost implications of the reforms.

In spite of this widely accepted view of the importance of education, and in spite of a legislative framework which gives the Secretary of State a close controlling role,[1] the variety of educational provision among local authorities remains substantial. The range of per capita expenditure is very wide, and in one particular policy area, that of secondary reorganisation, the local authorities reveal dramatic differences. The figures for 1967 reveal that more than half of the county boroughs had no thirteen-year-olds in

Source: Noel Boaden, *Urban Policy-Making: Influences on County Boroughs in England and Wales*, Cambridge University Press (1971), 45–58.

such schools and the range among the remainder was from 95·0 per cent to 0·1 per cent. This variation was accentuated by the rather polarised distribution among these county boroughs. Similar variation may also be seen in other aspects of the educational system, and is most overtly recognised in the designation of educational priority areas by the Department of Education. This policy acknowledges the relative inadequacy of certain areas within certain authorities, and by so doing suggests obvious differences between authorities in terms of the problems faced, or in terms of the techniques used to deal with them, or both. Areas within authorities vary, but by implication, so do authorities. . . . The traditionalist who argues the strength of central control over local authorities has to explain this variation in terms of central decisions either to foster variety, or at least to permit it. The alternative explanation, which seems more probable, is that the centre cannot exercise such tight control over the localities in respect of some features of educational policy, and that consequently local factors have considerable impact on those policy areas. . . .

Thus it is most obvious that different education authorities are faced with different school populations, certainly in proportionate terms, and this must be a cardinal indicator of need. The number of children aged between five and fifteen does vary from place to place, and the compulsory nature of the educational service ensures that such differences will be translated into the policy process, at least in overall terms. . . . But while the age structure of the population creates an obvious need, it is less obvious which other features will be so directly relevant to the overall sense. In addition to its broad age basis, the service provides for the bulk of the school-age population, thus cutting across a number of major lines of cleavage which might be important. As a result the social composition of an authority will have less effect on overall spending. It may have greater consequences for the direction in which funds are spent and this may have further financial repercussions. Especially is this the case where grammar-school and sixth form places are much more costly than other forms of provision. Some kinds of school do cater disproportionately for some sections of the population and we will examine one of these later. The important point here is that the bulk of the education budget does not go on such schools and that the impact of this characteristic of the population may not, therefore, show in overall spending.

But these comments derive from viewing the education service as a personal one in terms of classification on the basis of need. ... There is [also] a distinct physical aspect to be considered, both in its own right but also as strongly reinforcing many of the more direct population pressures on the service. This dual impact is most obviously produced by the extent of physical school provision and its adequacy, and by the general condition of such facilities. The physical upheaval of urban-renewal programmes is one powerful factor in this connection. The pressure for new school buildings can be a major influence, particularly as there is usually no available alternative, however inadequate, where people are resettled. Even more obvious is the need created by crowded and dilapidated schools. The implications for school building are obvious, but there are innumerable related teaching and social problems which fall on the education authority. These may take the form of extended education welfare services, or of ancillary provision to create positive discrimination in favour of such schools. All of these are relevant but all are difficult to evaluate and to measure. Inevitably this makes them difficult to incorporate in our analysis and they will only receive passing attention. They would, however, merit detailed consideration elsewhere.

If needs are important, in any of the ways outlined, so too may disposition be important in an area where expenditure is heavy and issues often highly controversial. This is certainly true in party political terms, this being one of the few services in which party conflict is widely acknowledged.[2] It may be objected that the compulsory nature of the service reduces local autonomy and that this seriously dilutes party differences. However, the variation in expenditure which has been shown suggests that this is rather an hypothesis to be tested than an established fact. Certainly party appears to have influenced one major piece of educational policy-making in terms of secondary reorganisation. The government circular 10/65 allowed a good deal of discretion to local education authorities about both the timing and the content of their reorganisation plans. Party control has been shown to be a very relevant factor in determining local reactions in this field, at least in terms of the submission of plans.[3] In fact the whole notion of a partnership between central government and local authorities in education implies local autonomy around which party might be important.

Given this, one might expect political differences to show

themselves in a number of ways. The scale of education spending and its impact on the overall scope of government suggest one basic difference. If our earlier point about Labour councils favouring government action is correct, then this should show in a greater commitment to a major service like education. They would be less interested in trimming the service to 'essentials'. This would be reinforced by other aspects of disposition. One might expect Labour councils to favour provision for the underprivileged sections of the community. In terms of need the source could become most significant in political terms, as is clear in the social arguments in favour of comprehensive schools. Not that all Labour authorities agree over how to help the disadvantaged, many favouring extended opportunities for grammar-school entry.[4] Similar arguments could be extended to other aspects of education, including ancillaries like school meals and medical services. These latter are rather marginal to this expensive service, but commitment to the lower-class sector has substantial overall cost implications. In the broadest sense it would involve spending in those parts of the service which cater for the majority of the school-age population, elite segments being only small in numbers.

This party distinction may thus be very indicative of collective councillor dispositions. Official and public attitudes are less easily summarised. Available evidence suggests that public knowledge of this service is low, though this is true of most services. It also shows that very few people involve themselves with the service in terms of enquiries or complaints.[5] This could be construed as reflecting a lack of interest in this sphere of local government action, but other information opens up other possibilities. Educational items do not occupy very prominent news positions and popular attitudes may be a reflection of the complexity of the service or the opacity of policy and decision processes.[6] In any event it is more surprising in a sphere where very severe rate implications might have been expected to generalise interest beyond the direct consumers of the service.

This individual lack of information and involvement may itself account for the emergence in recent years of a number of organisations concerned with educational problems. They have been concerned both to mobilise the public more fully and to press for certain kinds of policy. The Confederation for the Advancement of State Education and the Advisory Centre for

Education are two of the most firmly established. They do not seem to have been unduly successful but this probably reflects the very general nature of their aims. Organisations with more limited aims have been more successful. The Comprehensive Schools Committee, campaigning for that form of secondary school organisation, has been reasonably successful, though this may largely be due to the general tide of opinion flowing their way on that issue.

More interesting and important in general terms is the opposition to such reorganisation mounted in many localities, but most impressively in the London Borough of Enfield. A group of parents undertook a wide series of actions culminating in a High Court conflict with the Secretary of State for Education. Though they failed to prevent the move to comprehensives in the ultimate their campaign illustrates a number of important features. Obviously this will be a rare form of activity and will require people with high skills and resources, both of which were available in this case. At the same time, they operate most successfully on issues where opinion is divided and where procedures are complicated and opportunities for action frequent. Above all, this case would demonstrate the greater ease of preventive or delaying action compared with any positive efforts which might be called for. Local authority innovation has not been the subject of close scrutiny, but the inertia and caution of local councils is often noted and probably makes external pressure for innovation very difficult.

The pattern of relationships between the variables which have been outlined and per capita spending on education is shown in Table 1. This shows only the simple relationships between the variables, but a number of features become clear at once. In very broad terms the table gives support to the relationship between spending and needs, dispositions and resources which has been suggested.

The most obvious relationship in the table, coinciding with our expectation, is that between spending and the school-age population taken as a measure of need. This probably reflects the significance of the school sector in the total education service and the fact that this is the compulsory aspect of local education. This can have important implications for other aspects of the service, as is now being shown in the application of economies by education authorities which are primarily affecting further education, especially the non-vocational sectors. The other general indicator of need, social class composition, also shows a close relationship with spending. This suggests that social composition may have a greater and more general impact than we had suggested. Again this is a relationship with most significant implications.

These implications are mainly related to the other features connected with this kind of social composition. The incidence of other needs is likely to be greater in lower-class authorities, as we shall see, but above all they seem certain to have less resources with which to meet their needs. This is confirmed by our indicators of local resources which show that it is the poor authorities who spend most, despite their relative poverty. The somewhat contradictory nature of this relationship, like that with class, has special importance because of the great cost of education. An authority can only spend within its global budget and what it spends on education cannot go on other services. Central contributions obviously help poor authorities to discharge their heavy obligations, but still education decisions will have repercussions on other services. The relative significance of central finance will be taken up later.

Before looking more closely at the relationships just outlined, the strong correlation between disposition and spending must be emphasised. Labour councils do spend more than Conservative councils, indicating a much wider relationship between party and education than is usually observed. It is usually accepted that party control is related to specific educational questions like comprehensivisation, but not to the overall level of activity of the education authority. This narrower view of the relevance of party is probably a product of the tendency to focus on areas of public controversy and cleavage, effectively excluding much of the educational service. The relationship shown here indicates the significance of party control, which is ignored in most writing on the subject. While education may have a very professional element it is also related to party influence, reflecting the divergent values of the two parties.

Though it is not easy to take them into account, the table shows several relationships aimed at reflecting the impact of the bureaucracy and of the public. The significance of need would seem to imply an elaborate role for officers because of their technical preoccupation with such legal factors. The same would be true of the fact that education seems to flourish even where resources are scarce. If local authority departments do compete for resources, and this is most likely in the poorest areas, then education seems to do well, reflecting high performance by its officials as well as the parties.

Table 1 Simple correlations between per capita education spending and selected indicators of need, disposition and resources

Indicator	Correlation
Need	
Total population	0·074
Per cent of population aged 5–14	0·630
Per cent of population in social classes I & II	—0·462
Per cent of population in social classes IV & V	0·420
Disposition	
Councillors	
Per cent Labour membership on council	0·522
Public	
Per cent turn-out in local elections 1964	—0·038
Per cent turn-out in local elections 1965	—0·201
Officials	
Number of committees	0·069
Number of sub-committees	—0·080
Employment of an O and M officer	—0·047
Resources	
Rate levied	0·493
Per capita rateable value	—0·269
Level of rate deficiency grant	0·319

However acceptable at the intuitive level, these features are not reflected in the figures used in Table 1. Several indicators of officer autonomy fail to show any marked relationship. While this may invalidate the point just made, it should be interpreted cautiously as the figures are for the authority as a whole and not just for education. Thus to the extent that they imply bureaucratic influence, they do so for all departments alike. This means that the true impact of education officials may be lost in a combined figure reflecting the varied degree of official competence in different departments.

The same is true of the voting turn-out figures used to indicate public involvement. They probably reflect overall and rather unspecific tendencies which may only incidentally affect education. In any event they show only a very low order of relationship which is not surprising given many previous findings on public awareness of, and interest in, services generally. More precise indicators of group mobilisation and activity might of course reveal relationships with spending, but they are difficult to acquire on a reliable basis.

These simple correlations, however, reflect relationships which call for much closer examination. The relationship with party may be no more than a product of the fact that Labour councils tend to control working-class districts, and class may be the operative factor. Equally, the relationship between class composition and age structure raises the question of whether spending responds to class pressures or is really a result of the numerical pressure of a given school-age population. In the same way, lack of local resources is itself related to low social class composition with consequent problems in interpreting the relationship with local resources. These interrelationships are examined more fully in Tables 2 and 3 which show partial correlations between the main

Table 2 Partial correlations between per capita education spending and selected indicators of need, disposition and resources

		Controlling for				
Effect of	*Age 5–14*	*Class IV & V*	*Labour*	*Rate*	*Grant*	*Value*
Age 5–14	0·630	0·518	0·481	0·625	0·580	0·592
Class IV & V	0·024	0·420	0·084	0·324	0·310	0·339
Labour	0·271	0·351	0·522	0·390	0·450	0·466
Rate	0·484	0·421	0·343	0·493	0·419	0·437
Grant	0·111	0·118	0·123	0·147	0·319	0·181
Value	0·031	—0·056	—0·048	—0·092	—0·030	—0·269

variables involved. These indicate the degree to which any one of our factors retains its relationship with educational spending independently of each of the others.

Table 3 Partial correlations between per capita education spending and selected indicators of need, disposition and resources

Effect of	Controlling for					
	Age 5–14 & Class IV & V	Age 5–14 Labour	Age 5–14 Grant	Class IV & V & Labour	Class IV & V & Grant	Labour & Grant
Age 5–14				0·495	0·517	0·470
Class IV & V		—0·156	—0·025			0·041
Labour	0·309		0·251		0·345	
Grant	0·111	0·037		0·099		

These partial correlations immediately answer a number of the questions just raised. Most obvious, but most significant, is the fact of need. Given a population structure in which the younger age groups are represented disproportionately, there will be greater spending on schools. This will apply whatever the class composition, party structure or level of resources in the area—that is, whatever the dispositions and resources. This seems to be a product of the compulsory nature of the service which automatically converts the needs of the locality into effective demands for educational spending. While this is relatively obvious it raises a number of questions in an acute form. If the effect of need is felt irrespective of local resource levels, what are the implications for other services of the resultant shortage of resources? What variation might one expect in those areas of the education service which are non-compulsory (was it this factor which directed local attention to those aspects when cuts were called for)? Whatever the answers to such questions, the nature of the legislation appears to restrict local decisional autonomy to a degree. Though these are reasonably obvious facets of the education service, their implications for other services are significant. No other service is so clearly obligatory, and certainly none is as expensive, creating obvious scope for local initiatives.

From the tables it appears that the other indicator of need, class composition, does not exercise an independent effect. Its independent effect when local resources are controlled suggests that it may then be reflecting age structure or party control, both of which are closely related to class composition. This lack of independent effect would reflect our earlier expectation and confirms the fact that state school provision extends across class boundaries, particularly when the primary sector is included. Thus it seems that class has little effect on the total level of educational spending, though we shall later have call to look more closely at its particular effects.

Need, then, is the most obvious factor related to educational spending. In keeping with our model, however, and in spite of its compulsion, it does not operate alone. Disposition, conceived in party terms, is also related although the relationship is not so strong. Labour councils spend more whatever the context of need in which they find themselves, confirming their general orientation to government activity and to education in particular.

Finally, what do the tables tell us about the effect of local resources on this most expensive service? Using the level of rate deficiency grant as indicative of local resources, it is clear that this factor has little independent effect on the level of educational spending. Where need is present it will have to be met and resources must be found. Similarly, Labour councils, being disposed to spend on schools, are willing to find resources whatever their financial standing. This confirms the serious implications of this service for the pattern of service provided in other areas. It does not invalidate the resource element in our model but makes it more relevant in the wider context of the overall pattern of services. One would expect resources to impinge more directly on other services.

Thus we have a service in which needs and disposition produce a pressure for provision with resources automatically being channelled for this purpose. This suggests that finance may well be less salient to the setting of policies in this field despite its very considerable expense. Many decisions will in any case have only a marginal effect on the overall budget, unlike services where the same scale of item might have dramatic effect.

Two problems might now be raised. One concerns the relative efficiency with which funds are spent, though it has already been suggested that overall spending may be taken as a broad assessment of policy, allowing for variation in efficiency. In any event this is a difficult question which raises complex problems of educational values beyond the scope of the present enquiry. The other question is more amenable to discussion here and is concerned with the way in which educational spending is directed. Some aspects of spending are fairly directly controlled from outside, as has already been observed, but others might be considered. One important condition is that they must be rather broad policy matters if they are to be amenable to analysis with the kinds of variables being used here.[7]

One such area, though it is now becoming obscured by the move towards comprehensive schools, is the relative development of grammar schools in different localities. ... Taking the year 1965-6 as the observation period, which avoids the complication of increased comprehensivisation, the variation in percentage of grammar-school places was from almost 40 per cent to between 12 and 13 per cent. Given the permanent implications of their secondary education for most people's lives and the low level of later transfer to equivalent academic opportunities, this is a substantial difference and reveals an area of great local significance.

Once again, as with overall spending, one would expect a relationship between this figure and the age structure, though it may be the reverse of the earlier relationship. Grammar schools, even where most developed, never cater for even half of the secondary school population, and might depend for their development on the general impact of the remainder of the school system. Where there are large numbers of children to be catered for the grammar segment may be neglected somewhat. But whatever the overall implication of age structure it seems reasonable to assume that the class composition will be relevant in this case and constitute a clear need. Analysis of grammar-school intakes reveals the high degree to which they recruit from the middle class. Thus, given the basis of the current selection procedures and the broad wishes of parents from different classes, it is reasonable to expect that a larger middle-class population will create a need for more grammar schools.

Disposition on this factor also seems likely to be the reverse of that for education generally. Comment has already been made on the ambivalence displayed within the Labour Party towards grammar schools.[8] In spite of this, one would expect Labour councils to be less favourably disposed than Conservative ones; indeed some of the Labour spur towards comprehensive schools arises out of the differential grammar-school provision which we are discussing. In fact much of the divergence of Labour views at the local level may relate only to certain areas in which the grammar schools have been developed by the Labour council, with a consequent attachment to them and a wish to see them preserved. These are likely to be special cases, however, and one expects to find that Labour councils have developed the modern and technical schools more fully.

In terms of resources, one would not expect grammar provision to depend on the level of local resources. However large the provision of grammar-school places, they form only a small part of total spending. It may be that priorities within the overall pattern of education are significant, especially when cuts or extensions are being proposed, but for normal purposes this is less significant. Even if resources are not relevant, however, it seems likely that wealthy authorities will be more likely to have more grammar-school places because of the relation between the needs factors already discussed and the bases of local wealth.

As in the more general case, Table 4 shows the simple relationships between these selected variables and the number of grammar-school places. Before commenting on these, one other important point demands comment. This is the inverse relationship between the general educational spending and grammar-school provision $(r-0.148)$. Those factors related to high overall spending are inversely related to grammar provision, with the exception of the level of resources. This is possibly explained by the point, mentioned earlier, that pressures for basic spending allow few resources for use in special areas of narrow provision. More alarmingly, it indicates that those authorities who spend relatively little on education devote more of that spending to their grammar schools (assuming that more places do cost more to provide). The implications of this for secondary modern schools in such localities may be worth investigating. This relationship is somewhat akin to the recent case in which the government has diverted additional resources to selected areas within various local authorities, raising a number of questions about the previous allocations made by the local authorities themselves. In the same way that certain geographical sub-areas may be receiving disproportionately low allocations, so also may certain sections of the population, though the two are closely related in many cases.

Turning to the relationships in the table, they generally confirm the expectations just outlined. High social class composition and the presence of a low Labour percentage on the council do

Table 4 Simple correlations between per cent of thirteen-year-olds in grammar schools and selected indicators of need, disposition and resources

Indicator	Correlation
Need	
Population size	—0·119
Per cent of population aged 5–14	—0·254
Per cent of population in social classes I & II	0·302
Per cent of population in social classes IV & V	—0·212
Disposition	
Councillors	
Per cent Labour membership on council	—0·180
Public	
Per cent turn-out in local elections 1964	0·310
Per cent turn-out in local elections 1965	0·254
Officials	
Number of committees	0·310
Number of sub-committees	0·077
Employment of an O and M officer	0·105
Resources	
Rate levied	0·153
Level of rate deficiency grant	0·106
Per cent of rateable value high domestic properties	0·196

coincide with higher provision of grammar-school places. There is also the expected inverse relationship with the size of the school-age population, and the lowest order of relationship is with the index of local resources, though surprisingly the poorer authorities show a positive relation with grammar-school provision. This is the most problematic of the relationships, particularly as it conflicts in direction with that for social class composition, which would normally be inversely related to it. The explanation for this position may lie in the very low order of the relationship, but in any event should be clarified by the use of the partialling technique adopted in the earlier case. This will also serve as a check on the independence of the other relationships which is again confused by the interrelation among the independent variables.

Again, as in the general case, our measures of officer impact show virtually no relationship. This is not very surprising as this case is even more specific than the earlier one, with the indicators less valuable as a result. While this need not necessarily mean that officers are unimportant, it renders the question somewhat academic here.

The indicators of public disposition are more closely related and may repay further investigation. Electoral turn-out, though a feature related to social class, shows a relationship with grammar-school places. The literature on electoral behaviour suggests that causal relationships between turn-out and policy may be difficult to establish, but here we have some *prima facie* evidence for such a relationship in one part of a service. It will be interesting to see whether this maintains its relationship when other variables are taken into account.

Table 5   Partial correlations between per cent of thirteen-year-olds in grammar schools and selected indicators of need, disposition and resources

	Controlling for				
Effect of	*Age 5–14*	*Class I & II*	*Labour*	*Grant*	*Turn-out 1965*
Age 5–14	—0·254	—0·087	—0·189	—0·320	—0·198
Class I & II	0·190	0·302	0·262	0·388	0·221
Labour	—0·050	0·091	—0·180	—0·255	—0·097
Grant	0·226	0·275	0·206	0·106	0·115
Turn-out 1965	0·198	0·145	0·206	0·258	0·254

The partial correlations in Table 5 at once clarify the range of factors associated with this dependent variable. In the first place, the class factor maintains its association when the other variables are controlled. In particular when the negative factor or a large school population is withdrawn, class shows an even stronger relationship. This indicates the potential of a clear need in determining service levels where there are no strong competing needs to leave scope for disposition or resources to become influential. Obvious needs can be met without the problem of having to resolve competing priorities.

Disposition is more interesting here than it was in the earlier, more general case. Party does not show a very strong independent relationship with the number of grammar-school places. However, it is invariably a negative correlation showing the Conservative preference for grammar-school provision. Effectively, however, councillor disposition does not appear to be very prominent in this case. On the other hand, turn-out in local elections is consistently related to this dependent variable. This remains true when the other factors are controlled, though it is least marked where the control is for social class. No doubt this reflects the close relationship between class composition and electoral turn-out. While it is necessary to exercise care with this relationship, because turn-out is not a precise indicator of public disposition, it gives added support to the idea of public impact. If, as one would expect, electoral activity coincides with other activity in voluntary associations and the like, our findings would seem to be accurate. The actual influence process need not be electoral, of course, but examination of this more detailed problem is beyond the scope of our analysis.

Finally, resources show the opposite relationship to that which was hypothesised, though they were not given great emphasis in our analysis of a relatively cheap area of provision. The tables show that the poorer authorities provide more grammar-school places, particularly when the other variables are controlled. This relationship is most difficult to interpret as it seems most unlikely that the lack of resources causes this activity. It will clearly not prevent such provision of grammar schools, but it is likely that some other factor is at work in this case.

This relationship of grammar-school provision to a number of local factors is very important, though it relates to an educational form which is being superseded. This could make the question of comprehensivisation of much greater significance, partly because it is so important for the future of the educational system, and partly because it is such a clear-cut example of local policy-making. A detailed analysis will not be included here, however, as a number of case studies of the issue have been undertaken and a comparative study in some detail is now in preparation.[9] In addition, an analysis of submission of reorganisation plans has been done using the same analytical scheme as is being used here.[10]

The results of that study are probably worth summarising, however, as they give strong support to the general scheme. Submission of plans for secondary reorganisation was positively related to Labour Party control of the council. It was also related to the social composition of the local population, middle-class areas being less likely to submit plans, as one would expect. Resources showed little relation to submission, a product largely of the timing of the analysis (1966), which meant that this was a symbolic output for most local authorities. Activity on comprehensives is still not very apparent, as the recent Department of Education statistics show, and it may be that resources are very effective in terms of implementation of any plans.

Table 6 Partial correlations between per cent of thirteen-year-olds in grammar schools and selected indicators of need, disposition and resources

	Controlling for					
Effect of	*Age 5–14 & Class I & II*	*Age 5–14 & Labour*	*Age 5–14 & grant*	*Class I & II & Labour*	*Class I & II & grant*	*Labour & grant*
Age 5–14				—0·099	—0·136	—0·237
Class I & II		0·210	0·267			0·309
Labour	0·105		—0·122		0·049	
Grant	0·293	0·250		0·265		

There is no reason to pursue this topic further here as this summary is adequate for our immediate purposes, though it is an issue which should be investigated more closely. It is sufficiently clear that the patterns of relationship are similar for each of our dependent measures of educational activity. Obviously the very broad indicators being used mean that the most general dependent variable shows the closest relationship, and this is our major concern. More detailed factors could operate on particular aspects of the education service, though even in those our variables show considerable relationships. Certain broad features of party control, or disposition, of population character or need, and, to a more limited degree, of resources, do have a bearing on the extent and the direction of local educational activity. This is most significant in its own right, and receives added importance from the fact that this is a most expensive service, and may well affect the capacity for doing other things.

Notes

1 The Education Act 1944 says that the duty of the Secretary of State 'shall be to promote the education of the people of England and Wales and the progressive development of institutions devoted to that purpose, and to secure the effective execution by local authorities, under his control and direction, of the national policy for providing a varied and comprehensive educational service in every area'.

2 F. Bealey and D. J. Bartholomew, 'The local elections in Newcastle-under-Lyme, May 1968', *British Journal of Sociology*, 13, 3 and 4 (1962).

3 N. Boaden and R. R. Alford, 'Sources of diversity in English local government decisions', *Public Administration* (summer 1969).

4 For a review of the ambivalence shown by Labour politicians, see M. H. Parkinson, *The Labour Party and the Organization of Secondary Education, 1918–65* (London, 1970).

5 Maud Report, vol. 3, pp. 44, 50–51, 56.

6 *Ibid.*, pp. 26–7.

7 R. R. Alford, 'The comparative study of urban politics'.

8 M. H. Parkinson, *op. cit.*

9 R. Batley, H. Parris and O. O'Brien, *Going Comprehensive* (London, 1970).

10 Boaden and Alford, *op. cit.*

2.2 Which LEAs help children stay on at school?

Mike Reddin

The first step to doing something about education maintenance allowances, which are intended to help children in poor families to stay on at school, is to have some systematic information about the current level of awards. This is available for the first time now that some of the results of a Department of Education and Science study on EMAs, conducted early in 1971, have been published. The figures are set out in Table 1, showing for each local education authority in England and Wales the number of children getting awards, the percentage this represents of the potentially eligible pupils (those over the school-leaving age), and the average annual value of these payments. Finally, the authorities have been ranked according to the average value of the awards they have made. The figures show that twenty thousand pupils were getting awards on the date to which the census referred (December 1970). The average value of these awards was £72 a year and the average proportion of pupils benefiting was just under 4 per cent of the age group still in school. However, the averages conceal some very significant differences.

Wide variation between LEAs

Local authorities retain the right to pay such allowances at whatever level and on whatever terms they choose. As can be seen, they continue to exercise this dubious privilege of 'permissive variety'.

By following the ranking in the table, readers can see the wide variations in average payments. Thus at one extreme Burton-on-Trent is paying grants averaging £18 a year, while East Sussex pays £123. There's a similar disparity in the *proportion* of children getting grants. In West Suffolk 17 per cent of children over the

Source: *Where* (1972), 72, 250–2.

118

school-leaving age received EMAS, as against less than 0·5 per cent in Leicestershire and in Reading. The average value of EMAS in English county authorities was £68, in Welsh LEAS £52; in English boroughs £67, in the outer London boroughs £82 and for the ILEA £97.

Look behind the figures

But there are many more revealing characteristics behind these figures. For example, the ILEA comes well up the list of 'generosity' as measured by its average value award. But what sort of income does a family have in order to achieve an award at this average value of £97? A family with one sixteen-year-old child would receive this if its 'net' income was about £5 per week! (For gross income add on rent, tax and so on, to bring us up to, say, some £10.) How then do Londoners both stay alive and qualify for these awards? Presumably by not being in work.

Perhaps ironically, most LEAS view the unemployed man as 'poor', and getting social security benefits often means that an EMA at full value is granted to the family. Yet the same family, but with the father in full-time employment earning a wage at or about the same level as social security benefit, could (and the ILEA scales illustrate the point only too clearly) be entitled to no grant at all. Take the case of an unemployed man with a wife and child of sixteen. He would be entitled currently to supplementary benefit of £13·05p a week plus an allowance for rent and rates. If, however, the same income came from a wage packet, the recipient would have long forgone any EMA—in fact on the ILEA scales if his 'net' income passed £13·75p he would get no EMA even with five dependent children!

It must therefore be obvious that a very substantial proportion of awards must be going to non-wage-earners—the unemployed, the sick, or the families with only one parent who may not be able to go out to work. Otherwise one's poverty would need to be so grinding as to disappear beneath any conceivable rate of pay for the most menial of jobs. It would be quite easy to account for 99·5 per cent of the EMAS currently paid as a product of the current unemployment situation alone.

However, LEAS vary not only in their largesse in deciding the level of an EMA, but also in the number of children benefiting. Since in fact only very small sums are spent on EMAS in England

and Wales—an estimated £1·4 million on secondary school children in 1969/70 (compared with some £16 million on assistance with the cost of boarding education for pupils at independent and direct grant schools)—one might anticipate a pattern of either large average value awards to a few pupils or small awards to large numbers.

In fact there is no such simple pattern. Thus Durham makes awards with an average value of £94 to 14 per cent of its children, while Swansea offers £42 to 1 per cent. So obviously publicity, concern and deliberate decisions to be generous or mean will be and can be as significant as any variation in local wealth, poverty or unemployment. Certainly these figures on uptake tell us nothing about how many children are eligible for EMAS and fail to get them.

The poor don't qualify

It seems valid to conclude that these 'average award' figures may well, at this point in time, be atypically generous; that is, the number of children getting full value awards will be high as a result of their parent(s) being out of work, and receiving supplementary benefit. (It is interesting to note that the Supplementary Benefits Commission specifically disregards any income received from EMAS in the assessment of family income.) Consequently we may assume that awards made to the families and children of the working poor must be very low indeed to drag down the average to the levels shown and, if the ILEA figures are fairly typical (and my own research suggests they are not unrepresentative) *it is very unlikely that the working poor will qualify for benefit at all.*

Outdated levels of poverty

Certainly the old anomalies exist: wealth in EMA terms may mean incomes in excess of £10 a week. But in terms of university awards, such a level signifies 'poverty' and would qualify the applicant for a maximum value grant. Since EMAS were specifically designed to assist the poorer parents to keep their children at school (and thus presumably to have some chance at university entrance) it is ridiculous that the grants continue to exist as a gulf rather than a bridge between school and university. At least from the raising of the school leaving age family allowances will be extended for a further year to the benefit of that major group who now leave school at fifteen. But unless EMAs are also extended, and increased in value, many families are going to suffer badly financially, including those where the fifteen-year-old recipient will lose his EMA.

The 1957 Weaver Report recommended the rates of grant which were considered necessary. Today, updating those recommended values, we should be paying maxima of £130, £155 and £170 to fifteen- sixteen- and seventeen-year-olds respectively. But on the evidence of these figures we are not paying anything like as much to anything like as many of the children who need it.

Table 1 Spending on educational maintenance allowances: an LEA comparison[a]

For each local education authority we give here the number of pupils receiving EMAs (and the proportion this represents of pupils over school-leaving age), the average amount paid, and the LEA's place in the league table on average level of payment

Boroughs	Pupils		Payments	
Barnsley	52	(5·6%)	£64	62nd
Barrow	13	(1·5%)	£46	90th
Bath	32	(3·0%)	£65	59th
Birkenhead	23	(2·2%)	£69	47th
Birmingham	537	(4·1%)	£91	15th
Blackburn	28	(3·5%)	£79	32nd
Blackpool	30	(2·2%)	£80	30th
Bolton	83	(5·6%)	£78	34th
Bootle	37	(5·5%)	£66	55th
Bournemouth	100	(6·4%)	£59	75th
Bradford	109	(3·1%)	£78	34th
Brighton	87	(5·6%)	£86	23rd
Bristol	148	(2·9%)	£67	53rd
Burnley	34	(3·9%)	£68	50th
Burton-on-Trent	25	(3·0%)	£18	103rd
Bury	18	(4·0%)	£54	84th
Canterbury	21	(2·1%)	£72	42nd
Cardiff	70	(1·7%)	£49	88th
Carlisle	61	(6·5%)	£99	6th
Chester	10	(1·6%)	£100	5th
Coventry	66	(1·8%)	£41	95th
Darlington	56	(4·9%)	£97	9th

[a] Source: *Hansard*, vol. 836, col. 412: written answers to questions on 16 June 1972.

Table 1—*contd*

Boroughs	Pupils		Payments	
Derby	32	(1·8%)	£62	68th
Dewsbury	44	(8·7%)	£59	75th
Doncaster	54	(4·2%)	£64	62nd
Dudley	19	(1·2%)	£54	84th
Eastbourne	5	(0·9%)	£86	23rd
Exeter	21	(2·4%)	£58	78th
Gateshead	57	(7·3%)	£97	9th
Gloucester	56	(3·6%)	£64	62nd
Gt Yarmouth	77	(10·5%)	£64	62nd
Grimsby	44	(4·0%)	£66	55th
Halifax	58	(5·7%)	£66	55th
Hartlepool	89	(9·1%)	£96	11th
Hastings	32	(4·4%)	£96	11th
Huddersfield	32	(2·0%)	£67	53rd
Ipswich	101	(8·9%)	£71	43rd
Kingston (Hull)	302	(8·5%)	£59	75th
Leeds	469	(8·6%)	£51	87th
Leicester	68	(2·2%)	£63	67th
Lincoln	34	(3·3%)	£61	71st
Liverpool	534	(6·6%)	£28	100th
Luton	30	(1·6%)	£70	45th
Manchester	127	(2·0%)	£117	2nd
Merthyr Tydfil	28	(3·8%)	£21	102nd
Newcastle	310	(12·3%)	£84	26th
Newport (Mon)	31	(2·2%)	£49	88th
Northampton	18	(1·5%)	£45	91st
Norwich	86	(7·0%)	£58	78th
Nottingham	102	(3·4%)	£58	78th
Oldham	33	(4·2%)	£61	71st
Oxford	47	(4·0%)	£88	19th
Plymouth	67	(2·4%)	£41	95th
Portsmouth	136	(6·6%)	£83	28th
Preston	153	(14·1%)	£60	74th
Reading	7	(0·4%)	£61	71st
Rochdale	42	(3·8%)	£44	92nd
Rotherham	59	(6·1%)	£64	62nd
St Helens	40	(4·7%)	£62	68th
Salford	32	(3·0%)	£71	43rd
Sheffield	212	(3·7%)	£69	47th
Solihull	14	(0·9%)	£58	78th
Southampton	114	(3·7%)	£68	50th
Southend-on-Sea	66	(2·7%)	£94	13th
Southport	52	(5·7%)	£66	55th
South Shields	108	(8·8%)	£87	21st
Stockport	42	(3·0%)	£55	83rd
Stoke-on-Trent	104	(4·6%)	£76	37th
Sunderland	315	(12·9%)	£79	32nd

Boroughs	Pupils		Payments	
Swansea	23	(1·0%)	£42	94th
Teesside	255	(5·0%)	£80	30th
Torbay	46	(3·9%)	£54	84th
Tynemouth	74	(9·3%)	£99	6th
Wakefield	45	(10·1%)	£65	59th
Wallasey	36	(2·6%)	£74	39th
Walsall	61	(2·9%)	£39	98th
Warley	26	(1·7%)	£68	50th
Warrington	25	(3·7%)	£35	99th
West Bromwich	29	(1·8%)	£65	59th
Wigan	56	(9·2%)	£62	68th
Wolverhampton	183	(5·8%)	£69	47th
Worcester	8	(0·8%)	£44	92nd
York	94	(6·6%)	£56	82nd

London boroughs				
Barking	25	(1·6%)	£98	8th
Barnet	37	(0·7%)	£70	45th
Bexley	66	(2·4%)	£41	95th
Brent	53	(1·6%)	£91	15th
Bromley	58	(1·4%)	£85	25th
Croydon	76	(1·9%)	£93	14th
Ealing	97	(2·8%)	£103	4th
Enfield	45	(1·3%)	£84	26th
Haringey	63	(2·1%)	£87	21st
Harrow	182	(6·2%)	£26	101st
Havering	26	(0·7%)	£91	15th
Hillingdon	19	(0·6%)	£118	1st
Hounslow	44	(1·6%)	£76	37th
Kingston	31	(1·7%)	£90	18th
Merton	49	(2·0%)	£78	34th
Newham	67	(2·7%)	£74	39th
Redbridge	33	(1·3%)	£108	3rd
Richmond	27	(1·3%)	£88	19th
Sutton	29	(1·4%)	£83	28th
Waltham Forest	33	(1·2%)	£73	41st

Counties				
Anglesey	56	(6·8%)	£53	43rd
Beds	87	(3·3%)	£84	11th
Berkshire	62	(1·0%)	£70	24th
Brecon	32	(3·6%)	£53	43rd
Bucks	79	(1·1%)	£73	20th
Caernarvon	77	(4·7%)	£65	29th
Cambs and Ely	85	(2·7%)	£71	23rd
Cardiganshire	48	(4·3%)	£106	3rd

124 *Mike Reddin*

Table 1—*contd*

Counties	Pupils		Payments	
Carmarthen	103	(4·0%)	£42	51st
Cheshire	192	(1·6%)	£58	37th
Cornwall	196	(5·2%)	£38	55th
Cumberland	244	(8·0%)	£95	5th
Denbigh	287	(12·5%)	£36	57th
Derbyshire	289	(4·1%)	£91	7th
Devon	165	(4·0%)	£62	32nd
Dorset	94	(2·3%)	£74	19th
Durham	1,127	(14·0%)	£94	6th
Essex	255	(1·9%)	£86	9th
Flintshire	22	(1·0%)	£47	49th
Glamorgan	711	(7·5%)	£59	33rd
Gloucestershire	142	(2·2%)	£77	16th
Hampshire	221	(2·1%)	£72	21st
Herefordshire	45	(3·1%)	£54	42nd
Hertfordshire	280	(2·1%)	£78	15th
Huntingdonshire	29	(1·4%)	£82	13th
ILEA	1,732	(4·7%)	£97	4th
Isle of Wight	15	(1·3%)	£58	37th
Kent	522	(3·4%)	£72	21st
Lancashire	774	(3·4%)	£67	27th
Leicestershire	23	(0·4%)	£31	59th
Lincoln(H)	17	(1·5%)	£59	33rd
Lincoln (K)	26	(1·5%)	£52	45th
Lincoln (L)	48	(1·1%)	£46	50th
Merioneth	32	(5·6%)	£41	52nd
Monmouth	302	(6·8%)	£86	9th
Montgomeryshire	15	(2·3%)	£50	47th
Norfolk	106	(3·4%)	£68	26th
Northants	36	(1·3%)	£55	41st
Northumberland	557	(10·6%)	£83	12th
Nottingham	33	(0·5%)	£41	52nd
Oxfordshire	56	(2·1%)	£67	27th
Pembrokeshire	61	(3·6%)	£59	33rd
Radnorshire	7	(3·0%)	£37	56th
Rutland	5	(2·9%)	£76	17th
Shropshire	26	(0·7%)	£49	48th
Somerset	189	(3·3%)	£52	45th
Staffordshire	185	(2·5%)	£59	33rd
Suffolk (E)	88	(4·3%)	£56	40th
Suffolk (W)	225	(16·6%)	£58	37th
Surrey	118	(0·9%)	£87	8th
Sussex (E)	73	(1·7%)	£123	1st
Sussex (W)	47	(0·7%)	£81	14th
Warwickshire	123	(1·7%)	£64	30th
Westmorland	23	(2·4%)	£32	58th
Wiltshire	186	(3·3%)	£117	2nd

Counties	Pupils		Payments	
Worcestershire	87	(2·0%)	£76	17th
Yorkshire (E)	167	(5·5%)	£40	54th
Yorkshire (N)	125	(4·8%)	£64	30th
Yorkshire (W)	1,000	(5·3%)	£69	25th

2.3   North and south: the education split

George Taylor

Regional inequality hits hard in education. The northern regions of England, for example, are not seriously concerned with the divisive effects of public schools. More important, in their view, is increased nursery provision. Nor do they consider that expansion in higher education is as urgent as improvement in secondary education for all.

It is well known that the proportion of children staying on at school increases as one moves south. So also do average wages, earnings and incomes, the wealth of local authorities, length of education of the adult population and opportunities for varied employment. Travelling in the reverse direction, one can observe a gradual rise in the proportion of old school buildings and of free meals, in the extent of dereliction and of substandard and unfit housing, in the size of doctors' lists, in unemployment rates and in the proportion of families whose supplementary benefits are affected by the 'wage stop'. Lack of enthusiasm for extended school life is, therefore, only one characteristic among many which distinguish the northern regions from the rest of the country.

Defects in the total environment, and the economic difficulties of development areas (of which the northern region and Merseyside are the largest), are generally recognised. A lot is being done to assist them. But it was not until the publication of the Hunt report, on the intermediate ('grey') areas, that the deteriorating economic position of the north-west and of the Yorkshire and Humberside regions came home. Though the committee did not investigate standards of educational provision in the two regions, other sources suggest that their educational difficulties are partly the result and partly the cause of their economic problems.

Local authorities in the north-west ('the oldest industrial area in

Source: *New Society*, 4 March 1971, 346–7.

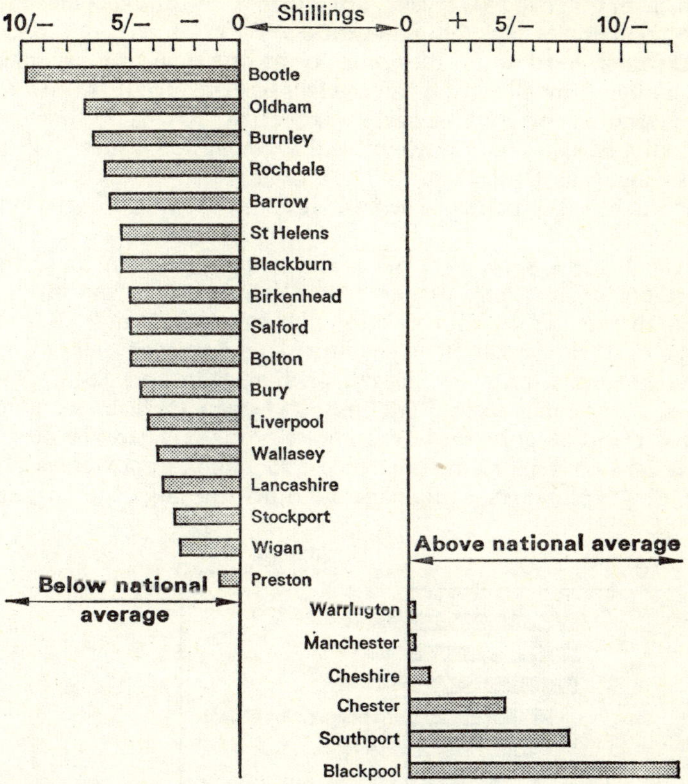

Figure of horizontal bar chart with scale at top:

10/—   5/—   —   0   Shillings   0   +   5/—   10/—

Bars extending to the left (Below national average):
Bootle
Oldham
Burnley
Rochdale
Barrow
St Helens
Blackburn
Birkenhead
Salford
Bolton
Bury
Liverpool
Wallasey
Lancashire
Stockport
Wigan
Preston

Below national average

Above national average

Bars extending to the right (Above national average):
Warrington
Manchester
Cheshire
Chester
Southport
Blackpool

Figure 1 North-western region
Variation of national average of rate-income per child (measured
by the product 1d rate per child) for LEAS
Figures in charts based on education statistics, 1966–7 (Institute
of Municipal Treasurers and Accountants)
Source: G. Taylor and N. Ayres, *Born and Bred Unequal* (Longmans,
1969).

the world') have all the signs of age: restricted income, obsolete
housing and schools, declining industry, dereliction and squalor.
The industrial West Riding—which includes the Yorkshire
coalfield—has similar conditions, though they are less concentrated in comparison with the south-east Lancashire conurbation.
Many of these regions' educational shortcomings, as well as

defects in other social services, are due to a low rate-income. This effectively limits expenditure on those services or parts of services over which local authorities have, or at one time had, complete discretion. How otherwise can the fact be explained that Bristol— an authority of long-standing prosperity—has 1,175 nursery- school places while Liverpool and Manchester—cities half as large again as Bristol—have 375 and 383 respectively? Or that Oxford has 327 places, whereas Huddersfield and Bootle have none?

The Figures show that most of the authorities in these two northern regions have a rate-income (measured by the product of a 1d rate per child) well below the national average. But the bulk of their education expenditure—on teachers' salaries, on student grants, on debt charges, on fuel, light and cleaning—is fixed by national scales. The only way open to them to match income and outgoings is to economise precisely where the need is greatest—on repairs, maintenance and minor improvements of buildings; on books, equipment and other learning materials; and

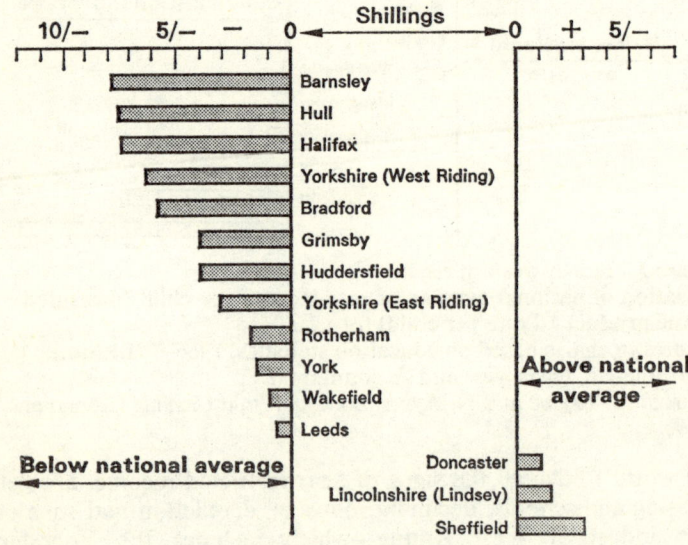

Figure 2   Yorkshire and Humberside region
Variation from national average of rate-income per child
(measured by the product 1d rate per child) for LEAS

on supporting out-of-school activities for those children unable to afford them.

Old buildings and a shortage of books and equipment do nothing to attract or retain good teachers, to promote curriculum reform, to encourage extended courses, or to enlist pupil and parent support. Such local authorities have other intractable problems. From the thirties onwards, most of them have had a shrinking population, not because of low birth-rates but because of net outward migration.

The effects are serious for two reasons. First there are empty school-places. So the 'roofs over heads' policy of successive governments has precluded replacing obsolete and unsuitable secondary schools. New capital investment in education has gone to areas of expanding population. Second, those who migrate are the young, the skilled and the highly educated. Professor A. J. Brown remarked, in his note of dissent to the Hunt report, that the north-west and Yorkshire and Humberside 'are heavy net exporters of people with education to the age of 20 or higher; Yorkshire and Humberside, in particular.'

The adults who remain in these regions, because of their own lack of it, tend to undervalue education. As parents, relatives, employers, managers and elected representatives, they influence both local authority education policy, and the attitudes towards education among the younger generation. They also tend to resist changes which are imperative if declining industry is to be replaced by enterprises that require new skills and modern methods of management. Moreover, with the flight of the better-educated, these regions reap no return on their investment in higher education with a more enlightened electorate.

What this means, in terms of parental support for the activities of a large comprehensive school, can be well illustrated by comparing Featherstone (a mining community in Yorkshire) with Hampstead. In Featherstone, we find the terminal education age of only 17 parents out of 1,000 was seventeen to nineteen. In Hampstead, the corresponding figure was ten times greater. The pattern of longer school life now corresponds much more closely with that for adult education.

Similar patterns emerge for the number of A-level passes and entrants to universities and, indeed, for all the various inequalities listed earlier. One exception is the greater proportion than elsewhere of students in Yorkshire pursuing full-time or part-time

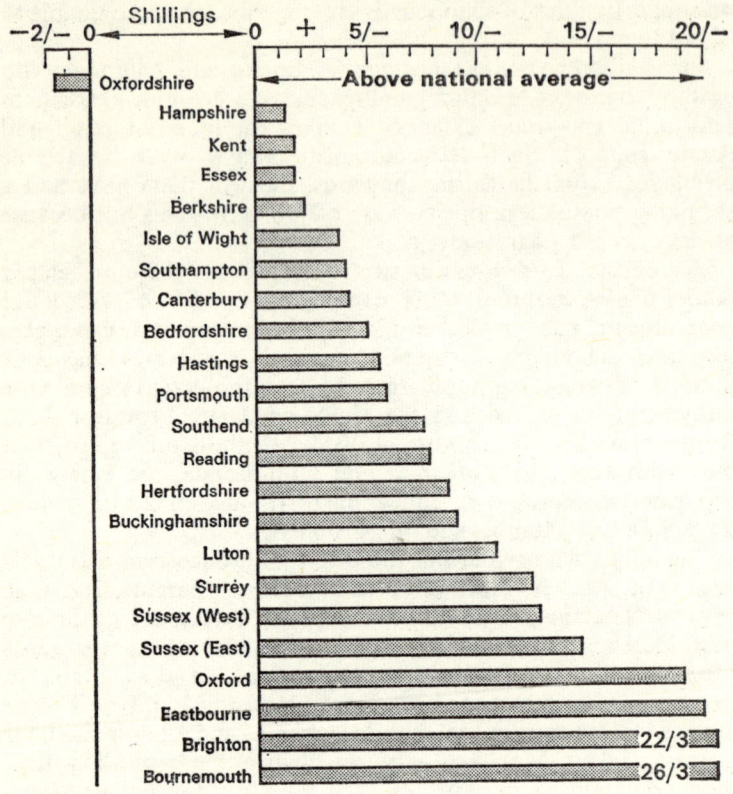

Figure 3   South-east region
Variation from national average from rate-income per child
(measured by the product 1d rate per child) for LEAS

courses in colleges of further education. It is hard to know whether
this arises from the attraction of vocational studies or from a
lack of opportunities at school. All-through comprehensive
schools may be right in the south-east; merging sixth forms with
colleges of further education may be more appropriate to local
circumstances in Yorkshire.

Even when the school-leaving age is raised and comprehensive
reorganisation completed, equality of educational opportunity
will be no nearer unless fresh decisions, however difficult, are

made on priorities for expenditure, and unless the financial resources of local authorities are more nearly related to their needs. Expansion in higher education is less important than higher standards of secondary education for the 90 per cent who do not go on to more advanced studies. It matters less than providing generous maintenance grants for young people who are willing to continue full-time education at school or college of education. Such measures are essential in the north-west and Yorkshire if the next generation is to cope with the changes that are now required to solve the regions' economic and social problems.

The major task, however, is to channel resources to areas of need. It is true that government grants narrow the gap between wealthy and poor authorities. But they do not produce equality of wealth, far less equality in relation to need. Do even the latest attempts to overcome this by redrawing boundaries go far enough? If there is today to be anything like equality of educational opportunity, immediate and drastic financial measures are needed. Many local authorities in the north are solvent only because they have few new schools (and therefore low debt charges), below-average numbers of children at school over the age of fifteen, and relatively few students at universities. If expenditure in these categories approached the national average, or the level in some south-eastern authorities, the demand on the rates would be beyond the capacity of ratepayers to pay.

Greater positive discrimination in the distribution of grants to authorities in need must inevitably mean less aid for other authorities. If redistribution is economically impracticable or politically unacceptable to either party when in power, then it would be as well to admit that equality of educational opportunity, though a laudable ideal, demands sacrifices from the fortunate that they are unwilling to make. Maybe Richard Hoggart is right in his view that 'the full implications of equality of opportunity would frighten most of us if we really faced them.'

2.4 Some intra-regional variations in educational provision and their bearing upon educational attainment— the case of the north-east

D. S. Byrne and W. Williamson

The purpose of this paper is to present some preliminary results of our research into the factors which influence the educational attainment of children in secondary schools and their patterns of uptake of further education. It seeks to demonstrate that the provision of educational resources by local education authorities, in so far as such provision is related to the wealth of each authority and the kinds of social policies pursued by each authority in the education field, is not only a neglected area of study but, more importantly, may be of greater significance in explaining variations in patterns of educational attainment than the better-documented factors associated with social class, school and family social structure.

The findings to be presented amount to no more than a research prospectus but they do lend support to our claim that whilst important advances have been made in such areas as the sociology of the family and social class, insofar as these bear upon educational attainment and the structure of educational opportunity, and whilst recent research efforts have concentrated on the sociology of the school, virtually nothing has been done on the sociology of the educational authority. This paper is an initial step into these hitherto uncharted waters.

Specifically the paper sets out to present a theoretical model of the way in which some variables of educational provision within a local authority area relate to educational attainment.

Educational attainment and the sociology of education

It is beyond the scope of this paper to summarize in any detail what achievements have been made by researchers into the problems of explaining why a significant proportion of children fail

Source: *Sociology* (1972), 6 (1), 71–87.

to extend their school careers beyond statutory age requirements. Twenty years of sustained educational research have pointed to the influence of family, class and community influences on patterns of educational attainment.[1] A series of official reports and Royal Commissions have lamented the failure of the schools to mobilize support for extended school careers, thus depriving the nation of its needed supply of educated manpower and the individual of a fuller life.[2]

Sociologists have attempted to clarify precisely what it is in the socio-cultural environment of the child—and particularly the working-class child—which limits educational aspirations and depresses learning ability.[3] Studies have been carried out on the relationship between the family and the school,[4] and on the effects of school organization on educational performance.[5] The effects of the peer group on a child's educational aspirations have also been examined in some detail.[6]

This research is cast in the mould of what we would like to call the 'stratification-education paradigm',[7] and whilst its policy implications have always been clear—in such fields as comprehensive reorganization and compensatory education—the extent to which educational attainment directly relates to the provision of educational resources in the local educational authority area has been scarcely examined. What we propose to show is that the provision of educational resources in an area may be a significant factor in explaining variations in school attainment of different social groups. Factors which can be associated with the socio-cultural learning environment of the child and the material situation of the family—social class factors—can be traced in their influence on educational policy and educational provision. ...

Models of determination of attainment

It seems appropriate, before going on ... to look at the basic 'theoretical' model which lends structure to this study. This is best done through an examination of other major sociological or socio-linguistic models of the determinants of attainment that have been developed in studies of the British educational system. Although certain elements in our model coincide with elements of earlier models, the explicit emphasis we place on the importance of policy, and on the operation of other factors through the intermediate variable of policy, represents a new conception of the processes under investigation.

Perhaps the most important basic element in sociological models of the determination of attainment has been the emphasis placed on social class. However, social class has never been considered to directly determine educational attainment but has been seen rather as operating through some intermediate variable. Douglas's work showed the high correlation between parental social class and the educational attainment of individual children. His subsequent analysis focussed on sociocultural aspects of the family, which he and others have related to class position. Bernstein's work on socio-linguistics has been used, however invalidly,[8] to reinforce a model of attainment determination which runs as follows:

Social class $\xrightarrow{+ve}$ familial socio-cultural intermediate variables $\xrightarrow{+ve}$ attainment

This has been the most important model of the determinant factors of attainment current in British educational sociology. The only major variation upon it has been the divorcing of familial socio-cultural variables from class determination in the work of Wiseman, especially in his research done for the Plowden Committee and described by one commentator as 'getting us away from the unhelpful categories of social class.'[9] Wiseman's model can be diagrammatically expressed thus:

Familial socio-cultural variables $\xrightarrow{+ve}$ attainment

Taylor and Ayres with their 'educational ecology' radically departed from this concern with socio-cultural factors.[10] They saw material environment as a major determinant of attainment, although they totally neglect the question of relationship between social class and this environment. Their (implicit) model would run thus:

Material environment $\xrightarrow{+ve}$ attainment

Eggleston introduces the notion of variation in provision as a determinant of attainment.[11] While his labelling of variables as 'administrative' lays a stress on the determinant nature of patterns of provision, his concern with such variables as age of school buildings includes an element on 'resource' determination in his model. It must be stressed that Eggleston's was a dual model in that, running alongside his administrative/resource determination, is a conception of the determinant status of high socio-economic class, although the mode of operation of this determinant variable is not specified explicitly. Thus Eggleston's models can be expressed as follows:

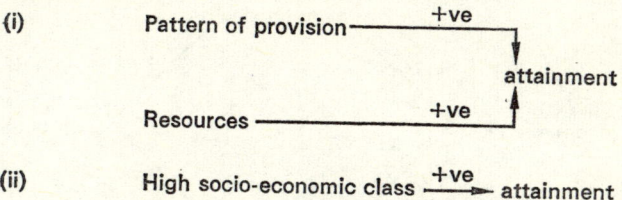

The hypothetical model we advance differs from all these discussed above in a number of important respects. The first relates to the determinant status of social class. Although we see social class as a major determinant of educational attainment, we consider that at least a major part of its influence is likely to operate through other, so far unexamined, intermediate factors. In so far as high socio-economic class is a positive determinant of attainment, we see this as being a consequence of the interrelationship between high social class *and* availability of resources on the one hand, and high social class and elite-orientated policy[12] (which will lead to high levels of attainment if attainment is defined in elitist terms) on the other. Elitist policy we see as being mediated through the political ethos of LEAs which is likely to be consequential on the social class background of the LEA. Thus *one* element in our model can be expressed as follows.

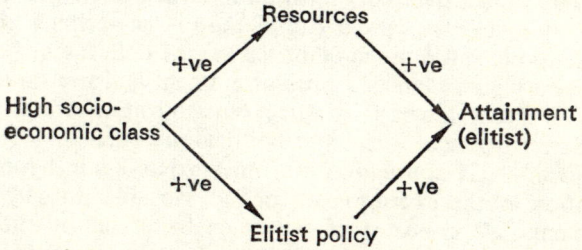

However, if we distinguish between 'resources', i.e. factors beyond the effective control of the LEA even over relatively long time periods, and policy and provisions, i.e. factors which are within LEA control, and if we consider what policy is mediated through local authority political control, then another element in our model relates to the positively determinant effects of *low* socio-economic class. Thus:

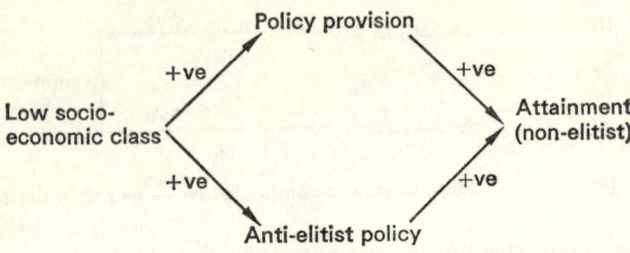

In other words, we might expect that low socio-economic class will be a determinant of a high level of 'provision' which will determine higher levels of attainment. At the same time, we might expect that low socio-economic class is likely to be related to anti-elitist policies on the part of the LEA, an ethos which will be negatively correlated with attainment if we define attainment in elitist terms; but it is likely to be positively related to alternative, non-elitist definitions of attainment.[13]

Now Eggleston related attainment to patterns of provision of secondary schooling and it must be accepted that 'patterns of provision' are very much a consequence of local authority policy particularly as regards policies of comprehensive reorganization. But this is not a major problem for our exploratory study in that the north-east, in the period under analysis, was not an area in which comprehensive reorganization had had any significant impact. Moreover, we would argue that it is perhaps generally possible to place too much emphasis on the determinant effect of administrative reorganization on attainment and too little on the 'policy' element inherent in such reorganization which has its origins we suspect in social and political pressures.

To justify this contention we must expand our hypothetical conception of the operation of 'policy' variables in determining attainment. We conceive of policy as being set by the power centres in the LEA[14] in response to socio-political pressures that are primarily of social class origin, and that manifest themselves through political organization. We see the most important 'policy' dichotomy as being between those authorities who have an elitist orientation and those with an egalitarian bias. The policy orientation of the LEA manifests itself in practice through a variety of mechanisms, the most important of these very probably comprising the promotions procedure for head teachers and the allocations of resources between different schools.

To take the latter first, we consider it likely that authorities with an elitist orientation will tend to concentrate available resources on their 'sponsored elite'. On the other hand, authorities with an egalitarian policy will aim at territorial justice in the distribution of resources and even attempt 'positive discrimination'. Our research design incorporates at least an attempt to assess the validity of this contention. As regards the internal transmission of ideology within an LEA through promotions procedure and the like, these processes are beyond the immediate scope of this study but represent a logical development from it. It is extremely likely that 'policy' factors of this form will assume even greater importance in the wake of an 'administrative' comprehensive reorganization of an LEA's secondary school system, in that they are likely to be major determinants of the *internal* organizational form of the comprehensive schools. However, the best we can do within the framework of the present enquiry is to look at the resource distribution factors and their effects on attainment, bearing in mind that these represent underlying policy commitments which are likely also to be manifest through this class of variables left uninvestigated.

The findings given in Table 1 on the interrelationship between the resource and policy provision variables for LEAs in the northeast tend to confirm the model of the role of 'policy' as determinant of attainment. If we examine the correlations between low social class and resource variables we find that d [old penny] rate per pupil and the proportion in social class D/E are significantly and highly *negatively* correlated (r^2 M 0·62). However, the proportion in social class D/E is equally highly and significantly positively correlated with the policy provision variable, rate-fund equivalent; i.e. with a measure of proportionate importance LEAS assign to their educational activities (r^2 M 0·60). While, as one might expect, there is a negative relationship between available wealth of an LEA and the proportion of its constituents in the lowest social classes, there is a strong positive relationship between the proportion in the social classes D/E and the proportionate financial importance the LEA attaches to education. It is an importance which, on careful inspection, seems to be independent

Table 1 Resource variables and educational provision: north-eastern planning region: zero order, product moment correlation coefficients r^2

	d rate per pupil	Rate-fund proportion	P/C expenditure	Pooled primary	Pooled secondary	Proportion in social class A/B	Proportion in social class D/E	Primary over-crowding	Secondary over-crowding
d rate per pupil	X	0·8281	0·17	0·19	0·28	0·02	0·62	0·12	0·14
Rate-fund proportion	0·83	X	0·003	0·33	0·25	0·01	0·60	0·12	0·01
P/C expenditure	0·17	0·003	X	0·09	0·07	0·06	0·08	0·12	0·27
Pooled primary	0·19	0·33	0·09	X	0·02	0·07	0·16	0·33	0·08
Pooled secondary	0·25	0·24	0·07	0·02	X	0·26	0·40	0·006	0·01
Proportion in social class A/B	0·03	0·01	0·06	0·07	0·26	X	0·14	0·21	0·06
Proportion in social class D/E	0·62	0·60	0·08	0·16	0·40	0·14	X	0·09	0·04
Primary overcrowding	0·12	0·12	0·01	0·34	0·006	0·21	0·09	X	0·05
Secondary overcrowding	0·14	0·01	0·27	0·08	0·01	0·06	0·05	0·05	X

of LEA size and therefore *not due* to rich, large LEAs having responsibilities not possessed by small, poor ones. With regard to patterns of expenditure, low social class is positively correlated with pooled primary expenditure but *negatively* and highly correlated with pooled secondary expenditure ($r^2 = 0.40$). However high social class, i.e. proportion in social class A/B, is not significantly correlated with pooled primary expenditure but is significantly and positively correlated with pooled secondary expenditure ($r^2 = 0.26$).

The policy provision variable, rate fund proportion, is significantly and positively correlated with pooled primary expenditure ($r^2 = 0.32$) but negatively correlated with pooled secondary expenditure ($r^2 = 0.24$). What these results indicate, then, is that LEAS which devote a larger proportion of their income to education, spend their money preferentially on primary education. As might be expected, pooled expenditure in primary schools is significantly and negatively correlated with primary overcrowding ($r^2 = 0.34$). Thus the proportionate importance which an LEA attaches to its educational activities is negatively correlated with the resources of the LEA ($r^2 = 0.828$).

If we 'express' these findings in diagrammatic terms, then we have the following:

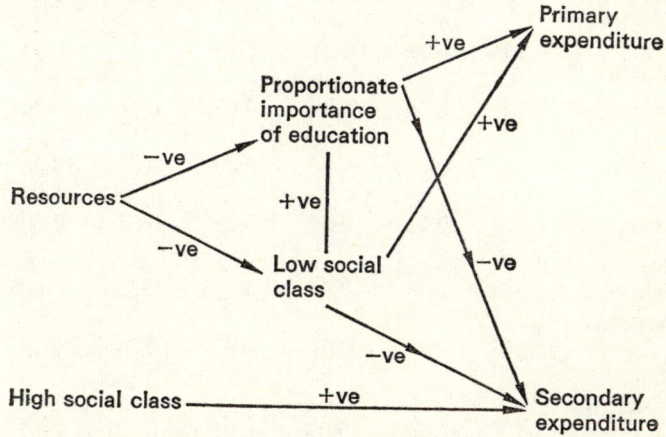

In other words, those authorities with a high proportion in low social classes resident within their area both devote a higher proportion of their income to education than do authorities with higher social class constituencies, and spend their money on primary education rather than on secondary education, the reverse being true of the 'high social class' authorities.

These findings can certainly be interpreted as support for the idea of the determinant role of elitist and anti-elitist policies which we advanced in our model, since expenditure on univer-salist primary education is indubitably more egalitarian in its consequences than expenditure on secondary education, especially when there remains a strong selective element in the secondary sector.

If we now turn to look at our findings (Table 2) about the rela-tionship between various indices of attainment and resources, provision and social class variables, we find a similar pattern. If

Table 2 Measures of attainment and educational provision: north-eastern planning region: zero order, product moment correlation coefficients r^2

	University	Further educa-tion (I)	Further educa-tion (II)	Teacher training	5th form	6th form
d rate p/p	0·06	0·33	0·11	0·18	0·22	0·25
Rate-fund prop.	0·005	0·09	0·34	0·30	0·09	0·13
P/C expenditure	0·12	0·54	0·23	0·005	0·28	0·08
Pooled primary	0·03	0·003	0·34	0·08	0·004	0·06
Pooled secondary	0·008	0·22	0·04	0·33	0·04	0·0001
Social class A/B	0·18	0·27	0·03	0·003	0·56	0·005
Social class D/E	0·007	0·19	0·01	0·02	0·24	0·29
Primary overcrowd-ing	0·0003	0·001	0·05	0·01	0·02	0·30
Secondary overcrowd-ing	0·48	0·36	0·10	0·03	0·17	0·29

we look first at staying-on indices; the proportion of students who stay on until their sixteenth birthday is positively correlated with the resource index, d rate per pupil ($r^2 = 0.22$), with per capita expenditure by the LEA on each pupil for which the LEA is responsible ($r^2 = 0.28$) and with the proportion in social class A/B ($r^2 = 0.56$). Staying on for the fifth form is negatively correlated with the proportion of social class D/E ($r^2 = 0.24$). It would seem that the major determinant of staying on is high social class but that higher rates of expenditure per pupil, stemming from higher resources, play a mediating role.

Thus these findings suggest a model of the following form:

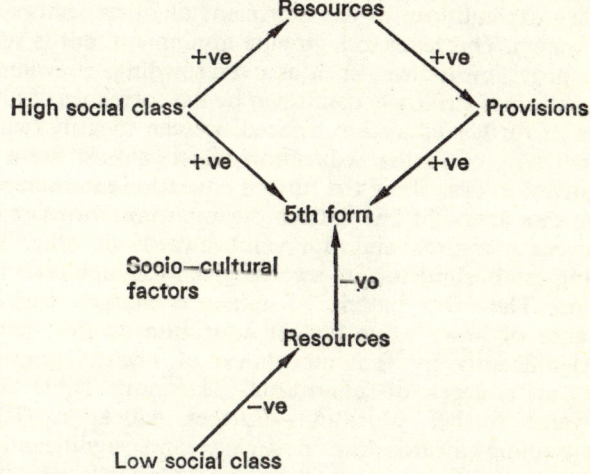

Although these models are here only suggested, rather than tested by partial correlation techniques, the very high positive correlation between high social class and 5th form staying on suggests that there the socio-cultural mode of effect of high social class is important. This is not the case with the findings relating to the correlation of staying on until seventeen with resource, provision and social class indices. Staying on until seventeen is positively correlated with primary overcrowding and secondary overcrowding and negatively correlated with proportion in social class D/E. Given that the overcrowding indices are not significantly correlated with social class D/E, this suggests a model of the following form:

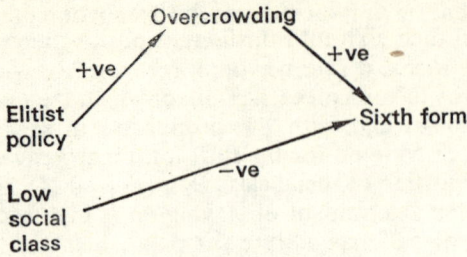

Or, in other words, it suggests that certain LEAS concentrate resources on secondary expenditure, in particular on 'elite' secondary expenditure, to the detriment of other sectors of the school system. This leads to high elite attainment, but is reflected in poor provision indices, such as overcrowding, elsewhere.

This pattern is strikingly confirmed by the correlates of different patterns of further education. Indeed, we can identify two significant patterns of further education which almost seem to be 'alternatives' in describing the further education attainment from different LEA areas. In one pattern the important forms of uptake are university awards and full value awards at other further education establishments, i.e. awards given for high level further education. The other pattern of uptake is characterized by the importance of lesser value further education awards, and even more significantly by the importance of awards granted for studies, at colleges of education. Thus, in Table 2 both lesser value further education—Further education (II)—and teacher-training awards are positively and significantly correlated with rate-fund proportion, i.e. proportionate importance of educational expenditure for the LEA ($r^2 = 0.34$ and $r^2 = 0.30$ respectively). The only other significant correlations for these two variables are that further education (II) is significantly and positively 'correlated' with pooled primary expenditure ($r^2 = 0.34$) and teacher training is negatively correlated with pooled secondary expenditure ($r^2 = 0.33$). Thus, these two types of attainment are correlated with the variables which are of importance for the 'poor' egalitarian LEAS.

University awards per 1,000 age group and high grade further education follow a diametrically opposed pattern. High grade, further education (I) awards are positively and significantly correlated with d rate per pupil, i.e. resources ($r^2 = 0.33$), with per capita expenditure per pupil, a variable including a considerable resource element ($r^2 = 0.84$), with proportion in social class A/B ($r^2 = 0.27$), and with secondary overcrowding ($r^2 = 0.36$). University awards are significantly and positively correlated with secondary overcrowding ($r^2 = 0.48$).

This pattern of correlation is markedly similar to the two patterns established for correlation between resource variables. It would seem that poor local authorities, with high proportions of social class D/E, spending a larger proportion of their resources on education, 'produce' teachers and students who pursue low grade further education courses. Richer local authorities with greater resources and larger proportions in social class A/B seem to have an elitist policy, spending their money on a sponsored[15] elite of pupils who 'attain' in sixth form, university and high grade further education courses at the expense of scarcity of resources elsewhere, and, in particular, of high levels of overcrowding.

Thus, one is led to the following models:

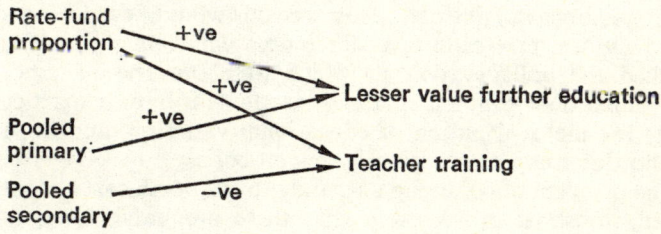

and

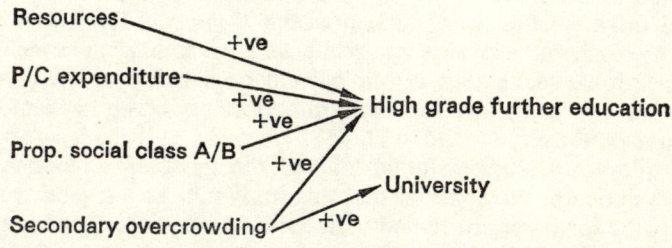

Thus the two 'policy' models of LEAs, i.e. those of the poor LEA with an egalitarian policy and the richer LEA with an elitist policy, seem to hold not only for patterns of resource distribution between school-types, but for the type of further education attainment—with the elite authorities producing children who attain in elite terms i.e. university and high grade further education, and the egalitarian authorities producing children attaining in lower grade further education training patterns.

Conclusion

This study has been specifically confined to LEAs within the north-east region, the only exception being the County Borough of Carlisle, which, however, in many respects is a north-eastern town. The Cumberland and Westmorland LEAs, although lying within the NEPC area have been excluded because of their overwhelmingly rural character. Results generated are therefore only applicable to the predominantly urban areas of the NEPC. This 'regionalism' is intentional. It would have been comparatively simple to extend the scope of the study to every LEA in England and Wales, since the analysis has been conducted with, in the main, readily available data. However this would have introduced socio-cultural and economic differences which might well have masked the policy variations which were our special concern. We think that regional analyses of this form have particular value for the explanation of educational variation, and hope to extend this study on a region by region basis.

The problem of confining our study to the north-east has introduced statistical problems in that there are only eleven LEAs and therefore only eleven cases. Despite this, a very high level of significance in results has been obtained. All results, i.e. r^2s, quoted in the body of the text are significant at the 90 per cent level and almost all are significant at the 95 per cent level. Scattergrams confirm these patterns. While we have somewhat stretched correlational techniques in our current application of them, we feel that this is justified in a study that does not claim to be more than exploratory.

Exploratory studies should lay out the guides for reconnaissance in depth. We consider that this study indicates several fruitful paths for those concerned with the influence of local policy in education in this country. One is the natural, region by region, extension of the current analysis which we have already suggested. Another is research in depth into the operations of particular

LEAS, to explore policy and modes of policy enactment, transmission of policy conceptions etc. As we stated at the beginning of this article, the sociology of education in this country has fruitfully concerned itself with the influence of family, language, culture and national policy, but the crucial local level has been almost entirely neglected. We hope this present study does something to redress the balance.

Notes

1 See, for example, P. W. Musgrave, *The Sociology of Education* (London, Methuen, 1965); J. W. B. Douglas, *The Home and the School: A study of Ability and Attainment in the Primary School* (London, MacGibbon & Kee, 1964); O. Banks, *The Sociology of Education* (London, Batsford, 1968); D. F. Swift (ed.), *Basic Readings in the Sociology of Education* (London, Routledge & Kegan Paul, 1970).

2 See, for example, Central Advisory Council, *Early Leaving* (HMSO, 1954); Central Advisory Council for Education, *15 to 18* (HMSO, 1960); Committee on Higher Education, *Higher Education* (HMSO, 1963), Appendix 1.

3 See for a review of some of the literature on this problem, D. Lawton, *Social Class, Language and Education* (London, Routledge & Kegan Paul, 1968); S. Wiseman, *Education and Environment* (Manchester University Press, 1964).

4 Douglas, *op. cit.*

5 See, for example, B. Jackson, *Streaming: An Educational System in Miniature* (London, Routledge & Kegan Paul, 1964); D. Hargreaves, *Social Relations in a Secondary School* (London: Routledge & Kegan Paul, 1967).

6 Unfortunately, on this problem, the literature is largely American. See, for example, J. S. Coleman, *The Adolescent Society* (Chicago, Free Press, 1961). For Britain, see J. Webb, 'The sociology of a school', *British Journal of Sociology*, 13, 3 (1962) 264–72; B. N. Sugarman, 'Involvement in youth culture, academic achievement and conformity in school', *British Journal of sociology*, 18, 2, (1967) 151–64.

7 The concept of 'paradigm' derives from T. S. Kuhn, *The Structure of Scientific Revolutions* (University of Chicago Press, 1962).

8 See B. Bernstein, 'A critique of the concept of compensatory education' in D. Rubinstein and C. Stoneman (eds), *Education for Democracy* (Penguin, 1970).

9 Howard Glennester, 'The Plowden research', *Journal of the Royal Statistical Society*, Series A, Part 2, 1969.

10 G. Taylor and N. Ayres, *Born and Bred Unequal* (London, Longmans, 1969).

11 John S. Eggleston, 'Some environmental correlates of extended secondary education' in Swift, *Basic Readings in the Sociology of Education.*

12 See, for example, R. H. Turner, 'Sponsored and contest mobility and the school system', *American Sociological Review*, 25, 5, (1960).

13 Elitist definitions of attainment are rooted in culturally specific criteria concerning positions reached in the occupational educational hierarchy.

This means they are concerned with only a minority of the products of the school system. A non-elitist definition would be concerned with the total output of the educational system – with *all* children rather than merely the academic minority. It can be hypothesized that elitist educational policies, whilst promoting the attainment of the few, depress the potential attainment of the majority. Equally, non-elitist policies will improve the performance of all at the expense of the performance of a select few.

14 See the Maud Committee Report, *The Management of Local Government* (HMSO, 1967).

15 Turner, *op. cit.* .

Introduction to Section 3

New ideas for city schools

Strategies such as compensatory education and the redistribution of resources are, arguably, only new formulae for fairer competition within an unchanged elite-selecting education system (Halsey, 1.6). In the search for 'educational roads to equality', a number of educationists have recently proposed a radical reorientation towards education based in and on individual communities; only through community-based education, they argue, can the majority acquire the necessary knowledge, understanding and skills to change their environment.

Cities are unique in the diversity of both population and social problems. The charge is often made that there is a wide gulf between what goes on in school and the social reality found outside it, and this gap is seen at its widest in urban schools (Fantini and Weinstein, 3.1). The urban school curriculum rarely includes the features of city life that are part of the urban child's experience. On these grounds, Fantini and Weinstein justify the need for a special urban curriculum which would incorporate, rather than reject, urban phenomena.

Illich (3.2) contends that both social reality and our ability to imagine educational change have become dominated by the notion of 'schooling'. Schools are seen as the only agencies of learning. But salvation, in Illich's view, lies in the disestablishment of obligatory schooling as a specialized institution. Instead, learning should take place in the general context of society, making use of the resources it offers.

'Deschooling' in the sense of totally abandoning schools is less popular than the idea of 'reschooling'—retaining the institutional framework, but making far greater use of community resources that already exist.[1]

Cities in particular, because of their size, density and diversity, contain vast untapped resources in terms of education 'objects' (e.g. libraries, factories, streets) and people with skills they could teach. Gumbert (3.3) suggests ways in which many of the current functions of schools—such as skill learning and peer activities—could be redistributed among other institutions in the city. Freed from such functions, schools would be able to carry out their specialized task of intellectual development more effectively; school buildings would become merely a base, and school teachers would become educational leaders, 'enablers' and guides.

Newmann and Oliver (3.4) consider that education has three important facets—systematic instruction, action and reflection—which should occur concurrently at all stages of learning. Like Gumbert (3.3) they suggest that the school is the most appropriate context only for the first of these facets, and that the community provides a better context for the other two. They also argue strongly that community-based education does not equip students only for life in one community; community problems are sufficiently generalizable for it to be valid in any environment.

Besides appearing educationally desirable, 're-schooling' is also financially attractive. Expenditure on the traditional school system has escalated in a vicious spiral of supply and demand, without noticeably reducing its inequalities. Money now poured into schools could, it is argued, be more profitably used to exploit existing community resources in a variety of ways for educational purposes (Illich, 3.2; Gumbert, 3.3). It is worth noting that the Parkway Program in Philadelphia (3.5)—an example of reschooling in practice, which employs community resources—was established partly because funds were insufficient to provide the necessary extra school in the traditional style.

The remaining papers in this section relate to experiments in community education in this country. Midwinter (3.6), one of its foremost proponents, describes some of the ideas and strategies developed by the Liverpool EPA Project Team at primary school level.[2] In this extract he stresses that the two main facets of a community—social and economic—should be reflected in schools by community management and various links with industry; but above all he emphasizes the fundamental importance of improving parental and public knowledge of school activities so that parents and others can better support and participate in the children's education.

This emphasis is repeated in the plans for the Cheetham/

Crumpsall Education Project in Manchester (3.7): 'the relief [of "disadvantage"] in school, and beyond, is intimately affected by parental attitudes to education and therefore by the place of the school in the community'. And so, in an attempt to fuse school and community, a campus with educational and leisure facilities for all age-groups has been designed as the focal point of the area.

Hatch and Moylan (3.8), however, compare the rhetoric of community education potential with existing practice, in particular at secondary level, and conclude that so far the practice has only realized a fraction of its potential.

Notes

1 See also James Coleman, 'How do the Young Become Adults?' (3.1) in *Cities, Communities and the Young: Readings in Urban Education*, vol. 1.

2 This extract has been included as an example of practice, and encompasses only a fraction of Midwinter's views on community education. For a fuller exposition see Eric Midwinter, *Projections* (Ward Lock Educational, 1972); *Priority Education* (Penguin, 1972); and *Patterns of Community Education* (Ward Lock Educational, 1973.)

3.1 What is urban about an urban school?

Mario D. Fantini and Gerald Weinstein

If we were to choose the one characteristic of an urban context that has priority for schools it would be stated as follows:

The urban context is one in which *there is persistent stress imposed by intensely concentrated social realities.* Although all schools operate in a context of social realities, those that are in smaller more homogeneous communities have much less tension because the schools reflect a reality that is more parallel to that of the surrounding community. In addition, in those communities there is not the intense concentration of so many varied realities—so many different slices of life. The urban school, located in an area of great density and diversity, finds itself at a convergence point of a whole array of realities.

While most schools have devotedly divorced themselves from direct confrontations with social reality, the urban school stands out as most absurd in its emulation of the way reality is reflected in suburban schools. But, before we go into what the school is or is not doing, we must take a hard look at the urban social realities and the stress they impose.

Although there are numerous ways to describe and diagnose the persistent press of social realities in urban areas, time and space force us to limit this particular discussion. However, from reading what some of the 'experts' in urban diagnosis have written and by using our own perceptions and experiences, we would like to single out those aspects that have a clearer (for us) relationship to educational prescriptions.

It will be necessary to describe briefly some of the concepts that shape our perceptions and help us diagnose the urban scene. Our general framework for examining the urban scene is this: How does the press of urban social realities affect certain basic human issues?

Source: Mario D. Fantini and Gerald Weinstein, *Making Urban Schools Work*, New York, Holt (1968), 3–10, 24–9.

Human beings have a combination of personal issues with which they continually attempt to deal in some satisfactory manner. Many of these issues are common enough to be designated as a pattern – '*human* issue.' Although these human issues have been labeled through the years in a variety of different ways (needs, wants, concerns, drives, and so forth), all of these different labels have something in common.

These human issues can generally be grouped into issues revolving around safety, security, or survival, which include most of the physical needs—food, clothing, shelter, health—as well as the emotional needs for safety and security. A separate grouping can be made of those issues dealing with the psychosocial needs of love, recognition, status, affiliation and potency, agency or effect. In addition a third grouping may be made: one dealing with aesthetic, knowledge-seeking, spiritual, and self-actualizing issues. Once some of these issues are described, one can look at the cities with the question: What are the physical and psychosocial characteristics of city life and what effect do they have on its inhabitants in their attempts to work through the issues just described?

For the purpose of this writing we intend to deal with the middle range of issues described, the psychosocial group, and to limit even those to the issues of identity, connectedness or affiliation, and power (potency—agency—effect), and then to proceed to outline some of the effects of urban life on these issues.

By *identity* issues, we mean those aspects of a person's behavior which aim at providing him with a sense of worth. This area includes all the questions pertaining to the process of self-evaluation and the consequences of these evaluations. It is referred to by such terms as self-image, self-concept, identity, self-awareness, self-esteem, ego, ego-strength, and the like. All of these surround the basic questions: Who am I? What am I worth?

By *connectedness* issues we mean those aspects of a person's behavior which aim at providing him with a sense of positive affiliation with others. This is the relations-with-others domain, ranging from the primary face-to-face relations to secondary relations with less direct groups. Connectedness issues involve the questions: To whom does the individual feel an allegiance? To whom does he feel he belongs? What are people to him? Who are the significant others? How does he relate? With whom does he *integrate*?

By *power* issues we mean those aspects of a person's behavior which aim at providing him with a sense of control or influence over what is happening and will happen to him. Does the individual feel that he has a significant part to play in the construction of situations that will affect him? If he does, does he act in accordance with these feelings?

Although these issues are usually integrated and less distinct as discrete personal arenas in individuals, we think it is helpful to keep them separate as we now examine some of the social realities of the urban context and their relation to these issues.

Density and loss of identity

To what extent do the urban realities contribute to the identity crisis of the city dweller? Do I really count? Do I have any importance? Am I being lost in the massive shuffle of the big city life? These are often the unverbalized questions of the city dwellers—all of which may be condensed into: How does the city affect my perceptions of myself?

Everyone knows that cities are crowded, that space is at a premium, that it is difficult to get away from crowds of hustling, bustling people. Everywhere there are lines of people waiting. Subway trains provide for some of the most physically intimate rides obtainable anywhere. But what is the persistent stress on the individual confronted with great numbers of people? We would contend that the result is greater depersonalization, less empathy, greater feelings of loneliness and anonymity, and a general hardening or mechanization of relationships with people.

Varied comments of urban dwellers reflect this description:

I don't feel sorry for nobody. When you been around this town as long as I've been and ya seen all the nuts and kooks, it just runs off your back like water.

How can I possibly count as anything important when I've never felt more lonely in my life than when I moved to the city? Everyone seems to be in such a hurry to get to his own hidden little world. Strange to feel so lonely when there are so many people around.

People living in extremely close physical contact with one another and highly dependent, yet remaining isolated in general from one another—a sea of unknown faces—is just one of the paradoxes of the urban social reality of size and density. Impersonal relationships are numerous here, and the brief casual contrasts between persons allow in most instances for the communication of only superficial information. Yet, on the basis of this limited information, people evaluate and rank others. Standardized, superficial criteria for stratifying people thus evolve according to address, speech, manners, skin color, dress, and so forth.[1] There are too many people to absorb as individuals; therefore, a categorical depersonalized shorthand becomes reinforced.

Within the urban school itself, depersonalization is dramatically evident. Class size has rarely been pared down, in spite of 'average' numbers issued in board of education reports. Having *every* child study the same thing at the same time for the same length of time is the rule. Teachers rarely live in the same community in which they teach, and thus parents and teachers are strangers. Because of the great numbers of children, cumulative records and reports in effect become the 'children' about whom standardized decisions are made. Personalizing education would mean fouling up the machinery of the organization and by all means the machinery comes before the individual or else we would have chaos.

This problem of depersonalization brings us to our next major social reality of the urban area.

Bureaucratization and powerlessness

In spite of Mayor Lindsay's pronouncement that New York City shall be known as Fun City, living there has been like being a member of 'Strike-of-the-Month-Club.' In the last three years the city has had subway, newspaper, hospital workers', teachers', garage, taxicab, and, most recently, garbage workers' strikes. Many of these caused considerable inconvenience to the urban residents. What struck us the authors, however, was the degree of nonchalance with which the citizens endured these events with an 'Oh, well, it will be over soon' attitude. It was almost as if people were being reminded that this was the price they had to pay for living in Fun City—or for that matter, in any large city. James Reston, in an editorial in *The New York Times*, was astounded at the complacent and passive reaction of the New York citizenry. 'The force [the bureaucracy] is so powerful,' he writes, 'that they are beyond reason or persuasion or control. Power will tell in the end, they seem to be saying, and the people are merely spectators and victims in the struggle.'[2] 'You can't fight City Hall' is the dominant theme. The bigger the city, the less feeling of control, so why bother?

Anyone who has gone through the experience of trying to get help on a problem from a large city agency and of then being passed from one official to another has an emotional sense of the castrating effect of such an experience. The public is regarded by frustrated bureaucratic clerks as an imposition, an obstacle, a digression from their work, which is, ironically, to serve the public. . . .

Many people question public institutions as to who serves whom. The verdict rendered most often in that is reality the client is at the service of the institution. Thus 'You can't fight City Hall' has become 'You can't fight the Board of Education.' As cogs in a gigantic machinery, administrators, teachers, children, and parents are rendered powerless in persistent ways.

The following statements help to sum up this powerlessness vis-à-vis bureaucracy and urban living: 'For satisfaction and growth, people need to engage in active interchange with their environment; to use it, organize it, even destroy it. . . . [their] physical surroundings [and institutions][3] should be accessible and open-ended . . .'[4] The present urban social reality is very far from this ideal.

Diversity and disconnectedness

To which extent does the city create a context for connectedness between different people? Does it engender a sense of community in which its variety of people see each other as important and related to one another? Does it create a sense of belonging?

Of all the social realities faced by the urban dwellers and especially the urban school, the tremendous diversity of people looms as the most crucial distinction. Because so many different kinds of people, attitudes, perceptions, values, and habits are concentrated in a limited geographical area, this may be cited as one of the most unique aspects of an urban environment.

It is one thing, however, to know that diversity is a fact of urban life; it is quite another to realize how diversity is viewed by the urban resident. To a few, diversity provides an exciting possibility for enrichment and expansion of one's own perceptions and experiences through a kind of cross-fertilizing interaction between different groups of people. These are the few who thrive on variety and find it nourishing. But we think that this attitude is not the one prevalent in the city. More often diversity is viewed as threatening, and at best as novel or interesting but certainly not anything one would consciously seek to develop. It is in the city, typically, that the great potential for cross-fertilization lies and yet the distinct ethnic and racial turfs are entered by others only when absolutely necessary. It seems as if the only meeting ground between these diverse groups is in the restaurant—but then only recipes and foods cross-fertilize, not the people. Physical and psychological boundaries that keep people disconnected and alienated from one another are as well maintained as the Berlin Wall.

The urban school, meanwhile, has always considered itself the great homogenizer. It has taken great masses of diverse people and acculturated them to the middle-class mainstream. Whether or not specifically articulated as such, this is what the mission of the school was and is. Only *now* something seems to be going wrong. The acculturation mission is having tremendous bumps and wobbles. Many of the processes established by the school are intended to stamp out diversity, both cultural and individual, so that the urban school actually alienates diverse pupils and keeps them disconnected from the school. Until recently, for example, it was illegal in New York for a teacher in a school to speak in Spanish to Spanish-speaking pupils except in foreign language classes.

If we now go back to our initial characterization of the urban milieu—which was stated as 'the persistent stress imposed by intensely concentrated social realities'—we can summarize in this way: density and size, bureaucracy, and diversity are social realities which persistently lay stress on the individual's concern for identity, power, and connectedness. Certainly there are other ways to select and categorize social realities; however, we think this will serve our present purposes.

The stresses we have been discussing also imply that a city dweller has less opportunity to ignore social realities. He is exposed to them whether he wants to be or not. He is close to crime, riots, poverty, muggings, alcoholics—they are constantly making themselves felt—and he cannot remain totally impervious to them. So it is with children in the urban school: The urban school has attempted to shy away from things going on in the real world which are part of an urban child's experience. Thus there is dichotomy and tension between the child's urban curriculum and the school's more antiseptic curriculum—a dichotomy that usually leads the urban child to label the school's curriculum as 'phony.'

We have been saving a final descriptive characterization for last in order to emphasize it. What we have been discussing up to now are some of the effects of urbanization on the 'average' resident—who could very well be middle-class and white. Depersonalization, anonymity, isolation, powerlessness, can be and *are* felt by people whose bellies are relatively full, who have steady incomes, and who have not been discriminated against by society. Now, however, it is becoming more evident that increasingly the 'average' city dweller is more likely to be poor and discriminated against. Public schools in large cities are basically the habitat of the socioeconomically disadvantaged and will become more so. Therefore if the characteristics of urban stress are felt by those who are relatively well-off, we must magnify those stresses, perhaps double or triple them, when applying them to the disadvantaged resident. We must also magnify those stresses when applying them to the urban public school itself. The urban school thus finds itself in the center of a situation where the black demands for power, identity, and connectedness are hammering on its doors with ever-increasing insistence.

A model of an urban school

After all this description of urban realities and analysis of their effects, what kind of prescription for the urban school is possible? According to the diagnosis given thus far, we shall offer a suggestion for a beginning model of an urban school that is directly connected with the issues we have raised. Therefore, corresponding to the limits we have given ourselves, the model would have to meet the following criteria:

1 Social reality and the school's curriculum have to be intrinsically connected.

    a. The school must acknowledge the realities by setting up a structure in which children are engaged in the examination of these realities.

    b. Children will learn the skills and behaviors needed to influence social realities.

    c. The skills and behaviors for social change will be applied by the children to the social realities.

2 Power, identity, and connectedness have to become a legitimized basis for curriculum development with the aim of expanding the repertoire of responses children have in dealing with these concerns.

3 Diversity, both cultural and individual, and its potential for cross-fertilization has to be encouraged and expanded through educational objectives and organization that allow and legitimize such an aim.

4 The school and the community it serves have to exist less as separate entities and instead develop responsibilities and lines of authority that are more integrated and shared.

Our construction of the model will have four major directions: (1) to consider an expansion and change in form of educational objectives; (2) to chart succinctly what a school that follows through on these objectives would look like organizationally; (3) to explore more fully some of the unique aspects of such a school; (4) to consider the relationship of this school to what society demands. In addition, after constructing the model we will address ourselves briefly to the questions of scheduling, staffing, and teacher training.

The objectives

'A' Objectives

For a starter we can begin with four kinds of objectives, only one set of which is presently legitimized in the schools.

The legitimate ones ('A' objectives), as we have repeatedly indicated, are those that are geared to the attainment of academic skills and subject matter content. These are the objectives that rule the educational roost (in spite of the fact that they have not succeeded in achieving many of our broader educational aims). These are the objectives that almost all educational 'innovations' are turned into. When these are the sole objectives of education all descriptions and diagnoses of any group of people or of any area (for example, urban) become very difficult, because they must be squeezed into subject-matter goals. If we discuss power, identity, diversity, connectedness, and all the other issues we have mentioned, it becomes quite a challenge to try to fit those issues into teaching tasks that have as their aims getting children:

1 to read, to compute, to outline
2 to know the causes of the Civil War

3 to become familiar with the geography of Latin America
4 to know the parts of speech
5 to know the material that constitutes the Earth's crust.

We certainly do not intend to deny the value of such tool skills and knowledge, but we find it difficult to relate sociopsychological descriptions to such objectives. In fact, we think this is a major reason for so many urban teachers becoming annoyed with consultants and with special resource people who feed teachers descriptions and analyses of their pupils. For they, the teachers, are constantly being put in the position of implementing a description when none of their teaching tasks have any intrinsic relation to those descriptions.

We have consistently had our knuckles rapped for the off-handed way we treat 'A' objectives. However, we did not care much, because the objectives we were most interested in have been, and still are treated in an off-handed way by those in the educational power structure. It was not until we were reprimanded by our colleague Bruce Joyce that we began to reconsider. Joyce, in his book *Alternative Models of Elementary Education*, has cogently spread out a menu of academic strategies from which objectives might be derived.[5] He lists as educational strategies those that deal with:

1 Symbolic-technical proficiency (reading, arithmetic, and so forth).

2 Information from selected disciplines (commonly, history and geography).

3 Structure of knowledge (concepts from disciplines).

4 Modes of inquiry (how scholars think).

5 Broad philosophical schools or problems (aesthetics, ethics, and so on).

It is fairly clear to us that, in reality, schools concern themselves largely with Strategies 1 and 2, 'Symbolic-technical proficiency' and 'Information from selected disciplines.' Given *only* these two strategies, we can reiterate our frustration in trying to relate sociopsychological description to them. However, using a combination of the last three strategies on the list makes it easier to relate them to our diagnosis. If we use Strategies 3 through 5 in order to develop academic objectives we would begin by raising such questions as:

a. What *concepts* from what disciplines, or what *philosophical schools of thought* have the greatest priority for the urban issues as we have defined them?

or

b. What *modes of inquiry* from what kinds of scholars would have the greatest priority?

Thus, while still acknowledging the importance of and including skills and subject achievement objectives as a portion of the schools' responsibility, we would like to suggest three more sets of objectives:

'B' Objectives

1 to have the children acquire the skills of negotiating with adults

2 to have the children devise a variety of strategies for getting something they want

3 to have the children learn to identify the real power sources in their community

4 to have the children develop the skills of organizing people in order to create some change in their immediate social realities

5 to have the children learn to use all forms of media in order to gain support for some social action they intend to take

6 to have the children develop general skills for constructive social action such as:[6]

a. the ability to define clearly the objectives of social action

b. the ability to evaluate the existing situation, to identify obstacles to the goal, and to identify the available resources for overcoming these obstacles

c. the ability to analyze and to generate alternative measures for action, and to predict the various outcomes of each alternative

d. the ability to select the most valuable of these alternatives and to test them through action

e. the ability to evaluate the tested procedure and to revise strategies, thus beginning the cycle again.[7]

If curriculums were developed with these types of objectives as their focus, we would begin to see a more intrinsic linkage between a teaching task and descriptions of powerlessness.

'C' Objectives

1 to have the children become aware of how with whom they live and where they live influence how they perceive themselves

2 to have the children learn how society's definitions of groups of people affect the way they judge themselves

3 to have the children analyze the criteria they are using for self-judgement in terms of its objective base

4 to have the children become more capable of predicting their own behavior

5 to have the children expand their repertoire of responses to situations

6 to have the children see themselves as more differentiated 'subselves'[8]

7 to have the children discover strengths, talents, and interests within themselves of which they may not now be aware.

Although these objectives are crudely stated, we hope that one can begin to see their relationship with the descriptions of the urban dweller's concern for identity.

'D' objectives

1 to expand the child's repertoire for interaction with others

2 to expand the child's repertoire for interaction with more kinds of others

3 to expand one's capacity for self-disclosure to others

4 to expand one's capacity for taking the risks in going out to others unilaterally

5 to expand one's circle of significant identifications

6 to expand one's ability to 'experience other people as they really are, *i.e.*, to become able to really listen, to really develop a kind of third ear for the music that he's playing as well as the particular notes and words—what he's trying to say as well as what he is actually saying in words.'[9]

One can begin to see the relationship between 'D' objectives and a concern for connectedness. Moreover, this set of objectives is particularly poignant in a society that has been diagnosed as 'white racist' by the President's Commission on Civil Disorders.[10]

When one thinks of all the energy that has gone into the curriculum reform movement without even considering curriculum that might achieve the types of objectives listed in these last three categories, one begins to wonder if we are really serious about dealing with the basic concerns of our society. . . .

Notes

1 See James M. Beshar, *Urban Social Structure*, New York, Free Press, 1962, p. 46.
2 'New York: The city that quit,' editorial by James Reston, *The New York Times*, 22 October 1965.
3 Authors' insertion.
4 From the chapter by Kevin Lynch, 'The city as environment' in *Cities* (a *Scientific American* book), New York, Knopf-Random House, 1966, p. 194.
5 Boston, Ginn, 1969.
6 These are basically problem-solving and scientific method skills, but here they are applied directly to social action.
7 Fantini and Weinstein, *The Disadvantage: Challenged to Education*, New York, Harper & Row, 1968, p. 436.
8 Briefly, a subself may be thought of as one of the many characters of the self, each of which plays different roles and whose interaction with one another constitutes a unified self-image. Sample characters or subself voices heard during a specific situation might be: (1) the critic subself, (2) the loving subself, (3) the hurt, sorrowful child subself, (4) the protecting subself, (5) the observing subself. The concept of subselves is derived from Dr Stewart Shapiro, whose article 'Transactional aspects of ego therapy,' *Journal of Psychology* (1963), pp. 487–9, explains the term more fully.
9 Abraham H. Maslow, *Eupsychian Management*, Homewood, Ill., Richard D. Irwin and Dorsey Press, 1965, p. 168.
10 *Report of the National Advisory Commission on Civil Disorders*, New York, Bantam Books, 1968.

3.2 Why we must disestablish school

Ivan Illich

... Not only education but social reality itself has become schooled. It costs roughly the same to school both rich and poor in the same dependency. The yearly expenditure per pupil in the slums and in the rich suburbs of any one of twenty US cities lies in the same range—and sometimes is favorable to the poor.[1] Rich and poor alike depend on schools and hospitals which guide their lives, form their world view, and define for them what is legitimate and what is not. Both view doctoring oneself as irresponsible, learning on one's own as unreliable, and community organization, when not paid for by those in authority, as a form of aggression or subversion. For both groups the reliance on institutional treatment renders independent accomplishment suspect. ...

Once basic needs have been translated by a society into demands for scientifically produced commodities, poverty is defined by standards which the technocrats can change at will. Poverty then refers to those who have fallen behind an advertised ideal of consumption in some important respect. In Mexico the poor are those who lack three years of schooling, and in New York they are those who lack twelve.

The poor have always been socially powerless. The increasing reliance on institutional care adds a new dimension to their helplessness: psychological impotence, the inability to fend for themselves. Peasants on the high plateau of the Andes are exploited by the landlord and the merchant—once they settle in Lima they are, in addition, dependent on political bosses, and disabled by their lack of schooling. Modernized poverty combines the lack of power over circumstances with a loss of personal potency. This modernization of poverty is a world-wide phenomenon, and lies at the root of contemporary underdevelopment.

Source: Ivan Illich, *Deschooling Society*, Calder & Boyars (1971), 1–24 (extracts).

Of course it appears under different guises in rich and in poor countries.

It is probably most intensely felt in US cities. Nowhere else is poverty treated at greater cost. Nowhere else does the treatment of poverty produce so much dependence, anger, frustration, and further demands. And nowhere else should it be so evident that poverty—once it has become modernized—has become resistant to treatment with dollars alone and requires an institutional revolution.

Today in the United States the black and even the migrant can aspire to a level of professional treatment which would have been unthinkable two generations ago, and which seems grotesque to most people in the Third World. For instance, the US poor can count on a truant officer to return their children to school until they reach seventeen, or on a doctor to assign them to a hospital bed which costs sixty dollars per day—the equivalent of three months' income for a majority of the people in the world. But such care only makes them dependent on more treatment, and renders them increasingly incapable of organizing their own lives around their own communities. . . .

It should be obvious that even with schools of equal quality a poor child can seldom catch up with a rich one. Even if they attend equal schools and begin at the same age, poor children lack most of the educational opportunities which are casually available to the middle-class child. These advantages range from conversation and books in the home to vacation travel and a different sense of oneself, and apply, for the child who enjoys them, both in and out of school. So the poorer student will generally fall behind so long as he depends on school for advancement or learning. The poor need funds to enable them to learn, not to get certified for the treatment of their alleged disproportionate deficiencies. . . .

School appropriates the money, men, and good will available for education and in addition discourages other institutions from assuming educational tasks. Work, leisure, politics, city living, and even family life depend on schools for the habits and know-ledge they presuppose, instead of becoming themselves the means of education. Simultaneously both schools and the other institutions which depend on them are priced out of the market.

In the United States the per capita costs of schooling have risen almost as far as the cost of medical treatment. But increased treatment by both doctors and teachers has shown steadily declining results. Medical expenses concentrated on those above forty-five have doubled several times over a period of forty years with a resulting 3 per cent increase in life expectancy in men. The increase in educational expenditures has produced even stranger results; otherwise President Nixon could not have been moved this spring to promise that every child shall soon have the 'Right to Read' before leaving school.

In the United States it would take eighty billion dollars per year to provide what educators regard as equal treatment for all in grammar and high school. This is well over twice the $36 billion now being spent. Independent cost projections prepared at HEW [The Department of Health, Education and Welfare] and the University of Florida indicate that by 1974 the comparable figures will be $107 billion as against the $45 billion now projected and these figures wholly omit the enormous costs of what is called 'higher education,' for which demand is growing even faster. The United States, which spent nearly eighty billion dollars in 1969 for 'defense' including its deployment in Vietnam, is obviously too poor to provide equal schooling. The President's committee for the study of school finance should ask not how to support or how to trim such increasing costs, but how they can be avoided. . . .

Obligatory schooling inevitably polarizes a society; it also grades the nations of the world according to an international caste system. Countries are rated like castes whose educational dignity is determined by the average years of schooling of its citizens, a rating which is closely related to per capita gross national product, and much more painful.

The paradox of the schools is evident: increased expenditure escalates their destructiveness at home and abroad. This paradox must be made a public issue. It is now generally accepted that the physical environment will soon be destroyed by biochemical pollution unless we reverse current trends in the production of physical goods. It should also be recognized that social and personal life is threatened equally by HEW pollution, the inevitable by-product of obligatory and competitive consumption of welfare.

The escalation of the schools is as destructive as the escalation of weapons but less visibly so. Everywhere in the world school costs have risen faster than enrollments and faster than the GNP; everywhere expenditures on school fall even further behind the expectations of parents, teachers, and pupils. Everywhere this situation discourages both the motivation and the financing for large-scale planning for nonschooled learning. The United States is proving to the world that no country can be rich enough to afford a school system that meets the demands this same system creates simply by existing, because a successful school system schools parents and pupils to the supreme value of a larger school system, the cost of which increases disproportionately as higher grades are in demand and become scarce. . . .

Equal educational opportunity is, indeed, both a desirable and a feasible goal, but to equate this with obligatory schooling is to confuse salvation with the Church. School has become the world religion of a modernized proletariat, and makes futile promises of salvation to the poor of the technological age. The nation-state has adopted it, drafting all citizens into a graded curriculum leading to sequential diplomas not unlike the initiation rituals and hieratic promotions of former times. The modern state has assumed the duty of enforcing the judgment of its educators through well-meant truant officers and job requirements, much as did the Spanish kings who enforced the judgments of their theologians through the conquistadors and the Inquisition. . . .

A second major illusion on which the school system rests is that most learning is the result of teaching. Teaching, it is true, may contribute to certain kinds of learning under certain circumstances. But most people acquire most of their knowledge outside school, and in school only insofar as school, in a few rich countries, has become their place of confinement during an increasing part of their lives.

Most learning happens casually, and even most intentional learning is not the result of programmed instruction. Normal children learn their first language casually, although faster if their parents pay attention to them. Most people who learn a second language well do so as a result of odd circumstances and not of sequential teaching. They go to live with their grandparents, they travel, or they fall in love with a foreigner. Fluency in reading is also more often than not a result of such extracurricular activities. Most people who read widely, and with pleasure, merely believe that they learned to do so in school; when challenged, they easily discard this illusion.

But the fact that a great deal of learning even now seems to happen casually and as a by-product of some other activity defined as work or leisure does not mean that planned learning does not benefit from planned instruction and that both do not stand in need of improvement. The strongly motivated student who is faced with the task of acquiring a new and complex skill may benefit greatly from the discipline now associated with the old-fashioned schoolmaster who taught reading, Hebrew, catechism, or multiplication by rote. School has now made this kind of drill teaching rare and disreputable, yet there are many skills which a motivated student with normal aptitude can master in a matter of a few months if taught in this traditional way. This is as true of codes as of their encipherment; of second and third languages as of reading and writing; and equally of special languages such as algebra, computer programming, chemical analysis, or of manual skills like typing, watchmaking, plumbing, wiring, TV repair; or for that matter dancing, driving, and diving. . . .

Potential skill teachers are never scarce for long because, on the one hand, demand for a skill grows only with its performance within a community and, on the other, a man exercising a skill could also teach it. But, at present, those using skills which are in demand and do require a human teacher are discouraged from sharing these skills with others. This is done either by teachers who monopolize the licenses or by unions which protect their trade interests. Skill centers which would be judged by customers on their results, and not on the personnel they employ or the process they use, would open unsuspected working opportunities, frequently even for those who are now considered unemployable. Indeed, there is no reason why such skill centers should not be at the work place itself, with the employer and his work force supplying instruction as well as jobs to those who choose to use their educational credits in this way.

In 1956 there arose a need to teach Spanish quickly to several hundred teachers, social workers, and ministers from the New York Archdiocese so that they could communicate with Puerto Ricans. My friend Gerry Morris announced over a Spanish radio station that he needed native speakers from Harlem. Next day some two hundred teen-agers lined up in front of his office, and he selected four dozen of them—many of them school dropouts. He trained them in the use of the US Foreign Service Institute (FSI) Spanish manual, designed for use by linguists with graduate training, and within a week his teachers were on their own—each in charge of four New Yorkers who wanted to speak the language. Within six months the mission was accomplished. Cardinal Spellman could claim that he had 127 parishes in which at least three staff members could communicate in Spanish. No school program could have matched these results. . . .

The deschooling of society implies a recognition of the two-faced nature of learning. An insistence on skill drill alone could be a disaster; equal emphasis must be placed on other kinds of learning. But if schools are the wrong places for learning a skill, they are even worse places for getting an education. School does both tasks badly, partly because it does not distinguish between them. School is inefficient in skill instruction especially because it is curricular. In most schools a program which is meant to improve one skill is chained always to another irrelevant task. History is tied to advancement in math, and class attendance to the right to use the playground.

Schools are even less efficient in the arrangement of the circumstances which encourage the open-ended, exploratory use of acquired skills, for which I will reserve the term 'liberal education.' The main reason for this is that school is obligatory and becomes schooling for schooling's sake: an enforced stay in the company of teachers, which pays off in the doubtful privilege of more such company. Just as skill instruction must be freed from curricular restraints, so must liberal education be dissociated from obligatory attendance. Both skill-learning and education for inventive and creative behavior can be aided by institutional arrangement, but they are of a different, frequently opposed nature.

Most skills can be acquired and improved by drills, because skill implies the mastery of definable and predictable behavior. Skill instruction can rely, therefore, on the simulation of circumstances in which the skill will be used. Education in the exploratory and creative use of skill, however, cannot rely on drills. Education can be the outcome of instruction, though instruction of a kind fundamentally opposed to drill. It relies on the relationship between partners who already have some of the keys which give access to memories stored in and by the community. It relies on the critical intent of all those who use memories creatively. It relies on the surprise of the unexpected question which opens new doors for the inquirer and his partner. . . .

Contemporary society is the result of conscious designs, and educational opportunities must be designed into them. Our reliance on specialized, full-time instruction through school will now decrease, and we must find more ways to learn and teach: the educational quality of all institutions must increase again. But this is a very ambiguous forecast. It could mean that men in the modern city will be increasingly the victims of an effective process of total instruction and manipulation once they are deprived of even the tenuous pretense of critical independence which liberal schools now provide for at least some of their pupils. . . .

The major obstacle on the way to a society that truly educates was well defined by a black friend of mine in Chicago, who told me that our imagination was 'all schooled up.' We permit the state to ascertain the universal educational deficiencies of its citizens and establish one specialized agency to treat them. We thus share in the delusion that we can distinguish between what is necessary education for others and what is not, just as former generations established laws which defined what was sacred and what was profane. . . .

The very existence of obligatory schools divides any society into two realms: some time spans and processes and treatments and professions are 'academic' or 'pedagogic,' and others are not. The power of school thus to divide social reality has no boundaries: education becomes unworldly and the world becomes non-educational.

Reference

1 Penrose B. Jackson, *Trends in Elementary and Secondary Education Expenditures: Central City and Suburban Comparisons 1965 to 1968*, us Office of Education, Office of Program and Planning Evaluation, 1969.

3.3 The city as educator: how to be radical without even trying

Edgar B. Gumbert

It is the contention in this paper that a simple but effective change which could save the schools for the benefit of future generations would be for them to renounce their alleged power to do social good beyond themselves. They should be purged of their service and noneducational functions—e.g., custodial care and manpower supply and should withdraw from any specific social initiatives—from trying to shape social change. Schools on the whole are powerless to produce social development or to influence either its amount or its speed.

To claim otherwise involves both schooling and education in a double danger. In the first place, there is the possibility that public opinion will swing from expecting too much from the schools to denying their ability to provide any useful instruction. Thus disillusioned, the public might withdraw value from all school activities, some of which continue to be of worth. Indeed, the schools will grow in stature and esteem as intellectual institutions as their attempts to affect social issues in the world decline. That is to say, the less effective the school is as a social power, the more effective it will be as a pedagogical power. The school's power lies in its ability to help us engage in a variety of intellectual exploratory activities, at different levels of sophistication and inclusiveness, under the direction of educational leaders. The function of the reformed school should be to make a contribution to our powers of understanding and control over ourselves and our environment which could not be made as elegantly by any other institution. The school should help initiate us (see Peters, 1963; 1966, pp. 46–62) into the specialized discourses of the structures of knowledge—expressed in a variety of 'languages'—that are necessary for an understanding of the full meaning of human development.

Source: *Education and Urban Society* (1971), 4 (1), 8–17.

Their physical resources, the willingness of many excellent teachers to work in them, and some of their traditions favor retaining schools as one kind of educational agency. Taken together, these resources, teachers and traditions enable the schools to contribute to the improvement of our intellectual and creative powers. These powers are developed in our attempt to master materials. In the dynamic transactions between men and materials, both are shaped and defined. This 'struggle' gives form and meaning to our feelings and concepts. Discipline develops from our work with materials, as does our humanity. Freedom and dignity rest upon our access to materials and to tools—physical and symbolic—with which to fashion them. The schools can contribute to our development by providing materials, tools, leaders, and a setting, *when and how we need them.*

The second danger attached to making exaggerated claims about the power of schools to effect broad social reform is that, if social energies were focused on school reform alone, our attention would be distracted from changes that are urgently needed in virtually all other social institutions. Problems which seem to be school problems frequently are social or economic problems—problems of housing, of town planning, of transportation, for example.

There is a limit to what we can expect from tinkering with the school system. The massive federal investment in schooling in the sixties brought about few of the consequences so ardently desired by its supporters. A feverish search for even more funds to solve the problems would be tragically misplaced. Instead of patching up the traditional school system with the help of enormous funds, we should radically change the schools by giving them limited and clearly defined functions. This new radical school would be austere, modest, simple, direct, trusting, at once reverent and irreverent toward the mysteries of knowledge and of ignorance. It would not be part of a system in the sense that the school is today; consequently it would not need the administrator-ridden, inflated bureaucratic machinery that we have currently. Instead of patching up the old conveyance or of making it even more luxurious, which would limit the roads on which we can travel and the places to which we can go, we should now park it, get out, and honorably walk. This makes more experience possible. We might need assistance from time to time to get us to where we want to go; therefore we might need a pilot or driver. But his influence over us would be temporary and according to our needs; we would be travelling on our schedule, not on one drawn up by some other person for his profit or for his bookkeeping convenience. If applied to schooling, this analogy presents a picture quite different from what now exists.

Educational reform: the networks in cities

Obviously our efforts must not be solely to improve schools and schooling; they must also be to change the conditions under which and the agencies through which education takes place. The specialized function of intellectual instruction in the schools can develop only on the basis of widely diffused general education. One radical reform calls for another. In this case, the radical departure consists of unlocking and using rather than wasting the enormous and powerful educational resources we already have. Many of the functions of schools as they now are constituted— e.g., skill learnings and peer activities—could be redistributed among other institutions which now exist, particularly in cities.

Within the city there are what Ivan Illich (1970b: 7/1-7/38) calls 'educational networks' of fantastic richness and variety waiting to be unlocked and utilized. Illich's four networks are: (1) educational objects—e.g., botanical gardens, libraries, museums, shops, and factories; (2) skill models—e.g., persons who can teach a foreign language or playing a musical instrument; (3) peer matches —persons who are interested at a given time in a selected problem or topic; and (4) educational leaders who can assist in exploratory activities, already referred to.

Public funds for education which now go almost entirely to schools could be distributed in such a way that they would better 'exploit' for educational purposes these other already existing community resources. For example, annual educational expenditures, in amounts publicly and officially agreed upon, could be distributed directly to individual learners in the form of educational vouchers, which could be exchanged for the educational goods and services the learners desire. Moreover, tax advantages could be given to jewellers, rare book collectors, seamstresses, oriental rug merchants, or to other specialists who undertook to devote time to instruction in their fields. Some individuals, organizations, and businesses no doubt would provide educational materials and services free.

Virtually everybody in the community could take on educational responsibilities. Instead of infrequent field trips from schools, learners would return to schools for varying lengths of time. Minibuses which would individualize point-to-point transportation to educational resources could easily be made available. Precincts for walking, cycling, or even for animal carts could be created.

Given these new experiences with authority and with community, it is possible that the schools in the city would be reawakened and their intellectual tasks strengthened. Both education and schooling in this case could contribute to an 'awareness of new levels of human potential and the use of one's creative powers to foster human life' (Illich, 1970a, p. 166).

The first three networks exist largely or entirely outside schools and their control. Most time would be spent, and probably most learning would occur, in them. The fourth network exists both within and without the schools as they are discussed above. Although less time might be spent in exploratory activities, they are more powerful, because it is primarily through them that we are rendered able to unlock and to use with more awareness and adroitness the resources of the other three.

The educational power and potential of the city

The city itself can be seen as an educational object. It provides for its inhabitants, young and old, an education of both the intellect and the emotions which is far more immediate and dramatic in its effects than an education provided by formal schooling. It would be difficult to argue that any other single area of land offers as wide a scope for learning and for shaping the lives of men as do cities. Schools can be ascetic, as suggested in this paper, because cities are opulent.

Cities contain many of the best—and the worst—elements of our cultural heritage; they are centers for the fusion of the past, present, and future, the old and the new. The constant interplay of contrasting elements can enhance and help expand our intellectual activities. Many enlivening experiences are available. Untold pleasures, adventures—and escapes—suggest themselves. Different life styles conflict and compete with each other for credibility and acceptance. Social class, race, and ethnicity, for example, are complex social forces with which it is edifying to deal. The character and quality of these forces are subjects of considerable importance, for they play a prominent role in the formation of our personalities and intellects. The personality must find 'new moorings' in the city (Illich, 1970a, p. 146). 'Urbanization for the individual,' Illich points out (ibid), 'means the search for new coordinates to his most intimate feelings and drives.' In effect, cities can afford us new insights into social actualities and social possibilities. These new perspectives in turn make it possible for us to increase our comprehension of and our control over our own lives.

The architecture of a city exerts a constant and significant influence on the life styles of its inhabitants. Buildings are valuable items in a network of educational objects; at the same time, they provide the infrastructure for other educational networks. That is to say, urban architecture and design are educative as both content and form.

As educational objects, city buildings are documents linking us to our past. They can be thought of as palimpsests—records of time and change. Like public records, they should be available to all without privilege or prejudice. Everybody can learn to 'read' them. Anything which denies us this connection with our past is in part an attack on our person and our property—on our psychological health and our cultural heritage.

As infrastructure architecture provides the 'permanent setting of a culture against which its social drama can be played out with the fullest help to the actors' (Mumford, 1952, p. 111). Le Corbusier (1964, p. 25) claimed that 'civic spirit can be born of living architecture.' Lewis Mumford (Howe, 1971, p. 68) has suggested that 'perhaps the best definition of the city in its higher aspects is that it is a place designed to offer the widest facilities for significant conversation.' Urban structure—architectural forms, their uses, and the spatial relationships among them—obviously can either help or hinder movement and meeting, contact, and communication. If it fosters conversation, then it is in the broadest and best sense educative. For by meeting and by talking we continuously create and recreate social life and reality. Urban structure thus is one of the single most important influences on the quality and scope of the four educational networks discussed above and on the ease and frequency with which they are used. As these networks, when taken together, have unrivalled educational power, urban structure is an indispensable component of the foundations of education.

The density of a city—an outgrowth of structure—also is an important ingredient in its educational value. It clearly has important social consequences. The quality of human relations changes in a dense city society. Individual expression and eccentricity, rather than conformity and homogeneity, can develop. Deviant and diverse subcultures, such as bohemian and student groups, are more likely to emerge; movement among and mingling within them is made easier. Human mix stimulates awareness and increases our ability to communicate with each other. Richard Sennett (1970, p. 68) holds that

In the dense, diverse communities the process of making multiple contacts would burst the boundaries of thinking couched in homogeneous small group terms. Since urban space would be free for all manner of incursion, the neat categories of spatial experience in cities – such as home, school, work, shopping, parks and playgrounds – could not be maintained. Men would find community problems and community experiences, as well as community conflicts, not limited to the sphere of their own small jobs, just as the region where a man lived would not be immune to a diverse circle of influences and modes of life.

In dense societies, city streets are important educational objects. The streets of Paris or Florence or Vienna, for example, invite people to stroll about, with or without aim or purpose, to take in rather than to reject impressions, to think, to feel, to enjoy, to mix, to see, and be seen—in short, to celebrate existence. As Bernard Rudofsky (1969) has pointed out, classrooms cannot compete with streets for many important kinds of learning experiences. The ancients knew this. The great teachers of Greece preferred to talk and to instruct while walking in the streets. The Stoics took their name from stoa, the protected walkways on which they liked to teach. The Romans, too, used porticos as educational centers. The visual pleasures of walking, the opportunities for coming into contact with other people, the awareness of community when on the streets—all can enhance our humanity.

In addition to being educational objects in their own right, streets are vital networks taking us to other important educational objects—to parks and squares, to markets, to libraries and museums, to shops, cinemas, and theatres, to restaurants, pubs, and cafes, to schools and universities.

A. E. Parr (1967, p. 3) has stated so well some of the things we have in mind that it is worth quoting him at some length:

Until I reached the age of five we lived a short commuter distance outside of a town of about 75,000 on the west coast of Norway. Not as a chore, but as an eagerly desired pleasure, I was fairly regularly entrusted with the task of buying fish and bringing it home alone. This involved the following: walking to the station in five to ten minutes; buying ticket; watching train with coal-burning steam locomotive pull in; boarding train; riding across long bridge over shallows separating smallboat harbor ... from ship's harbor ... including small naval base with torpedo boats; continuing through a tunnel; leaving train at terminal, sometimes dawdling to look at railroad equipment; walking by and sometimes entering fisheries museum; passing central town park where military band played during midday break; strolling by central shopping and business district, or alternatively, passing fire station with horses at ease under suspended harnesses, ready to go, and continuing past centuries old town hall and other ancient buildings; exploration of fish market and fishing fleet; selection of fish; haggling about price; purchase and return home.

When I was five we moved into the town itself, and I started to kindergarten and elementary school soon after. The days would go as follows: off to school with the other children joining the morning stream of white-collar pedestrian males ranging from clerks to ship-owners, usually not walking with our elders but unavoidably exposed to overhearing adult conversation and observing adult behavior; soon passing a small botanical garden and greenhouse and a large building housing a substantial museum of natural history and a fair museum of history and ethnography; passing, also, a great architectural variety of residences; then the railroad terminal and the building opposite which houses the fisheries museum previously mentioned, and also, on higher floors, a museum of decorative arts, a small city art gallery and the exhibition halls of the art association; past the central park with the music stand to the school, which shared a block with the fire station, city prison and an historic but still functioning public building. These were the days of two work periods with a long mid-day break. During the break the morning route was reversed, with stops to listen to the military band, to pay visits to museums ... and to seek other adventures. At this time the stream would include some women, and it would cross a flow of blue-collar workers moving in the other direction. In the afternoon the pedestrian procession would go back again, but now with a considerable number of wives on errands of their own, starting out with, or more or less at the same time as their husbands and proceeding to the same parts of town, sometimes accompanied by their children, there being no afternoon elementary school. When spending free time in our own neighborhood, I had only about 300 feet to walk to watch activities in a booming shipyard; about 1,000 feet farther along came the public aquarium; and immediately beyond that was the seawater moat protecting the naval station, where sticklebacks nested in the seaweeds; sculpins, gobies and small flounders darted about and could be watched for hours. In another direction it was about 300 feet to ferry stairs where I could fish, about 600 feet to a large dock and coal depot, and many rocky, still vacant lots to explore. There were also frequent visits, unaccompanied, back to the natural history and the history museum. This is actually only a very incomplete list of how things were around 1905–7.

It seems, then, that radical changes in education should begin with a reform of schooling along the lines indicated above and with changes in the texture and density of our cities. They should take into account the way our streets and other educational objects are made available to us. That is to say, radical changes in education involve nothing more nor less than rearranging our cities so as to release their educational powers. We should try to create again, in principle although obviously not in all details, urban communities where people can have the kinds of experiences that Parr describes, communities where children and adults can live, work, play, and learn together.

The task obviously will not be easy. Ideological and material forces have fused to create formidable barriers to developing and using the educational potential of cities.

References

Howe, I. (1971) 'The city in literature,' *Commentary*, 51 (May), 61–8.
Illich, I. D. (1970a) *Celebration of Awareness: A Call for Institutional Revolution*, New York, Doubleday.
Illich, I. D. (1970b) Ciclo Lectures, summer. Mexico, Centro Intercultural de Documentacion (CIDOC cuaderno 1007).
Illich, I. D. (1971) 'Education without school: how it can be done,' *New York Review of Books* 12 (7 January, 25–31).
Le Corbusier (1964) *The Radiant City*, New York, Orion.
Mumford, L. (1952) *Art and Technics*, Columbia University Press.
Parr, A. E. (1967) 'The child in the city: urbanity and the urban scene,' *Landscape* (spring), 3–5.
Peters, R. S. (1963) *Education as Initiation*, London, Evans.
Peters, R. S. (1966) *Ethics and Education*, London, Allen & Unwin.
Rudofsky, B. (1969) *Streets for People: A Primer for Americans*, New York, Doubleday.
Sennett, R. (1970) 'Urban peace through disorder or the uses of anarchy,' *Psychology Today* 6 (November), 66–9.

3.4   A proposal for education in community

Fred M. Newmann and Donald W. Oliver

Since we believe that efforts at reform have generally failed to consider the fundamental importance of *contexts* in which education is pursued, we begin by conceptualizing alternative modes of, and environments for, learning. Imagine a hypothetical community in which learning is pursued in three quite different contexts: the 'school' context, the 'laboratory-studio-work' context, and the 'community seminar' context. Subjects or problems for study and also the relations between students and teachers would be construed quite differently in each of these contexts.[1]

The school context. There is a clear need for systematic instruction in basic literacy skills, health and hygiene, driver education, and the like. Learning of this sort is pre-planned, programmed, and formalized. The teacher has clear objectives or 'terminal behaviors' in mind as the products of instruction. Most of the activity in schools as we now know them falls in this category. This is not to suggest that school-based learning should continue to follow traditional subject matter lines, nor that instruction be didactic and rote. On the contrary, school learning should be problem-centred and exciting and should constantly consider reorganizing basic content to make it lead toward more powerful insights and understandings; for example, coordinate and symbol systems used in graphs, charts, and maps, might be combined with linguistic analysis and musical notation in teaching a course in symbolics. Technology has thrust upon us rich possibilities for more effective instruction through (a) greater opportunity for self-instruction, (b) availability of multi-media approaches, and (c) more accurate assessment of student needs and progress. Teaching within a school context may take many forms: tutorial between teacher and student, student with computer or programmed instruction, students in small groups, or large

Source: *Harvard Educational Review* (1967), 37 (1), 95–104.

groups watching films. The distinguishing feature of the school context is that it concerns itself only with those aspects of education involving systematic, planned instruction. It should be clear from the explanation of the following two contexts that we see this kind of learning as only *one* among three critical types.

Laboratory-studio-work context. In the laboratory context, the major objective is not formal instruction, but the completion of a significant task, the solution of problems which the learner wants to attack, regardless of educational by-products that dealing with the problem might bring. The physical location of the laboratory context might be a factory, art studio, hospital, library, science or industrial laboratory, political party headquarters, or government agency. The activity of participants would be governed, not by a skill or a product that is programmed for students to learn, but only by the developing nature of the problem-task itself. Such problems might include painting a picture, rebuilding a car, writing an essay, promoting a concert, organizing a protest demonstration, lobbying for legislation, selling insurance, programming a computer, acting in a play, nursing in a hospital, competing in a sport, participating in conservation and wildlife management, caring for children, planning and participating in a church service, broadcasting on radio and television, making a dress, printing a newspaper, making physical and chemical experiments, serving as a guide at the UN, organizing a raffle to raise money, or even creating instructional materials for use in a school context. Laboratories are contexts for learning in the midst of action; learning occurs not because it is planned, but only as an inevitable by-product of genuine participation in problem- and task-oriented activities. The laboratory is seen not primarily as apprenticeship or vocational training for breadwinning, but rather as the opportunity to satisfy broader humanistic and aesthetic goals. At present many adults are engaged in laboratory contexts—that is, their jobs—which are not recognized or supported for their educational value. Young people are deemed not 'ready' to participate until they first spend twelve to sixteen years in 'school.' We believe the laboratory offers important educational benefits at all ages; it should not be restricted to adults.

Community seminar context. The purpose of the seminar would be the reflective exploration of community issues and ultimate meanings in human experience. The seminar would provide an opportunity for the gathering of heterogeneous or homogeneous groups, for youth and/or adults, to examine and discuss issues of mutual concern. Seminars might begin by focusing on problems specific to members of the group (e.g., the meaning of productive work for people unemployed, retired, or dissatisfied with their jobs). Discussion might be stimulated by outside provocateurs who present new ways of viewing economic, ethical, or aesthetic questions. Seminars could have at their service a qualified resource staff that would gather information (readings, films, TV programs) and make arrangements for experiences, such as field trips, to observe unfamiliar ways of life, technological innovations, social problems in action. In addition to relatively specific problems (What kinds of working conditions are we entitled to?) and general public policy questions (How should the community be zoned?), we would hope that the seminars would concern themselves with the broadest questions raised in planning for education in community. Other possible topics include: understanding various conflicts between youth and adults, the functions of the family in modern society, attitudes toward nonconformity and deviance in the community, prejudice and pluralism among ethnic groups, changing mores in sex and religion, various approaches to child-rearing, the use of increased leisure, population control, protection of the consumer, moral implications of advances in biology (e.g., selective breeding), reconstruction of the political and legal system, evaluation of current programs sponsored by government and private agencies, creation of new professions and problems of vocational retraining. The major thrust of the seminars would be reflection and deliberation, though the questions discussed would be highly relevant to the laboratory context or the world of 'action'. Learning in the seminar would not be pre-planned, nor would there be specific tasks or problems to solve. Questions would be raised, investigated, and discussed—this process, regardless of numerous and unpredictable possible outcomes, is of high educational value. Generally both youth and adults are denied the kind of learning afforded by this context; the time of youth is monopolized by school, and that of adults by jobs or 'laboratories.'

Points of clarification. The contexts described above are intended to convey the major point that education consists of three important facets: systematic instruction, action, and reflection. The facets are not listed in order of importance, nor chronologically. All three should occur concurrently at all stages of life. A child learning how to read in a school context can participate in a laboratory project of building a model airplane (using the symbolic skills acquired in 'school'); he can also discuss with children and adults in a seminar what to do about noise control for the local airport. An adult interested in politics might study government systematically in school; he might participate in the 'laboratory' of a political campaign; and in the community seminar, he might lead discussions on political organization appropriate for the modern community. While some communities may choose to place most young children in the school context and allocate much of adult education to the seminar, we see no logical reason for this particular arrangement. Our scheme allows for various mixtures of the three components to be tailored to the needs of various stages of life or to the unique requirements of different types of communities.

Who would fill the leadership roles in such an educational scheme? If formal school comprises only one-third of the educational program, will professional educators be put out of work? Possibly, but not necessarily. Those most qualified to carry on instruction may well be teachers and educators currently working in schools. Thus many teachers and administrators would stay in schools (although advances in technology suggest radical changes in their roles and jobs even if they do stay there). Since learning in school would occupy only a small portion of the student's day—perhaps three hours—one might expect school staffs to dwindle. If, however, adults also used the school for instruction, then the school's student population would increase, even though any given student spent only a small amount of time there. The demand for professional educators would remain high.

Leaders in the laboratory contexts would be experienced persons in the various laboratory areas (engineers, lawyers, mechanics, poets, politicians, athletes, secretaries) who would be given released time to take on educational responsibility for youth and adults interested in laboratory activity. It is possible that professional educationists can be converted into laboratory leaders; for example, an English teacher could take on apprentices in the writing of poetry, but in his laboratory role, he would be interested primarily in the creation and analysis of artistic works, not in teaching. The laboratory context would rely primarily upon private enterprise, government, the arts, labor, etc. to provide creative practitioners willing to assume on-the-job educational responsibility. If we are willing to recognize as teachers the vast number of talented practitioners in such fields, we shall approach a dramatic solution to the manpower problem of finding enough intelligent 'teachers.' By taking advantage of the educational value of the on-the-job activities, we may begin to break the strangle-hold by which the education profession has restricted our conception of education.

Community seminars could be run by professional educators, businessmen, politicians, parents, laborers, policemen, boy scouts, gang leaders, criminals, musicians, or journalists. The community seminar, perhaps more than the school or laboratory, raises the issue of incentive. What would induce people to participate in such activities? The success of such programs depends upon the willingness of various organizations to provide released time for leaders and participants. Financial arrangements must insure that such activities do not economically penalize participants. On the contrary, it would be reasonable to give monetary rewards for participation in educational activities. Paying people for undergoing training is already done on a large scale (neighborhood youth corps, Jobs Corps, scholarships and fellowships, prizes and rewards for high grades, in-training programs of businesses, etc.), and is quite consistent with the idea of making an investment in the development of human resources. We would assume that, given the time and money, the tasks and issues explored in these contexts could be sufficiently exciting to attract wide participation.

A community concerned with implementing some of these general ideas would require coordination of several resources, including private voluntary agencies such as churches, businesses, museums, and libraries, political parties, economic and political pressure groups, and social service organizations. It would require flexibility and attention to individual differences; yet to avoid the problems of fragmentation or specialization, it would have to facilitate participation in common experiences through which members could relate across economic, racial, political, ethnic, or occupational lines.

Implementing a program along these lines seems at first glance an administrator's nightmare, involving the coordination of disparate agencies and the cooperation of people with conflicting vested interests. Will colleges recognize the value of laboratory and seminar experience in their admissions policy? Would the education establishment be willing to relinquish much of its control over the learning of youth? Would business accept for employment people with varying, rather than standardized educational backgrounds? Who would have the power to accredit educational programs, and what new criteria would be needed? At the moment, we have no satisfactory answers for such problems, and we recognize the difficulty of putting some of these ideas into practice. It is possible that, in implementing the three contexts, an educational bureaucracy as rigid as the present one would evolve, with tight scheduling and compartmentalization equal to, or worse than, the current system. All we can say at this point is that the implementation must be guided by serious attention to criteria for building community, else the purpose of educational change will be defeated. It thus becomes clear that when we speak of educational change, we speak of social and community change —a process for which few people have useful administrative guidelines.

Moreover, we hesitate to suggest specific plans or models, because we feel these should arise from the basic concerns of particular communities. We envision no national model that could be replicated across the land. Instead, there should develop a plurality of structures and programs. Jencks (1966) has suggested ways in which private groups could compete with each other and with the public education establishment by offering qualitatively different types of education, sensitive to community needs. In a single community, schools, laboratories, and seminars might be run by businesses, parents' groups, teachers, and churches—each competing with each other for students. It should be possible to fund competing enterprises without allowing a single centralized bureaucracy to gain total control. In some communities, literacy training may be a major problem (e.g., an urban slum); in others technical re-training (e.g., an area with a rapidly growing electronics industry); other areas may have particularly acute problems in human relations, or even in the use of leisure time.

Basing education on the needs of particular communities does not imply that students (youth and adults) are being trained for life within that community only. On the contrary, with communication and transportation breakthroughs likely to continue, all communities are becoming more dependent upon each other; their problems are therefore increasingly generalizable. The production of a TV program to publicize the plight of migrant workers involves the same considerations as producing a program to plead for better equipment for the local football team. Organizing tenants to protest against landlords involves processes similar to organizing real estate brokers to protest to Congress. Painting a picture of harvest time is in many ways similar to painting a scene of industrial smokestacks. A discussion of the boring process of cotton picking may be helpful in a later discussion on the meaning of work in an assembly-line. We see no reason to be alarmed that a community's education be focused on critical contemporary issues. If critical, they are, by definition, of relevance to other communities in other times.

... [This tri-school] proposal is not offered as a panacea; it is not intended as a model of community itself. We see the three contexts as vehicles that may broaden our search for solutions. (The existing schooling establishment generally inhibits and stifles that search.) The contexts of *action* and community *reflection* provide alternative techniques of search not ordinarily available in present schooling. Recognizing the educational value of these activities may help to nourish common commitments. The sense of community may also be improved by the dissolution of artificial barriers that tend to fragment certain experiences— barriers based on age, ethnicity, occupation, and especially the distinction between students and those who participate in 'real life.' We clearly recognize the dilemma between allowing for flexibility and diversity on the one hand, and the need to increase communication among different styles of life on the other; but the proposal argues that attacking this dilemma be acknowledged as an educational activity to be supported and encouraged; it also suggests new contexts in which this attack may be pursued. Conventional educational reforms largely ignore such problems by restricting their concept of education to formal instruction.

Assuming that one could find a community willing to alter its patterns of education along some of the general lines mentioned above, where would it turn for direction? Much of its work would move over uncharted waters. There are, however, a number of educational experiments that could be used as possible illustrations of the broader view. Such projects are not necessarily aimed at the construction of community; their efforts may focus on narrower educational matters. Nevertheless, they represent interesting approaches that could be adapted to particular community needs. The following examples have come to our attention, but we feel certain they comprise only a small portion of the total available catalogue. Additional examples should be sought and recorded.

Some examples

In connection with Harvard's Research and Development Center, Robert Belenky, James Reed, and Jonathan J. Clark have instituted a combination preschool and school study group, which we would consider an excellent example of a laboratory activity. Four kinds of people are involved: university educationists, mothers, youths, and young children from a lower-class ghetto in Boston (consisting of two public housing projects: one white and one Negro). Under the supervision of the educationists and mothers, the youths teach young children in a basement recreation room of the Negro project. The educationists and mothers take field trips to explore a variety of the more progressive schools in the greater Boston area to provide information from which to discuss the kind of school experience they would like for their children. There is hope that these discussions will lead to constructive dialogue with the formal school establishment, and, if need be, political and social action to bring about a change in the formal schools. One member of the educationist group is from the ghetto, an artist skilled also in methods of social action and protest. Rather than viewing this project as an educational program to improve formal education, i.e., the schools, one might view this as a continuing educational program in its own right. Rather than construing this kind of activity as mainly temporary, compensatory, or rehabilitative (though it may in fact be the latter), why not consider this as one of a number of normal educational opportunities in which adults and youth might choose to engage?

A second example is a radio club sponsored by an electronics firm in Concord, Massachusetts. Two days a week a group of youths comes to the main factory and works with engineers and technicians, building ham radio sets, exploring radio theory, and exchanging technical information. Presently this club is extra-curricular, piled on top of what for many high school students is an already overburdensome amount of school work. Why not include adult 'hams' as well as young people? Why not construe this as a genuine educational setting and allow the participants to account this time against the school or work responsibilities in their normal schedules?

Some churches are becoming increasingly involved in activities designed to restore community in urban areas. While many of their efforts may be seen as traditional welfare and settlement house services having relatively small influence, others reveal a broader concern for the total pathology in community. Church-sponsored projects have combined the buying and renovating of slum housing for low-income people with manpower training and protests for civil and consumer rights. The Urban Training Center for Christian Mission in Chicago participates in a number of such activities and uses these programs as major parts of a training process for prospective ministers. Trainees live in the slums with the poor (they are given only a few cents for several days), and they participate in action projects like the above as workers for various sponsoring groups. After periods of intensive involvement working in the community, the seminarians withdraw for reflection and deliberation. They are temporarily released from immediate pressures of the day, given time for study and discussion of general issues. The UTC's approach combines the laboratory with the community seminar context and seems to have success in both areas.

Another church-sponsored project illustrates a type of community seminar. Sponsored by the Presbytery of Detroit, the Episcopal Diocese of Michigan, and the Michigan Conference of the United Church of Christ, the Detroit Industrial Mission (DIM) sends clergymen into industrial plants to initiate contacts with men who organize small discussion groups among the workers. Topics are drawn from concerns of the workers themselves. The mission does not preach any particular point of view, but attempts to foster better communication and deeper levels of understanding among all groups in industry. The responsibility of staff members is merely to arrange opportunities for men to say to each other what they think about human and ethical issues that occur in the plant. This illustration has a number of interesting characteristics: (a) it was initiated and carried out by a private, voluntary group, without public funds or public officials; (b) its purpose was to provide neither vocational training nor an opportunity to philosophize about 'great books,' but rather to raise fundamental questions of immediate relevance and importance; (c) the 'teachers' operate from a clear ideological base but are not interested in evangelical conversion; (d) the 'students' are not seen as preparing for some distant goal, but as learning to make better decisions here and now; and (e) there are no sharp age or status distinctions—men at different points in their careers talk sincerely with one another.

The Highlander Folk School, in the Cumberland Mountains of Tennessee, began in the Depression as a labor school to teach workers in the South how to organize and run unions. Often the center of controversy, it offers another example of an environment of reflection directly related to community action. A nonprofit institution supported by private donations and foundation grants, Highlander runs resident adult education programs, teaching adults how to teach others to deal with social problems. The programs consist mainly of workshops arranged in response to specific pressing issues. For example, in 1960, the Student Non-violent Coordinating Committee asked for help in evaluating their own future program. A workshop was held, yielding the decision to concentrate upon voter registration. The School is the scene of many workshops related to civil rights issues and has always been racially integrated. The emphasis is not only on the making of policy decisions, but also on leadership training and the dissem-ination of knowledge gained through the Highlander programs. Concerned with the most explosive of social issues, the School has been attacked in the courts (the state revoked its charter), invest-igated for subversive activities, and destroyed by fire. Similar institutions could be developed as retreat seminars, not limited to a single community, but available as resources to many.

Conclusion

The deliberate effort to view education in community from three vantage points and to look for contexts, outside of the formal school, where people learn is only the first step in any important effort at educational reform—but it is the hardest. After one wrenches oneself loose from the paralyzingly constricted posture that all true education must be programed, planned, compulsory, and public, and it must all happen in schools, one's imagination trips over a host of exciting places for youth and adults to learn, by themselves, and in association with one another. Only after this first step has been taken do really important questions of educational policy arise (Thelen, 1960, pp. 13–14):

What does the educational system have to do with the system of government, of economics, of politics? It is all very well to say that education is for the purpose of maintaining our nation or developing a world order, but what does that mean? Does it mean that every individual must be made literate, wise, loyal and conforming? ... Is a school a cultural island, separated from the community mainland by the same kind of things that separates fantasy from real life? Does the school lead or follow the community or both? We hear a lot about the need to 'involve' citizens in school problems. Who, how, why? Is it just to keep them quiet? or to manipulate them into contributing more money? Is school supposed to 'induct youth into the community'? What does that mean? ... Can the school do the job alone? Or is the school only one part of a community-wide educational system which exists in fact whether the school board knows it or not?

Critics of this position tend to ask for specific blueprints and definite answers to such policy questions. They ask for outlines, schedules and programs, raising such issues as: How much time would students spend in school? Would the rest of their time be completely free or planned and supervized in some way? Who would pay for extra-curricular activities? How could adults be released from their jobs to take responsibility for community education? How would legal authority be allocated among community agencies? Would state departments of education change their requirements? Would colleges accept students with this sort of education? Would the students perform better on standard tests and attain standards of 'excellence' comparable, for example, to European education? Can we demonstrate that education organized around these ideas would have any real pay-off in later life?

To answer such questions directly at this point would be inappropriate. Until people in a community have argued about and accepted some of the premises in this paper and are vitally concerned with implementation for their particular situation, it would be foolhardy for armchair professors to prescribe programs. Providing blueprints in the abstract, not tied to a specific situation, would be inconsistent with our premise that education should arise from real needs and issues within community, not from the drawing boards of distant national planners.

We are chastised for evading the issue of practicality, as critics throw up their hands in despair with our 'unrealistic,' 'unfeasible' ideas. This basic criticism and questions like the above reflect a commitment by critics to the present system, a reluctance to search for fundamental deficiencies in the status quo. The major issue from our point of view is not our inability to give blueprints and specific answers to such questions; financial, logistic, and administrative problems of plural educational contexts are relatively minor difficulties. Instead, the major issue is whether or not we can find people willing to begin serious discussion on premises and ideas rather than only on blueprints and programs. The next step lies not in a more concrete plan, but in a *search for a group of people*, some 'missing community', with the courage and energy to re-examine how education, most broadly conceived as the interaction between reflection and action, can invigorate the lives of all its citizens.

Note

1 These 'three contexts' are discussed in a mimeographed document, 'Walden III,' by Joseph C. Grannis and Donald W. Oliver, presented to a seminar at the Harvard Graduate School of Education, 1965. Similar ideas are also contained in an earlier paper by Grannis (1964).

References

Grannis, J. C. (1964) 'Team teaching and the curriculum' in J. T. Shaplin and H. F. Olds, Jr (eds), *Team Teaching*, New York, Harper & Row.

Jencks, C. (1966) 'Is the public school obsolete?' *Public Interest* (winter issue), 18–27.

Thelen, H. A. (1960) *Education and the Human Quest*, New York, Harper & Row.

3.5 The Parkway Program

Patricia Farrington, Gwynn Pritchard and John Raynor

This article is a revised version of the Broadcast Notes for Television Programme 2 in the Open University course, 'The Curriculum: Context, Design and Development' (E283). Most of the views in quotes come from recorded material (not all of which were finally used in the programme).

The Parkway Program cannot be pinned down in a single description. Anything that is written therefore reflects the Program at a particular time and from a particular viewpoint. This article is based on interviews during a four-day visit in October, 1971, together with information from the Program itself and from the book written by the first Director of the Program, The School Without Walls *by John Bremer and Michael von Moschzisker.*

What is the Parkway Program?

The Parkway Program in Philadelphia is an experimental high school opened in 1969 that has no traditional school building of its own, but encourages its students to find their classrooms, much of their curriculum and many of their teachers from among the resources of their urban community.[1] John Bremer, the first Director of the Program, has said that because Parkway has no space of its own, students must 'take the initiative, go out into the city and make the city their curriculum by making it their campus.' At Parkway, learning can take place anywhere in the city that is convenient, appropriate or helpful. Bremer considered that the city was an essential part of Parkway's curriculum (Bremer and von Moschzisker (1971), pp. 46–7):

> Every student must come to know the city, the complex of places, processes and people with which he lives. He must know it for what it is, understand it in terms of what it can do, and respect it for what it could be . . . Simple city skills come hard at first, but students rapidly

189

catch on and also acquire the courage to attempt more imaginative projects. What is public space? Who can reasonably be expected to help us? How do we ask? When? Where? What organizations of men are there in the city? What do they do? Why? ... The answers to such questions may seem simple, but they are not simple, and certainly not to students—particularly to students from minority groups. They all need to acquire the skills of dealing with the city, to gain a small measure of power over it, for without this they cannot make a contribution.

How does Parkway match up to these aspirations? Of the many innovative features at Parkway, three will be examined here: the administrative organization of the school, the use of community teachers, and the emphasis on student responsibility. Before coming to these features, it should be noted that Parkway is a school within the Philadelphia education system, and students there are expected to meet the requirements of the State of Pennsylvania if they wish to graduate. And although there is a wide variety of courses taught by community teachers from cultural institutions, social service agencies and city departments, as well as individual volunteers, parents and students, there is a permanent, full-time teaching staff plus university interns[2] who offer a large programme of courses in basic skills, traditional academic subjects and others. Parkway could exist on its own resources as a traditional school, but as the innovative Parkway Program, its success undoubtedly depends on the urban community maintaining its support and actively engaging in its work.

Parkway's unique position in the Philadelphia school system

Parkway should first be seen in the context of the Philadelphia school system as a whole. Philadelphia is the fourth largest city in the United States and has the problems of most large American cities. Budget cuts have meant serious overcrowding in the city's schools. Most of the high schools in Philadelphia have between 3,000 and 5,000 students and there are sometimes as many as fifty in a class. One of the Parkway parents said of her son at his previous high school, 'He was given a computerized roster and maybe he doesn't want what's on it. We went to see a counselor because he was being given a repeat math course. She hadn't the foggiest idea who our son was, nor whose adviser was in charge of him and she said, "I'll get back to you, but you know, I have 300 parents to see this week." I haven't heard a thing from that counselor yet.'

But the problem is more than that of school size. Rather it lies in the fact that many high school students reject traditional school values, become disenchanted with the curriculum and, as a result, drop out of the system. One of the features of high schools which Parkway students mention most often is the feeling that they are constantly in competition with each other. At Parkway, students generally feel that they can work together.

Although it was originally established on a Ford Foundation planning grant, Parkway is now publicly funded. It is, unexpectedly, a high school within the School District of Philadelphia and, as we have said, has to meet the same general requirements for graduation as all the other high schools. However, as the present Director, Dr Leonard B. Finkelstein, has said, 'We are able to do things that many of the other schools are unable to do because of, perhaps, the Board turning its head somewhat, or just because we want very much to try things in a way that they haven't been tried before and we've been given that opportunity.' Two possible reasons for Parkway's survival within the system are that it has no school buildings which require outlay or upkeep, and that it draws a number of high school dropouts nominally back into the education system.

It should be stressed that Parkway is not a special school for any particular group, such as the talented, the backward or the dropouts. The student body is chosen by lottery because there are far more applicants than places. At the time of writing, an equal number of places were given to the eight geographical school districts in the city, and a small percentage from suburban and parochial high schools. So, racially and intellectually, the student body is a heterogeneous mix, reflecting the mix of the city itself.

How does Parkway compare with other high schools in Philadelphia? A survey of the Program for the School District of Philadelphia carried out in 1970 was broadly favourable. In academic terms, they reported that of those who got their diplomas in 1970 and wanted to go on to college, all but one got places. It seems that Parkway offers to the student who wants it a range of positive learning experiences using community resources, and that in spite of a number of problems it is a viable alternative to the traditional high school. One thing is certain and that is that small classes and tutorial groups ensure individual attention, often on a one-to-one basis. Compared with classes of up to fifty in other high schools, classes in Parkway never have more than fifteen students. At the time of writing, the overall staff-student ratio was one to eight (including community teachers).

An outline of the early history of the Parkway Program[3]

The Parkway Program is a 'synthesis of two educational concepts which sustain and complement each other'. The first came from Clifford Brenner, an administrative assistant to Philadelphia's School Board. By 1967, it was clear that Philadelphia's schools were already seriously overcrowded, but a new building would have cost $15 million which the Board of Education[4] did not have. The School Administration Building overlooks the Benjamin Franklin Parkway, a mile-long boulevard lined with most of the city's cultural institutions. Looking out of his office window, Brenner realized that the Parkway could form the campus of a school, its institutions could be the classrooms—a completely new kind of school.

The board accepted the proposal in principle and, after various delays, they brought in John Bremer, an English educator who had been educational director of a community-controlled school experiment in New York. Taking Clifford Brenner's framework John Bremer set up a radical educational and administrative experiment. Before Bremer arrived, the proposed programme seemed a huge logistics problem: computers planning each student's timetable, buses shuttling them around, and lots of administrators checking on attendance.

First, Bremer's educational philosophy implied a concept of 'open education' involving the maximum use of community resources. Central to this was the use of community teachers to teach specialized courses. Further, parents were included in the educational process by being asked to comment on the Program and to give any help they could. Second, Bremer's philosophy centred on a belief in student responsibility. Students would plan their own timetable, walk or take public transport to wherever it was in the city that they were being taught. There would be no grades[5]—evaluation was to be on the basis of pass or fail. Students were to contribute to the process of evaluation by making comments on their own progress as well as that of the teacher and of the course to stand alongside the traditional comments by the teacher on the student.

In Bremer's view, the starting points of the concept of a 'school without walls', the use of community resources and student responsibility opened the way for a reformulation of what education means for the present-day urban student.

An outline of the administration of Parkway

Parkway does have a defined structure – it is just not a traditional school structure. In 1971–2 there were four separate, autonomous units in Parkway—Alpha, Beta, Gamma and Delta (names which do not imply any kind of ability grouping). Each unit has its own headquarters in different parts of the city. These headquarters only provide office space for the staff and a communal room and lockers for the students—all classes take place in community facilities ranging from an empty room in a prestige office block to a church hall. At the time of writing there was within each unit, consisting of up to 200 students, a staff of ten full-time certified teachers covering the variety of subject areas required by the state (see the Appendix on p. 202, *Note*, for the requirements of the Pennsylvania State Diploma). There are minimally an equal number of university interns. The staff divide their time between classroom teaching, student counselling and administration. The job of unit head is rotated among the staff. Each unit, as the present Director has said, 'develops its own curriculum, selects its own staff, handles its own problems of government and is related to the greater Parkway in terms of basic philosophy'. Each quarter,[6] the staff and students produce a course catalogue for their own unit (see the Appendix on p. 199 for the list of course offerings by the Beta unit for autumn 1971). There are problems with the use of temporary premises. At the time of writing, Beta for example, was housed in the office area of an abandoned warehouse.

All Parkway unit operations are co-ordinated by a small central staff working with the Director of the Program. This staff is primarily concerned with planning and development, communications between units, central liaison for community teachers, and public relations.

The *tutorial system* is the key part of the programme and the only compulsory element. The students are out in the city for a large part of their day so they must have a reference point, a place where they can go 'and put all their experience in some kind of context'. It is a support group of about fifteen students selected at random, together with a staff member and an intern. Students must attend their tutorial group regularly (a total of about four hours a week). Its purpose is to provide help for the student in planning his goals, choosing his courses of study, evaluating his work, and solving his problems as they come up. It is also a basic skills unit in which all students are provided with essential background in English and mathematics (in addition to the regular courses available). As well as this, the tutorial group acts as a communications unit: the tutorial leader keeps students' records and is in touch with their families. Since the group is determined by chance, the students have to learn to get along with others of different race, age, and background. Bremer felt that without the tutorial group, Parkway might not be a learning community, but a list of courses. With all these functions to fulfil, it is hardly surprising that the tutorial group is not always successful. It demands good leadership, and considerable co-operation from the students.

Each unit holds a *town meeting* when needed. It is a gathering of the student body and staff of the unit to discuss and try to solve problems of general concern to the community. A town meeting may be chaired by a teacher, an intern or a student. It has been said to provide 'lessons in both group organization and group frustration'. The learning of self-government by students used to being told what to do is not a tidy process, but forms a basic principle of the Program.

Management groups are student organizations which help provide services for the successful functioning of the Program. A specific problem is identified or a proposal agreed on, and a management group is formed to deal with it. Among other things, management groups have been formed for publishing a newspaper, social activities, public relations, and improving communications within and between units. The purpose is both to involve students in the administration of the Program and to provide them with an opportunity to develop leadership and management skills.

The use of community teachers at Parkway

About half the curriculum offerings at Parkway are provided by organizations and individuals in the community of Philadelphia, none of whom are paid for their services: the community has assumed some of the responsibility for educating its children. Parkway students can learn through direct experience in, for example, hospitals, offices, workshops and the mass media. The present director has said, 'I don't know that it must be that you have to have a school to have learning, nor that you have to have only a certified teacher who can teach.' Lisa Strick, the Information Officer who is also a staff teacher, has said, 'We make no distinction in terms of the validity of the learning experience that a student receives from one of our teachers and the learning experience which he has with the community person out in the city.'

Each quarter, the staff at Parkway try to find out the needs and interests of the students and then see how many can be met by the staff themselves. For the rest, staff, students or parents go out and find someone who is professionally qualified in the field and willing to give a course. A parent has described how her son got himself a chemistry course when the chemistry classes in Parkway were full, 'He's a senior and needs two more quarters of chemistry. He went to the University of Pennsylvania on his own and wandered into the laboratories. He just started talking to some graduate student there, who knew a fellow who had some time and he's got himself a course.' Many courses are also suggested by individuals who come to Parkway to offer their help.

Although community teachers undoubtedly enrich the range of curriculum experience for the students, this does not guarantee effective teaching. Do they know what will be of most benefit to the students? Are their methods of teaching appropriate? Do they know clearly enough the differences between their own expertise and the students' level? A psychiatrist who taught a class of Parkway students at Temple University at the time of writing did not think that level was a problem: 'All you have to do is begin where they are and show them how they can take the next step.' Although each community teacher has a staff liaison who will advise him on teaching and discipline problems, attendance records and evaluation, it would appear that evaluation of these volunteer teachers present difficulties.

One of the most interesting aspects of the innovation is the enthusiasm of many of the community teachers and their feeling that the students have taught them more than they have taught the students. Some find themselves becoming more tolerant of young people. Many take tremendous care over preparing their classes: the organizer of a course called 'Introduction to Civil Engineering' said that his boss, the director of the city engineering department, spent 'more time on his lecture to the Parkway kids than he did on preparing for a hostile City Council'.

The emphasis on student responsibility at Parkway

Basic to the whole idea of the Parkway curriculum is freedom for the student to find out what he wants to learn, but how does this autonomy square with the credit requirements for graduation in Pennsylvania?[7] According to Lisa Strick, 'The student must take four years of English and three years of social studies, two years of mathematics, one year of science. But the subjects are extremely broadly defined'. Depending on what a student's needs and interests are, credits in English could be in basic reading or basic composition. Or they could be in journalism at one of the city newspapers, television production or drama. As well as the curriculum offerings available, the student is also encouraged to take part in a programme of individual study in an area of his own interest in collaboration with other students if he wishes. The emphasis is on relevance to the student's needs and interests. One of the Parkway parents has said, 'Instead of having to line up with six hundred other kids to see the counselor once a year maybe, youngsters can sit down with their tutorial leader and figure out what credit they need, look at their own record and see what they have taken and start making choices.'

The students take an active role in the planning and administration of the autonomous unit they belong to, because it is their goals which must determine its future direction.

Part of the student's autonomy stems from the changing role of the teacher at Parkway. He is no longer an instructor, but a facilitator of learning, acting more as a resource for the student to turn to when in need of advice. Parkway teachers must believe that the individual student is central to the learning activity. The report of the survey of the Parkway Program for the School District of Philadelphia already mentioned summed it up: 'It takes time to become a Parkway teacher. Teachers are not used to freedom. Teachers are not used to giving pupils genuine responsibility. Teachers are not used to having students take leadership in planning lessons and courses. At Parkway, teachers learn all this by experience.'

There are problems, of course. One is truancy. As Lisa Strick has said:

> Periodically, attendance does become a problem here, particularly for the new student, who has recently escaped the confines of his traditional school and comes to Parkway on a lovely spring day and is on his way from City Hall up to the Art Museum and he has to pass the park. The fountain's going and it's warm and sometimes it seems like it would be a much better idea to go into the fountain for a bit of a splash rather than to go in and take his American history course or whatever ... Most of the students find, however, that constant non-attendance really works to nobody's disadvantage except their own.

Students know that credits depend to quite a large extent on attendance, and a high school diploma is necessary for almost any job apart from manual work.

Another problem is self-motivation and responsibility for choice. Students coming from the traditional high school are used to having marks and threats as motivation. Most need time to adjust and it can be chaotic for them for a while. Some cannot handle the freedom and responsibility and go back to their old schools. As one student put it, 'It's better than regular school, but it's tougher, because you're on your own. No one is going to tell you what to do and how to do it—you have to decide for yourself. And if you make the decision, you take the responsibility.'

Conclusion

Parkway raises several important questions that can only be explored briefly here. First, can an experiment such as Parkway take place within a different social and cultural context? In so far as cities in advanced industrial societies possess broadly similar features—cultural institutions, specialized occupations and professions, and general concentration of resources—such an experiment should be transferable to other urban situations. Parkway has, in fact, inspired other experiments within the school systems of some major cities in the United States, including the Metro School in Chicago. All these experiments are different from Parkway in one way or another, tailored as they are to local circumstances and needs. It is, of course, most unlikely that schools along the lines of Parkway will be widely adopted, so its value in educational change would seem to lie in the fact that it can serve as a model whose experimentation has implications for urban schooling in general.

Second, why is it that in Britain we are reluctant to experiment on this scale within the state system of education? Parkway, it should be remembered, exists within the Philadelphia school system, and as such can be regarded as an alternative school. If one likes, it is an experiment in 'reschooling'. In this sense, it must be contrasted with the free school movement which exists outside the system. In Britain, innovations of this kind have so far found their opportunities outside the established system as with the developing free school movement. There is a need for alternative programmes within the established system whose experimental approaches can feed ideas back into more orthodox schools.

Third, Parkway raises the question: what is a genuine community curriculum? A distinction has to be made between a community-located curriculum where learning can take place in any part of the city, and a community-based curriculum where much of the learning is about the city. A community-located curriculum which is not community-based fails to utilize the urban potential to its fullest extent. Parkway, we believe, has a genuine community curriculum because it is community-based to the extent that not only is the curriculum geared to living in the urban environment, but it also fully utilizes community resources —parents, specialists within the community and institutions within the city.

Fourth, in what ways does Parkway challenge established ideas in educational institutions? It implies a widening of the concept of a school and the present boundaries of the curriculum, and the roles of both student and teacher. Parkway challenges the traditional concept of a school, because it is open to the community and to new ideas, and it encourages openness between students, teachers, parents and the community. Parkway represents a movement towards different types of learning situations in which a self-determined curriculum is one of the principal features. Its emphasis is on using all available resources to provide an individual curriculum for each student which meets his needs and interests as far as possible. Parkway challenges the traditional role of the student as a passive receiver of learning. It gives the secondary school student as much freedom and responsibility as a college student. Parkway challenges the traditional role of the teacher. As we have said, he moves away from being an instructor towards being a facilitator of learning and a resource person.

Finally, Parkway raises the question of whether urban schools succeed only to the extent that they fit their students to cope effectively with an urban environment? If the philosophy of Parkway encourages self-reliance, initiative and open discussion, as well as understanding and knowledge of the city and its possibilities, then it seems likely that such students will be more effective in an urban society than those from the established school system as it is at present.

Appendix

BETA course catalogue offerings for autumn 1971

Note: This list represents courses offered by one unit during one quarter of the school year. Editorial comment is provided where course titles are not self-explanatory.

Social studies
Abnormal psychology (held at Temple University Department of Psychology)
American history since 1900
Assistant teacher for exceptional children (helping to teach mentally handicapped children)
Community organization (working with a community food co-op)
Consumer economics
Court watching (How does justice work in the community?)
Early childhood development
Economics
Government—change in America
History of architecture
Intern program (helping a teacher in an elementary school class)
Introduction to psychology
Introduction to 'sensitivity training' ('the group explores verbal and non-verbal methods of expanding self-awareness and other-awareness')
Introduction to sociology
Modern American history
Municipal affairs
Non-violence, revolution and power
Participation and observation with pre-school children
Physical city (survey of urban conditions with emphasis on the physical problems of urban environment)

Resolution of conflicts (community, racial, campus, commercial and
   labor)
The Russian Revolution
Scholastic Aptitude Test preparation (for college entrance)
Self-destruction (a study of mental health and suicide)
Theory of education: the learner *vs.* the schools
Working with adult basic education classes
World cultures
Volunteer work at Planned Parenthood

English language
Advanced English skills
Afro-American literature
Basic English
The Big City Library
The case for neglected humanities ('The course will endeavour to
   familiarize the student with some relatively obscure or misinterpreted
   methods of reacting and employing one's humanness in a life situa-
   tion. These methods will be taken from various cultural sources.')
Communications Resource Center (for students interested in careers in
   television, radio and newspapers)
Contemporary popular literature
Criticism of 20th-century literature
English
Geoffrey Chaucer: *The Canterbury Tales*
Hemingway: the man and the myth
Introduction to public speaking
The modern imagination (a multi-media forum on creativity)
Shakespeare
Survey of language (the role of language in everyday life)
Television and film production
Tutoring in reading
Tutoring and workshops in basic reading and writing
Verbal Scholastic Aptitude Test preparation (for college entrance)
The written word (to develop an awareness of the effect of the written
   word on emotion and judgment)

Foreign languages
Russian I
Spanish I
Spanish (intermediate and advanced)
Languages at South Philadelphia High School

Mathematics
Algebra I

Algebra II
Geometry
High math (algebra, geometry and trigonometry)
History of mathematics
Ideas in mathematics
Independent study in mathematics
Introduction to math
Introduction to symbolic logic
Math (intermediate)
Mathematics for computers
Modern geometry
Preparation for Scholastic Aptitude Test in math (college entrance)

Science
Biology
Geology
Program development in science (helping to develop activities in the
    community in the science area)
The zoo

Business
Accounting
Book-keeping
The copy-shop (learning how to use a spirit duplicator, mimeograph,
    etc.)
How to get a job and keep it (the course includes investigation of
    training opportunities and child labor laws, among other things)
Shorthand
Typewriting

Art and Shop
Architecture as a living experience
Art
Basic drawing
Can you talk to the younger generation? (observation of Museum of
    Art classes, discussion of teaching problems and organization of
    children's tours using the Museum and its objects as a teaching tool)
Cartooning
Color, design and collage
Drafting principle techniques
Fashion design
General shop (woodwork)
Graphic arts and communications
Graphics and the environment
Photography from the negative to the mounted picture

Portfolio review and constructive criticism (mainly for students apply-
ing to art school)
Re-discover the city landscape
Silkscreen, printmaking, drawing and design
Textile crafts
More than basic drawing
The anatomy of an institution (the function of an art museum)

Miscellaneous
a cappella chorale
Basic electricity I
Basic electricity II
Cooking and meal planning
Cosmology and the counter-culture
Dance
Home economics
Internship in camping (working with fifth- and sixth-grade children in
camping and survival techniques)
Moving your bod* (football, swimming, baseball, basketball, etc.)
Musical things
Musician's workshop
Music appreciation
Library intern course
Swimming

Note: In order to graduate from the Parkway Program with a Pennsylvania State Diploma, each student needs $18\frac{1}{2}$ credits. Each credit is
equal to 120 hours. The State requires that there be the distribution
which follows:

4 credits English
1 credit American history
$1\frac{1}{8}$ credits Social studies
$\frac{1}{3}$ credit Economics
$\frac{1}{2}$ credit World cultures
1 credit Science
2 credits Mathematics
$\frac{1}{2}$ credit Health
8 credits other.

*[This is not a misprint but colloquial American for 'body'.]

Notes

1 For a much more detailed, first-hand account of Parkway see John Bremer
and Michael von Moschzisker (1971).
2 University interns at Parkway are graduate or undergraduate students who
come for three months or more.

3 We would like to acknowledge the article by Henry Resnik, 'Parkway: a school without walls' in Ronald Gross and Paul Osterman (eds) (1971), as the source of information on the parts played by Clifford Brenner and John Bremer in the setting up of Parkway.
4 The Board of Education is a body elected by the voters of all school districts in the State, and responsible among other things for the hiring of teachers.
5 Grades are given on individual assignments and on completion of a course. The course grade is part of the student's permanent record. Grades can be numerical (1–100) or by letters, normally A, B, C, D and F representing excellent, above average, average, below average and fail. This system is used throughout American schools, in elementary school and college as well as in high school. Some places now give only two grades: pass and fail (as at Parkway).
6 At Parkway, the school year is divided into three 'quarters'.
7 In high school, a credit is given for satisfactory completion of a course; a certain number of credits in subject areas over a period of four years are required for graduation. Students at Parkway must meet the requirements of the State of Pennsylvania if they wish to graduate with a state diploma.

References

Bremer, John and von Moschzisker, Michael (1971), *The School Without Walls* New York, Rinehart & Winston.
Resnik, Henry (1971), 'Parkway: A school without walls', in Ronald Gross and Paul Osterman (eds), *High School*, New York, Simon and Schuster.

3.6 Community education and the urban primary school

Eric Midwinter

... It should never be forgotten that community education is a cradle to grave concept, that, in the school sense, it should best be seen as a three to sixteen/eighteen continuum and that, in general, it must give the education system globally to the people, with adult education well in evidence at all stages.

The primary school—home and school relations

It would be assumed that the school would deploy its plant for the benefit of its catchment area. It would be hoped that those concerned with school building would consider this point urgently and plan for purpose-built Community Schools. Beyond that, one might hope to see comprehensive programmes which incorporated new schools fluidly and openly into newly-developing environs. It would also be assumed that the 'open' school would play a fair part in the pre-school and post-school educational activities of the neighbourhood.

However, the main outgoing to communal commitment of the school would be in the field of improving parental and public knowledge of its activities, in order that parents and others might be better placed to support the children's education. This, substantially, is a public relations exercise, and we have indicated an approximate formula for conducting such an exercise.* Set out in logical progression, it might read:

1 *The publication.* Here, the emphasis is on the professional presentation of material into the home, and we have experimented with some success with the teacher-centred newsletter, the child-centred magazine, a mixture of these two, the one-off prospectus,

Source: Eric Midwinter, *Priority Education*, Penguin (1972), 164–8, 176–9.

* [*Editorial footnote:* This extract is taken from the author's account of the Liverpool E P A Project (1968–71), of which he was Director.]

the calendar, and the booklet based on a major piece of school-work such as a study of the locality. Expense forced the Project latterly to experiment with the common cover, 'Back Home' (now heading towards its eighth edition), which could be used either independently or as the backing or folder for school, class or individual material of all kinds. In Liverpool this was, with its 710,000 run, a popular addition to our help to many schools and, in the main, it was used with imagination and dash. It is obviously a task for the LEA or for the recommended 'project team' to produce for a given set of schools. It could even be produced on a national basis, and one might even foresee a triple layer—a national cover, a local contribution and a school insertion.

2 *The exposition.* It should be the duty of the Community School to sell its wares at natural focal points in its catchment area. The most obvious examples of this culled from our own experience are shops, department stores, public houses, doctors' surgeries, bingo halls, community centres, churches and factory canteens and social clubs. That in no way is an exclusive list, for supermarkets, public libraries, cinemas, races, football matches, holiday camps and many other social foci could be added. Exposition takes two forms—the straight exhibition and the 'live' demonstration—or, of course, a combine of the two. The latter has marvellous impact, especially when supported by hand-outs or other material. The former needs constant change to retain its attraction and the danger of children doing 'exhibition' work must be watched. In some ways, the 'live' demonstration is one of the freshest approaches in the school/community field and one worthy of some development.

The concept of exposition leads naturally to the 'Education Shop' idea, and the Project, in completing its operations, planned a collapsible kiosk for general use. It is felt that LEAS should look critically at such prototypes. 'Education Shops' have naturally been seen chiefly in the department store context, but there is no reason why they might not operate at other focal points, like the ones suggested above. Alternatively, it would be a tremendous boost if one or other of the large chain-stores undertook to establish an 'Education Shop' in each of its branches. There is little doubt of its value but it must be seen as a long term venture. As with any other social mechanism, it takes some getting adjusted to and people who have been disappointed with a week's experiment have entertained foolish hopes of the

'Education Shop' mechanism. Since the end of the Project, we have also looked closely at the practical implications of a mobile advisory service, and the results have been encouraging.

3 *The site improvement scheme.* By declaring war on their own site, teachers and children can demonstrate to the community their intention to look critically and positively at their surrounds. Playground wall-murals, litter campaigns, reclamation of bits of land for garden, roof and playground gardening, and interior decor, particularly in corridors, have been the principal illustrations of this. Ideally, they draw curricular and communal concerns together. Each piece of work grows from an intrinsic part of the syllabus, so that the adult observer, as well as noting the social value for the children and the community, is also vividly informed of what the school is attempting in a curricular sense and this, more direct, message is one worthy of further consideration. The scope for child-centred improvement schemes is broad and one should next perhaps consider a widening of this device beyond the school bounds. The Christmas decorations for a shopping precinct or a wasteland 'junk' sculpture enterprise are two examples which spring to mind.

4 *The parent in the process.* There is no gainsaying that, for full home/school inter-relation, the parent must eventually observe or, preferably, participate in the educational process. The Project has undeniably shown that the class is the most profitable focus for this exercise, with teacher and children inviting parents to join them regularly for half-day sessions. This began as 'coffee mornings', but widened encouragingly into the afternoon and evening. There were several permutations on the theme, but most schools plumped for the parents joining their children working in groups and the creation thereby of a valued social-cum-educational experience for everyone. The success of the evening efforts, when fathers and working mothers have an opportunity to engage themselves, might point the way to weekends as well as evenings as a viable time for schooling. Provided no increased overall burden was placed on teachers, some investigation of this possibility might be attempted, with parents and children (perhaps on some kind of roster basis) enjoying early evening and weekend school together. This, incidentally, could be the juncture at which to mention the need for holiday programmes in the Educational Priority Areas. Given a lack of leisure facilities and a paucity of traditional educational achievement in such areas, a strong argu-

ment could be made for holiday schooling, again provided teachers were not overburdened. An evening, weekend, holiday approach should necessarily imply a close look at teacher-commitments and conditions of service, but, in terms of parental involvement, it could be essential. We have recently experimented, with some success, in the holiday school field.

With instances such as the 'festival' theme, whereby parents were invited to school to help celebrate calendar occasions which had been the recent centre of interest for the children, parental and curricular probes have been drawn nearer. But the ultimate comes only when the parent undergoes the process with the child, in what we called parent-child projects. Experience with these was limited, but hopeful. Only four were attempted; success varied; but innumerable lessons were learned. Again, a series of evenings was tried as well as a run of afternoons, and, predictably, creative and local studies seemed most suitable. It would be a significant breakthrough if schools could be encouraged to float child-parent projects of this nature, possibly attempting, initially, to ensure that every parent has at least one chance of the experience during the child's stay at school. The usual warning must be appended. It could take a generation or more of hard slogging to adapt teachers and parents in general to this final step in the partnership.

There are, we have observed, no blanket answers to home and school relations. The project team would advise all teachers to examine themselves critically before embarking on one or another scheme, for their success often depends on teachers' temperaments and personalities. Nor did the team examine all the possibilities— one thinks of home visiting (as successfully developed by our colleagues in the West Riding Project), teacher residence in the area, parents spending a day in school in twos or threes, and so forth. It perhaps should be reiterated that parent associations, parents as teacher-auxiliary or 'parent power' was not part of the thinking in this first phase. It is the fathers and mothers in the learner-role that requires urgent remedy; as such, the teacher must be seen as critical. If one teacher can be converted to good home/school practice, thirty pairs of parents and their children could benefit. If one parent is converted and becomes a proselytizer of home/school practice at the school, it could, in fact, alienate teachers.

The rapport of school and home must, of course, be the rub of any community education programme. Every EPA school must be persuaded of the import of this truth. It is, in essence, a public relations venture and, as such, resources need to be diverted for the purpose. We recommended nationally that each EPA school should be subsidized with an annual public relations grant of £150, or 50p. *per capita*, whichever be the greater. In our experience, this would enable a school to publish material pleasingly with the aid of some common 'Back Home'-type folder; to mount a small set of exhibitions and demonstrations within its locale; to embark on and sustain a site-improvement scheme; and to float a thorough-going parental linkage through the school. This is not to limit the school to these four techniques we found most valuable, but it does offer some reasonable base for a monetary calculation. And if the agelong dichotomy of school and home in urban centres could be broken for £150 a year, it would be indeed a cheap invest-ment. . . .

The primary school and the community

In the home and school section, several facets of community rela-tions were touched upon, leaving, nonetheless, several others quite unexamined. From any number of possibilities the project did alight briefly on two very different community features and they require some specific comment. They are school management and the economy.

First, as to managers, the Community School requires com-munity management. It needs men and women who can act as interpreters, as bridges between the school and its locality. There is little evidence that the dominance of LEA elected members and nominees on managerial or governing bodies is able to perform this function, save in exceptional, all but accidental, cases.

Legislation should allow, as soon as possible, for a positive move towards 'community' boards of managers and pressure needs to be mounted nationally and locally to that end. A sug-gested panel of managers might read: headteacher, teacher rep-resentative, LEA officer, LEA elected representative or nominee as ratepayer watchdog, parent or parents, related commercial or industrial representative, where relevant, related college repre-sentative (perhaps replacing the conventional university delegate) with powers to co-opt up to three others able to meet or represent the particular interests of the individual school. A radical change in the structure of management must preface a radical change in the function of management. It is frequently difficult to find a parent who can name one manager of his child's school. Some schools are extremely fortunate in their managers and governors, but probably all would benefit from a face-lift. To assist in such a facelift, obligatory courses for school managers and governors should be arranged and lists of managers' names and addresses should be widely published among parents.

Secondly, as to the economy, the happy relations the Liverpool Project negotiated with the John Moores organization were a valid reminder that the community is an economic as well as a social one. We were rightly castigated for lack of follow-up of our initial overtures. This was accurate enough and we could only plead lack of time, money and expertise to excuse us. Our frankly underdeveloped connections with industry chiefly served to demonstrate the almost frightening potential of educational/economic rapport. The four main angles appeared to be straight material support, extended social relationships on a two-way basis, parental communication after the 'home is at work' aphorism, and, in the case of secondary education, vocational adjustment and the import of narrowing the chasm between school and work. Perhaps it should be added that there was no thought here of churning out suitably moulded factory-fodder; the belief was that, as a parallel to producing the thinking consumer and citizen, the Community School should attempt to produce the thinking producer and worker, able to participate as creatively in the workplace as in the residents' association.

As a foundation for this endeavour, schools and companies could be interlocked rather after the fashion of the college link-up. In some ways, the complex economy of most urban centres makes it impossible to negotiate a genuinely direct and integral connection, analogous with the mining village with its one colliery and three or four schools. It can normally be presumed that parents attached to one school rarely duplicate the pattern at work. Nevertheless, if a group of schools were variously associated with a group of commercial concerns, a criss-cross network could manifest itself beneficially. A broad programme could be planned of financial and resources support, of worker visits to types of schools, of varied exhibition/demonstration and 'Education Shop'-type activities, of school involvement in company sports, theatrical and other social occasions, and of a variegated pattern of pre-school-leaver experience. Together with a relevant business representation on school managerial governmental bodies, this could prove a tremendous advance in both the theory and practice of the Community School.

As with the college liaison schemes, such consummations do not spontaneously occur. Some kind of leg-man is required to forge such close and detailed links, and, yet again, he would ideally need to operate within a project team so that the school/ work action could be dovetailed carefully into the total programme. There are openings here for local business and industrial interests to finance industrial educational officers for this purpose.

It is difficult to overexaggerate the significance of this finding. The comment here is brief because, in substance, the evidence is slight. It is truer to say that the project team merely saw a glimmer of a bright potential. One must not be naïve. Few industrialists and employers and executives are as longsighted and as aware of their social responsibilities as were our business associates. It would be a laborious slog and often vain struggle against suspicion and short-term evaluations. One would need swiftly to draw the trades union movement into the reckoning and not be content with discussion with the management. It would be fraught with countless difficulties. Yet it cannot be gainsaid that if 'community' has meaning, it must include the economy and thus it is to the economy that community education must address itself. Given what one now sees as a remarkable, if somewhat inaccessible, potential, and granted the import one would now attach to the economic sector of the community, one might argue in retrospect that if a re-start of the Project were possible, a greater emphasis on this element would be the only basic change of strategy. Since the project ended, we have begun three schemes for unemployed school-leavers under the Government-sponsored 'Community Industry' programme, and we see this as a fruitful lead.

3.7 The Cheetham/Crumpsall Education Project

... the idea of the 'community school' and its relevance to the problems of compensatory education ... has been little explored in Britain as yet, but in Sweden at least very notable progress has been made. In that country it is taken as axiomatic today that the needs of schools, youth, further education, and the adult community must not be considered in isolation when new building is envisaged; planning must take account of the needs of all the various interests from the start. In Stockholm and its suburbs, and in cities such as Vasteras and Orebro, one may see splendid new accommodation designed for multiple usage. Various ministries and municipal departments have joined forces to provide a better public service at less cost. In a period when schools in Sweden are being reorganized on comprehensive lines, the opportunity is being seized to build educational and leisure facilities for people of all ages on a rational basis. ...

In England there is as yet little to match this kind of development. Sports centres are appearing in some places. The Forum Theatre at Billingham-on-Tees is part of a £1 million recreation unit which includes a swimming bath, learners' pool, and ice-rink, and the facilities are used by schools as well as by the public. The Dukeries Comprehensive School shares a campus with a college of further education; and Egremont School has been designed to offer educational and leisure facilities to the adult community as well as to pupils. The proposed educational and recreational centre for Dawley New Town is intended to link education with services to the general public.

There are other examples; but perhaps the most ambitious project so far is in Manchester, where plans are afoot to incorporate in a single institution school, further education, and com-

Source: *Cross'd with Adversity*, Schools Council Working Paper no. 27, Evans (1970), 134–40.

munity facilities. The need for an eight-form-entry comprehensive school for boys and girls in a part of the city which includes a good deal of very old housing resulted in proposals for a community school. The possible relation of this project to an existing plan to build a college of further education in the same district led to the suggestion that school and college might be brought together on adjacent sites, sharing some accommodation and certain services. The college was to be mainly for the 16 to 19 age-groups and would include courses in commerce, hairdressing, printing, liberal studies, science, and engineering. More detailed study indicated the possibility of substantial advantages in still closer integration. The Crowther Report had strongly advocated experiments in this direction for the 15 to 18 age-groups and the Manchester Cheetham/Crumpsall Education Project is now conceived as a single institution embracing the following features:

A school building (or buildings) for pupils up to the age of about 15

Here the younger pupils would be expected to spend the major part of their school week. It would be their home base, on which pastoral care would be centred. Nevertheless this building is not intended to house a separate school, but to be an integral part of the larger project. Pupils here would claim a share in the wider facilities of the campus—the playing-fields, the sports centre and the library for example. Perhaps even more significant would be the benefits accruing from their contact with the many facilities provided more particularly for older students, and from the possibilities of staff deployment, in appropriate circumstances, over the entire age range.

A centre building for young people beyond the age of 15 (whether in full-time or part-time education), which would also offer facilities for adult education classes and groups

The proposal to bring all the over-fifteens together aims to avoid the separation which is generally forced upon contemporaries at the school-leaving age. The fact that young people may be pursuing very different educational courses is not a good reason for enforcing divorce in other directions. There are very obvious arguments today in favour of continuing their opportunities for social contact at least.

The advantages of the proposal also include, of course, the more economical use of accommodation and equipment, the more profitable deployment of scarce teaching staff, and the prospect of a wider range of both academic and vocational courses in a larger establishment. Wasteful duplication of courses might be reduced, and some valuable classes which would have failed in college or school alone (for lack of numbers or staff) might be sustained. The virtues claimed for 'day-release' of some pupils from school to college would be built into the organization.

Proper provision for advanced academic work and for specialized further education courses would of course be essential. Yet even in this direction there could be mutual advantages; students following different disciplines might profit from the opportunity to see something of what various vocational courses demand of those who follow them.

The overriding reasons for the proposal to provide a common base for the 16- to 19-year-olds may be summarized as follows: When all young people in these age-groups are brought together a smoother transition seems likely between formal education and membership of the adult working community; more young people may be persuaded to stay longer in full-time education; best of all, a social atmosphere should be possible which could go far to bridge the gap between students who intend to go forward to higher education and their contemporaries who will follow other paths.

For drama, art, sports, and reference to books, students would turn mainly to the communal arts centre, the sports centre, the playing-fields, and the campus library, referred to below.

The '15 to 19' building would clearly be the venue for many adult non-vocational classes and groups in the evenings and at week-ends, and it is important that this fact should be taken into account in its design and furnishing. The need for quiet study rooms for adults living in poor housing conditions may be expected to increase as correspondence courses multiply (including courses associated with The Open University), and in this connexion facilities for practical work may be required. One might envisage also the use of central premises for the pursuit of individual interests and skills—for example, car maintenance, household repair work, or photography. In the campus library members of the public might learn a foreign language by using tape-recorders in booths provided for the purpose.

Other buildings, and playing-fields, for the use of pupils, students, and members of the local community

(i) A library and resources centre, staffed and serviced by the libraries department of the corporation, to serve school and college and to provide lending, reference, and study facilities for students of all ages.

The library would cater for serious reading by members of the public and the centre would also offer teachers resources of apparatus, materials and information for lesson and lecture preparation and demonstration.

The concept of a resource centre has great potential value in relation also to curriculum development and the in-service training of teachers.

(ii) A sports and recreation centre, with facilities for swimming, gymnastics, and indoor games. Changing rooms and showers could serve both indoor and outdoor players. In such a centre too, it often might prove possible to cater for the interests of minorities (archery? fencing?).

(iii) Recreation grounds and playing-fields designed to serve school, college, and community needs. This would be a focus for outdoor sporting activities, but people of all ages might find something to attract them into the open air; here mothers might bring their babies and a children's playground would be an attraction. Training sessions might be offered to local clubs and community groups both on the playing-fields and in the indoor centre, so that young people might find encouragement to carry forward interests and skills discovered at school.

It is most important that the construction of playing-fields is such as to ensure that they would in fact stand up to the uses envisaged for them.

(iv) An arts and social centre, incorporating a music and drama school and an assembly/concert hall, with ancillary workrooms, property stores, cloakrooms, etc., and refreshment facilities.

This would be a focus for the artistic activities of pupils and older students; it would open its doors for the productions of local societies; and it would provide a meeting place for parents and for the general public. An exhibition space here, for displays of many kinds (e.g. pictures, fashion, professional information, public notices) might prove a continuing attraction.

(v) A club house for older people, quietly situated yet within sight of community activity; perhaps near to the nursery unit (see below).

It is the experience of not a few schools that some of their most under-privileged pupils are among the most willing to take an interest in helping old people, and an old people's club could offer an outlet for enthusiasm of this kind.

(vi) Accommodation for youth work. The Cheetham/Crumpsall Project might well embrace more than one organized youth club for which premises will need to be provided. It should be remembered however that the sports centre, the arts centre, and indeed the main 15 to 19 building, would be expected to cater for many youth activities.

(vii) A short-stay residential block, for perhaps ten to twelve pupils. A week or two spent here, while children attend school in the normal way, might be regarded very much as a privilege and could offer a happy experience to boys and girls from homes of all kinds. The many facilities on the campus would be available to the children out of school hours. The wing might be of particular value in helping in cases of truancy or school-phobia, or where a sudden breakdown occurred in the family which yet did not seem to demand the longer-term care and protection afforded by the Children's Department.

An application for financial assistance under the Educational Priority Areas allocation, to build residential accommodation of this kind as part of the Cheetham/Crumpsall Project, has received approval from the Department of Education and Science.

(viii) A nursery care unit, professionally staffed but with occasional help from older pupils and students.

Such a unit could be of value in freeing young housewives to attend afternoon classes in further education. But it could also offer practical experience to students on nursery or home-making courses.

(ix) Accommodation for parents. This is very important. Not only should there be a pleasant reception area and interview rooms where staff and parents could meet, but parents should be encouraged to enjoy the facilities of the whole site and to engage in activities in support of the centre.

Other desirable developments are not difficult to imagine—an information centre or citizen's advice bureau, an education welfare centre, a health centre, and so on. The mere recital of possibilities may be considered by some to cast doubts upon the whole enterprise. No one supposes that money will be forthcoming today to carry out, in one place and at one time, all that has been suggested as desirable. Even the formidable obstacle of finance is not the only problem. There are for example the daunting difficulties of trying to synchronize the programmes of various corporation departments, of securing capital allocations at the right time, and of coordinating the submission and approval of plans involving more than one Government department.

Special difficulties arise in connexion with the proposals for the 16 to 19 age-groups. Are pupils and students to be regarded as coming under two codes—school and college—for teaching purposes? Disparate standards in matters of discipline, as for example between school pupils and day-release students, might not prove insuperable if (as would be hoped) emphasis is put upon the personal responsibility of young people for their own development. But other difficulties are of a different order. Schools Regulations and Further Education Regulations differ and are administered by different branches of the Department of Education and Science; building standards are different for schools and colleges; staffs are employed under different conditions of service and on different salary scales; examinations and examining bodies are largely distinct; and even within the local authority education office, school and further education matters are the responsibilities of different departments.

How might such a situation be resolved? The educational, social and financial advantages of unification seem quite compelling, yet the difficulties might to some appear insuperable. A great deal of thought has been given to the way in which such a centre ought to be managed. A single director, working with a board of governors representative of all the various interests associated with the project, seems essential if the project is to achieve its unifying function. He will need academic and administrative support, but there is no space here to enlarge further upon the management aspect. We come back to our original thesis. Disadvantage begins at home. Its relief in school, and beyond, is intimately affected by parental attitudes to education and therefore by the place of the school in the community. New schools and new colleges are being built all the time, and they cost a lot of money. Many of them, or large parts of them, will stand empty for much of their life. These are some of the basic reasons why a new assessment of neighbourhood planning in relation to school and college building is urgently necessary. Such a study might reveal the school as an essential part of a continuing process of education, rather than a finite episode. It might show how buildings of different kinds, the responsibility of various corporation departments (and even perhaps of private interests), might be designed and positioned so as to be of the utmost convenience and service. The exercise of extracting the possible from a shopping list of the desirable seems very well worthwhile.

One other aspect should be mentioned. Behind all the thinking on Cheetham/Crumpsall is the idea that the education department would rely greatly upon the services and professional advice of several other corporation departments. The library and resource centre, for example, would be administered by the city librarian, the sports centre by the baths superintendent to the corporation, the playing-fields by the director of parks. The director of the education centre would call upon the services of these and the other departments concerned for a considerable part of the work of the centre. In all this the support of chief officers is already assured. It is a new conception of joint action.

We believe that the problems we have outlined are not insuperable; that the time is ripe for an experiment in education of this kind; that it would command the interest and support of very many people; and that means should be found to ensure that regulations and existing practices are not allowed to stand in the way of its realization.

3.8   The role of the community school

Stephen Hatch and Sue Moylan

... In essence, the community school attempts to extend the role of the school and blur the division between school and community. But this objective can be tackled in either a radical or a moderate way. Because there is so much confusion about the meaning of the concept, the various interpretations need to be disentangled. Eric Midwinter (1972), taking the radical viewpoint, thinks the community school is 'a thoroughgoing device to identify school and community in every aspect of the life of each for the better health of both', a 'new concept of providing children with an equality of opportunity' and 'the one alternative in the major urban centres to threatened dislocation and breakdown'. Dennis Marsden (1971), in support, thinks the community school offers 'a whole range of educational innovations and teaching methods and relationships with the outside world which will bring about a new ethos and a new view of the child'. Translated into practice, the radical approach would involve a far-reaching, two-way process. On the one hand, the school would go out into the community, becoming something of a community development agency. Some of the more imaginative community service schemes, for example, may start with digging old people's gardens, but widen out into involvement with the community on a range of local issues, from slum clearance to youth employment. On the other hand, the community would come into the school in the form, first, of radical alternatives to the curriculum, to suit the needs of the community rather than the demands of the General Certificate of Education; and, second, in the form of local involvement in the government of the school, with the ultimate idea of communal control.

On a more moderate level, the community school, as outlined in the Plowden report (Central Advisory Council for Education,

Source: *New Society*, 21 September 1972, 550–2.

1967), is simply 'a school which is open beyond the ordinary school hours for the use of children, their parents and, exceptionally, for other members of the community. 'Cyril Poster (1968) considers that 'recognition by the school of its place in the community will have its effect on the curriculum, where social relevance is desirable, and on the responsibility and participation not only of parents and pupils but also of the wider public. In return for the services and facilities which the school is able to offer the community, the school would benefit by sharing of community facilities.'

But what of the existing practice in this country? What relationship does it, in fact, bear to these different expressions of the potentialities of the community school? Existing community schools mostly serve rural areas like Cambridgeshire, Cumberland and Leicestershire. There are only a few in urban areas, though several are now planned or being built, particularly in deprived neighbourhoods. In addition, a number of primary schools associated with Educational Priority Area projects have developed in a community approach—the best known being in Liverpool.

This article is mainly concerned with secondary schools. Evidence from some of the better known ones is summarised in Table 1.

As Table 1 shows, all community schools encourage dual use of gym, classrooms, swimming baths, workshops and other facilities. But with few exceptions this is *dual* use, not *shared* use. That is to say, local people make use of facilities when the pupils do not need them. Another universal characteristic is the stress on relationships with parents. Efforts are made to contact parents over and above the usual parent/teacher associations and parents' meetings, like the groups being pioneered in each of the local villages at Swavesey.

Initiative for school and community activities generally lies with the staff, and there is sometimes difficulty in getting people to attend the variously named committees to which the community users could send representatives. There is very little local involvement in the government of the schools. Nowhere were extra powers delegated to the governors, and only at Swavesey was there a departure from the normal system of appointing governors, in that one governor was chosen by the PTA and another by the community association.

Equally significant is the sparse effort to give what goes on

Table 1 Facilities and participation in community schools

	Lawrence Weston Bristol	Les Quennevals Jersey	Sheppey Kent	Swavesey Cambridge	Wyndham Cumberland
Community use of facilities					
library	yes	yes	no	yes	yes
youth club	yes	no	yes	yes	yes
sports	yes	yes	yes	yes	yes
evening classes	yes	yes	yes	yes	yes
Additional daytime provisions					
preschool	yes	yes	yes	yes	yes
extended day for pupils	yes	yes	yes	no	no
elderly	no	yes	no	yes	no
Mechanisms for local participation					
parent-teacher associations, etc.	yes	yes	yes	yes	yes
representation on governing body	no	no	no	yes	no
Pupils and community					
adaptations to curriculum	yes	no	yes	no	no
community service scheme	yes	no	yes	no	no

	Lawrence Weston Bristol	Les Quennevals Jersey	Sheppey Kent	Swavesey Cambridge	Wyndham Cumberland
Intake all pupils from neighbour- hood	yes	no	yes	no	yes

inside the school a community orientation. Sheppey is embarking on a local studies course and Lawrence Weston had similar ideas, but nowhere is there evidence of the radical transformation of the curriculum advocated by Midwinter. Likewise, community service schemes do exist, but these seem to be marginal, rather than central to the schools' activities. In many places they just serve to occupy the non-exam streams.

Existing community schools are undoubtedly far removed from those schools with a high wall round them and a sign saying 'Parents not allowed beyond this point.' The community is encouraged to use the facilities, and generally the more middle class people do so. These schools also tend to be progressive on other issues, such as discipline and streaming. Nevertheless, there are many progressive secondary schools that stress parent–teacher relationships and have evening classes on the premises. There seems little difference between such schools and ones that style themselves as community schools. Admirable and valuable as existing community schools are, essentially they represent moderate enlightenment. They are not as yet the radical alternative sometimes claimed nor the answer to educational inequalities and inner city deprivations.

Could they become these things? The problem of difficult schools in deprived areas can be put like this. Middle-class teachers live far away and come to the school from nine till four to try to impart to their pupils a middle-class set of skills, values and ways of behaving. Prestige within the school, and priority in the allocation of resources, tends to go to the thin cream of potential GCE successes. The bulk of the pupils find these priorities and values alien and realise that they're never going to make it on middle-class terms; so they reject the educational offering. In so doing they receive the tacit support of their parents.

To a very large extent, this tension is inescapable. It reflects the structure of our society and the role of the education system as the method of allocating or withholding opportunities. Let no one pretend it can simply be wished away. For many of the skills and experiences children need in order to function effectively in our society are those labelled middle class. But what is important is this: in a community school there could be more common ground between teachers and taught. The school could be, and, what is more, could be seen to be, on the side of the local community.

All deprived areas have a considerable range of problems, to some extent susceptible to community action of one form or another. These problems are associated with preschool provision, play facilities for children, clearance and redevelopment, housing, traffic and so on. One of the community school's jobs might be to help local people tackle these problems. This is partly a matter of what the children are taught, partly of voluntary work by older children, partly of facilities that the school can make available to local people—but it is also a matter of active involvement of teachers with local adults.

The other side of the coin is the curriculum. Nowadays there is a growing interest in local study projects. Instead of saying, 'this is a deprived neighbourhood: so let us direct the children's attention outside it', teachers could say, 'this area has problems: how can we cope with them more effectively?' For example, redevelopment could be studied in school, and children could learn what rights people have when it happens, and the action they can take to improve their position. Local institutions and situations can be used in a host of different ways, as has been shown by Eric Midwinter (1972), as a starting off point for much school work.

To make progress with a radical community approach, certain conditions are necessary. The school needs to be identified with a given area and take nearly all, if not all, the children from that area. This involves some curtailment of parental choice, and defining a comprehensive school as one which recruits all the children from an area rather than one with a 'balanced' intake in terms of intelligence and social class. Such a recruitment policy can only be justified if accompanied by a policy of positive discrimination, such that schools which are disadvantaged in terms of facilities and intake receive priority in the allocation of resources.

To achieve a proper integration of activities, responsibility needs to be decentralised on the headmaster: if the adult education, or youth, side of the school is separately accountable to a different part of the local education authority's bureaucracy, spin off from one to the other will be difficult. The head, in turn, has to accept a much wider role. Even more important is the challenge to the role of the ordinary teacher, for what is at stake is the teacher's mastery in his own house. Whatever the formal arrangements for school government, the logic of a community approach means giving priority to the community's own definition of its needs, not to the teacher's view of what education should be. In middle class areas the ensuing tensions may well be manageable: less so in the inner city. But if one declares that our society is over-segmented, one must recognise that the professions are themselves segments, and may stand in the way of reviving grass-roots community life.

So the radicals in the community school movement have set their sights on some urgent and basic issues. But there are real difficulties in their path which need to be faced. Otherwise, like so many laudable new enterprises, the community school will be guilty of pretending that major problems can be resolved by no more than a little oil in the wheels.

References

Central Advisory Council for Education (England) (1967), *Children and their Primary Schools* (Plowden Report), HMSO.

Corbett, A. (1969) 'Community school', *New Society*, vol. 13, no. 335.

Marsden, D. (1971) *Politics, Equality and Comprehensives*, Fabian Society.

Midwinter, E. (1972) *Projections*, Ward Lock Educational.

Poster, C. (1968) 'The head and the community school', in B. Allen (ed.), *Headship in the 1970s*, Oxford, Blackwell.

Ree, H. (1969) 'Henry Morris assessed', *New Society*, vol. 14, no. 367.

Introduction to Section 4

Curriculum considerations

In any society, the objectives and content of the curriculum both derive from and sustain the culture of that society. Traditionally, the distinction (in terms of values, knowledge, and skills) drawn between cultural universals and the cultural specialities of dominant groups has been reflected in two types of curriculum: 'common education' for all and 'special education' for a social and/or vocational elite (Smith, Stanley and Shores, 4.1). Curriculum change within this framework is essentially liberal: the distinguishing line is re-drawn, rather than abolished. However, the discussion of social and educational equality in sections 1 to 3 has implied both the need and the general direction of more fundamental curriculum change.

Skilbeck (4.2) discusses some of the basic issues in the deliberate planning of change. The question of *who* participates in the determining of curriculum content is fundamental and Skilbeck argues that the content and influence of the curriculum are such that parents, pupils and the general public should be involved in its determination, not just the single sub-group called educationists. There is no single simple solution; the nature of the strategy must vary according to the kinds, numbers and status of the participants, and also the material constraints and opportunities of different situations. Skilbeck sees teachers as the common element in this diversity, and suggests ways in which they could become more effective *agents* of change.

The need for diversity in both curriculum content and pedagogy to take into account particular environmental and individual characteristics (in other words, 'a relevant education') is the theme of the remaining articles in this section.

Midwinter (4.3) cites the example of humanities in the urban school curriculum; method may have changed in recent years, but the content—faraway people and places—has remained substantially the same. Like Skilbeck (4.2), Midwinter stresses the need for concurrent reform in content and method. He argues that the teacher's task is not escapism, but equipping children to tackle the reality of growing up and living in city centres and corporation estates; not the communication of traditional beliefs, but the open-ended examination of values, standards and codes of conduct.

The call for content relevant to circumstance, and the challenge through education of the social status quo are both repeated in Hamilton's account of the growing demand for black studies in the USA (4.4), although in this case the content is more overtly political, and the impetus has come from the black students themselves.

Taba and Elkins (4.5) outline some alternative teaching strategies for use with 'disadvantaged' pupils, for whom conventional learning experiences and motivational devices have become patently inappropriate.

4.1 Cultural roots of the curriculum

B. Othaniel Smith, William O. Stanley and J. Harlan Shores

If an observer looks at the curriculum of the school in any society, he will find, either stated or implied, a set of educational objectives, a body of subject matter, a list of exercises or activities to be performed, and a way of determining whether or not the objectives have been reached by the students. He will find also some kind of control which the teacher is required to exercise over the learners. These things comprising the curriculum are always, in every society, derived from the culture. The objectives stressed will be those that reflect the controlling ideas and sentiments contained in the universals. The subject matter will tend to be that which is believed to embrace the most significant ideas and most generally used knowledges and skills. The way in which the learners are controlled will reflect the prevailing methods of social control of the society at large. As the instrument of society for the education of the young, the curriculum will reflect the ideals, knowledges, and skills that are believed to be significant, or that are related to the common activities of the members of society. The curriculum is, therefore, interwoven with the social fabric that sustains it.

In every society a distinction is made between the curriculum of common education and that of special education. Common education will be based upon the universal elements of the culture and such aspects of the specialities as are of general concern. Special education will be based largely upon the dominant specialities of the culture. It will be designed to train the individual for a particular social or vocational position.

Source: B. Othaniel Smith, William O. Stanley and J. Harlan Shores, *Fundamentals of Curriculum Development*, New York, Harcourt Brace & World (1957), 8–12.

Common education based upon cultural universals

Common education is concerned with the problem of maintaining the society as a closely knit and well-integrated unit. It is only natural, therefore, that the rules and knowledges by which the people as a whole regulate their conduct and anticipate the behavior of one another should be its principal content. Not all the universals, however, will be contained in the common curriculum. It will ordinarily not incorporate such superficial elements as the method of greeting friends or the way to tie shoes. As a rule, these things are left to the individual to acquire informally and often unconsciously through participation in the common life of the people. Instead, the curriculum will tend to emphasize the more fundamental universals, or cultural core, such as the values, sentiments, knowledges, and skills that provide society with stability and vitality and individuals with the motivations and deep-lying controls of conduct.

The heart of the universals, as already pointed out, is the standards and knowledges by which the people decide what is right and wrong, good and evil, beautiful and ugly, true and false, appropriate and inappropriate in all sorts of activities—political, economic, aesthetic, educational, or what not. These standards constitute the moral content of the society. Next to them in importance are the knowledges and skills that have to do with the control and improvement of the common activities of the people such as their political and economic behavior. Together these constitute the subject matter of common education.

Special education related to the specialties of the culture

Returning now to special education, it is to be remembered that the specialties of a culture are usually those ways of thinking and acting associated either with vocational groups or social classes, or both. Hence special education may follow the interests of either one or both of these special groups. In societies having a recognized social elite, it will be found that instruments of education will be set aside for training the immature members of the elite group in the special points of view and patterns of conduct of these privileged adults. The presence of *exclusive* private or finishing schools is evidence of the existence of an elite class having particular outlooks, polite manners, and behavioral patterns which it wishes to maintain. Indeed, the existence of such classes has led in some nations to the creation of dual educational systems—one for the folk and another for the upper classes. For this reason higher forms of education, including secondary as well as higher schools, have tended historically to be designed for the privileged few. Even in the more democratically inclined countries, where a single educational ladder has been adopted, the curriculum of the upper rungs reflects a privileged origin.

Education for vocational purposes is always correlated with the needs of persons of particular socio-economic level. Hence it is sometimes difficult to distinguish from that form of special education designed to equip the individual to occupy a particular position in society. The sons of upper-class families in western nations who go to private schools, or to publicly supported schools specially designed for them, in order to pursue the so-called 'cultural' subjects—not to mention programs leading to 'higher' professions—are thereby being trained for upper-class vocations. This type of training usually is just as vocational for them as study of how to read blueprints would be for a prospective plumber, because the so-called 'cultural' courses prepare them for domestic governmental positions, for foreign diplomatic service, or for positions in industrial bureaucracies. In any case, the display of relatively useless knowledge, information, and skills, marking their possessor as a member of the leisure class, will be of inestimable value, for it gains admission to the polite circles of other countries as well as his own.

The point of this discussion is not that all vocational education is class education. Only in societies where certain vocations are associated with particular social classes will this tend to be true. Social systems that emphasize an open-door policy for all occupations—making it possible for every individual irrespective of race, creed, or social background to acquire the knowledges and skills he is capable and desirous of obtaining—will reduce the chances that some occupations will be monopolized by privileged classes. In these societies vocational education will be least associated with class education.

Class education sometimes confused with common education

Not only is there a tendency for class education to be confused with vocational training, but also with common education. When a society passes from a class to a classless system (or to one in which classes exist only in a loose sense), the educational ideals and programs designed in the earlier phase for the education of the upper classes tend to persist in the later phase, under the guise of general or common education. It is for this reason that the curriculum of the American high schools, as well as that of American colleges, has been so slow to adjust to the demands of mass education. Thorstein Veblen, about fifty years ago, made it clear that remnants of the leisure class educational program persisted in schools and colleges.[1] These remnants may still be detected today.

Moreover, the colleges tend on the whole to continue to provide vocational programs under the banner of liberal education. A former president of Harvard University—James B. Conant—has aptly phrased this point.[2]

> By and large, the general education which our conventional four-year liberal arts colleges provide in one form or another is given as a background for two vocations—the learned professions and the managerial positions in business. This type of education, however much it may be improved (and it will be improved greatly in the coming years, I feel sure), cannot be considered apart from the vocations for which it prepares. In short, it has no over-all general validity for it cannot be considered apart from the clientele for which it has been developed over the years.

It is disturbing that in the United States, where the prevailing social creed denies the desirability of social classes, there should be social groups trying to reinstate and bolster up outworn systems of class education in the name of general or liberal education. Few things have encumbered thinking about the development of a more adequate program of common education in the United States, as well as in other countries, so much as adherence to educational ideas brought over from the class system of past cultural phases.

References

1 Thorstein Veblen, *The Theory of the Leisure Class*, Kelley (1899).
2 James Bryant Conant, 'Public Education and the structure of American society,' *Teachers College Record*, vol. 47, no. 3 (1945), pp. 164–5.

4.2 Strategies of curriculum change

Malcolm Skilbeck

There are a number of presuppositions written into the notion of strategies of curriculum innovation which need to be explored if we are to reach even tentative conclusions about how the curriculum might best be changed. Most important perhaps of these presuppositions is that of the worthwhileness of the 'strategic approach' to the problem of developing the curriculum. Talk of strategies of curriculum innovation can easily be taken to imply a preference for deliberate, pre-designed changes over those that occur in a more evolutionary and organic way.

This chapter will deal mainly with some of the basic issues that arise in thinking about and discussing strategies conceived as deliberate, preplanned changes. However, education changes in many different ways and it ought not to be too readily assumed that the full personal commitment of a perceptive, intelligent teacher to ongoing classroom processes results in curriculum development that is inferior to those changes which result from advance planning and calculation. These two types of approach may be crudely polarized as the intuitive and the rational. There is no good reason to suppose that in education the time has come to discard intuitive approaches. This is not to say that we should avoid the effort to elucidate the means by which intuitive teachers achieve results nor that we should overlook the need to establish criteria for judging the value and effectiveness of intuitive approaches.

This is one preliminary point about the significance of the strategic approach. A second point concerns the presumption that curriculum change should be embarked upon in the manner of a painter scraping the pigments off a canvas and starting afresh. The curriculum, as will be noted below, has to do with the stuff of

Source: *Curriculum Organization and Design*, ed. Jack Walton, Ward Lock Educational (1971), 27–37.

human experience. We should be wary both in talking about changing and modifying experience, and in adopting a technical stance, a preoccupation with means, in discussing such modifications. We cannot be confident that we know how to change experience for the better, either as a question of technique or as a question of value. In Susan Sontag's phrase, strategies for improving experience are more delicate, subtle, complex and morally charged than is appreciated by many contemporary writers on organization, administration and decision-taking in education. While the emphasis of the following discussion is on a certain set of procedures, I should like to set that discussion from the outset in the wider context of the diversity of valid teaching procedures and the moral implications and consequences of any set of proposals for modifying and directing human experience.

Over the past ten years or so, it has become widely accepted that educational changes of a quite substantial kind are desirable and indeed unavoidable. At first, these changes, in so far as they relate to the curriculum, were thought of mainly in terms of particular changes in subject matter, e.g. the replacement of mathematics by new mathematics, the introduction of neo-Darwinian biology, the replacement of descriptive citizenship courses by analytical social science and so forth.[1] Alongside this preoccupation with updated subject matter and the academic concerns this expressed, there developed a new emphasis on how children learn, the virtues of activity, discovery, inquiry methods (e.g. Nuffield Junior Science), the shortcomings of traditional notions of readiness and new ways of breaking down and organizing subject matter.[2] This emphasis was probably largely due to Piaget's work, or perhaps it would be more accurate to say that the relatively quiescent tradition of progressive education, which had always stressed the active role children and groups of children play in their own learning, was revitalized by an infusion of Piagetian thought.[3]

In America, it was Jerome Bruner in the late 1950s who most conspicuously linked the academic interest in updated content with the more pedagogical interest in learning and teaching, and who argued, as had John Dewey before him, that a reform of curriculum content and changes in learning and teaching procedures should go hand in hand. (Bruner's essay on Dewey reveals his debt.[4]) What Bruner also achieved, and again in the tradition of pragmatism, or experimentalism, of which Dewey was the chief exponent, was a widespread recognition that curriculum change should not be thought of as an occasional shot in the arm but as a continuous process of practice, reflection and renewal requiring the establishment and development of new kinds of educational institutions and teaching roles. Of these institutions, I need only mention in this country the Schools Council and the teachers centres, which might be thought to represent respectively the determination to establish a national, unifying forum for the shaping of overall curriculum and examination policies, and the recognition that national policies are of no use unless there is a network of diffusion agencies, or centres for the discussion of the new policies. This of course is pulling together rather too neatly and tidily two large ideas and their corresponding institutions. In practice there is as yet no overall national curriculum policy, only a coordinating and funding institution in which future development of the whole school curriculum can be discussed and in some measure guided. Also, teachers centres are not simply diffusion agencies through which national policies are reticulated to the masses. But they are at least, like the Schools Council, expressive of the belief that the large changes which are widely felt to be needed in the school curriculum require more than goodwill, enthusiasm, research or even money—that they require the invention of new and more or less permanent institutions, themselves committed to inquiry, criticism, discussion and diffusion. Many more examples could be given of this relationship which is being established between new ideas and relevant agencies for implementing them—including of course the traditional institutions designed for this purpose and acting in this way over a long period, notably the colleges of education.[5] But I do not wish to examine the various ways in which the institutionalizing of innovation is occurring, only to note that powerful new institutions have come into existence as part of what might be called the curriculum reform movement and that these institutions serve to remind us that curriculum innovation is now a permanent feature or a conditioning factor in education in this country.

This does not mean of course that the institutions are necessarily adequate for their purpose, nor that more and different kinds of institutions are not needed, nor indeed that any and every innovation in the curriculum is worthwhile simply because some thought has been given to the procedural means whereby it might be implemented. John White's criticism of Schools Council development projects is a useful reminder that educational values are not to be equated exactly with influential, and in certain senses success-ful, institutional devices.[6] We may not care for many of the changes that are occurring and often we may feel that many of those changes we do like are a reminder of old ideas rather than something fundamentally new and different. Nevertheless there is, I believe, a perceptible, recognizable ground swell of innovation and this may be expected to grow much stronger and more powerful, to the point where teachers will feel challenged as part of their profes-sional role to know what they think about, for example, primary French, humanities in the early secondary years, general studies in the sixth, science for young school leavers and so forth. And to know what they think not merely in the abstract but in relation to their own teaching and the variety of options open to them.

I shall return later to this point about the variety of options open to them, because I want to draw attention to the difficult challenge facing teachers when they will be asked to choose amongst the various curriculum packages, kits and thematic courses which will become available in profusion over the next five or ten years, as the sixty-odd Schools Council project teams disgorge their materials. But before we come to this I should like to return for a moment to my title and to consider the notion of a *strategy* of curriculum innovation.

There is no single recognizable strategy of curriculum innova-tion in the sense that research, study and experience have yielded a set of imperatives or even guidelines for action.[7] The world itself is perhaps unfortunate in an educational context not only because, as Joslyn Owen has pointed out, it has overtones of military control[8] but also because it communicates—and alto-gether too pretentiously—a sense of settled and tried procedures which will work, if only we handle them properly.

From a review of literature and research[9] I have reached the conclusion that several thousand years of practice, a rather lesser period of theory and a half century of research have not yet yielded a single over-arching strategy for curriculum innovation which rises much above the level of platitude and commonsense! This may appear a somewhat disconcerting or at any rate an idiosyncratic expression of opinion and it may appear to leave me with nothing else to say on this subject. What I intend by this expression of opinion is not an end to discussion and a return to routine methods, but that we should not look for simple panaceas or single solutions to the problem of setting about to change the curriculum. Furthermore we should be ready to observe and inquire, in the manner recommended by Bacon, to try to find out how people do in fact proceed to change the curriculum, whether they are successful, what their criteria of success are and to what ends they seek to make certain changes. From such inquiries we can begin to build some ideas that might eventually yield powerful strategies. (Similar sorts of inquiries in relation to teaching methods are recommended by P. Levy.[10])

I propose now to consider some of the ideas that occur to me, in a very personal way, out of a consideration of curriculum innovation as I understand it. Then I shall conclude by offering a simple set of proposals for school based curriculum development. As far as possible I shall try to avoid a technical vocabulary but I shall make reference to sources where this vocabulary is freely employed.

The curriculum may be looked at in several ways. From the teacher's point of view it is several things: the totality of ideas, methodologies and materials provided by his school of which he lays claim to his part: his subject or, in the case of the primary teacher, his age group, with which he feels more or less at home. This is his piece of professional estate, in which he has invested his professional competence, his standing as a member of the teaching community, and into which he himself was initiated as student in college or university. From a slightly different standpoint—perhaps that of the head, or the director of studies, or the head of a department or a division—the curriculum is a plan or a scheme, a concrete, practical expression of the educational aspirations of the teacher, the way or ways in which he formulates, expresses and acts out his educational ideology or belief system, whether this be his own creation—e.g. the very independent minded primary head—or his more subservient response to the requirements of the examination syllabus.

From the pupil's point of view, the curriculum may be all kinds of other things—as shown in the responses of pupils as reported in *Enquiry I: The Young School Leaver*. For him, curriculum may signify teacher's whim or enthusiasm, or what has vocational potential, or the shifting pattern of experiences whereby class music blends into discussion and that in turn into group work in science and that into individual assignments on themes or so called projects.

Parents, again, may think of curriculum as meaning all the

subjects or as the impenetrable vagaries of an undifferentiated timetable, and will compare this with their own schooldays or with what they hear is happening in other schools. Similarly employers, local authority inspectors and HMIs, college lecturers and other interested parties will have different views about what is meant by the term 'curriculum' and about the value of the various enterprises that go under that title.

Now the questions arise, whose view of the curriculum is the right one and by whose authority do and should changes in the curriculum occur? These are very large and difficult questions. A simple set of answers, and one we are all familiar with, runs like this 'The curriculum is the responsibility of the school, particularly of the teachers. Their views as to what it consists of and should consist of are those of the professionals and the experts, and they should have the authority to decide what should be taught and by what means.' In fact we recognize all kinds of constraints: not class teachers—i.e. those who do the teaching—but heads have the greatest authority, but their authority is also affected by various constraints: the pressures of external examinations, of parents, of employers, the exigencies of the teaching strength available, the limitations in physical resources, plant, equipment, etc. Any discussion of strategies of curriculum development would have to sort out these factors and attempt to show how they do and should operate differentially in various situations. For example a secondary teacher may have very good reasons for wishing to combine his history with someone else's geography, but he may well find himself in a situation where the geographer is reluctant, or where timetabling restrictions make blocked time very difficult to arrange, or where the head, reflecting parents, is doubtful about the effects of this on examination results.[11] My point here is that no strategy could adequately proceed unless it were based on a very careful appraisal of constraints and opportunities. These constraints and opportunities are what I describe as 'the situation' and they may be thought of as:

1 materials, equipment and money, actually and potentially available
2 political factors, including the pattern of authority relationships within the school and between the school and the forces impinging upon it from its environment
3 skills, knowledge and personalities of the teaching participants
4 aptitudes, abilities, interests and defined educational needs of the pupils.

Of course one may proceed without consciously attending to one or more of these factors, but I should have thought the likelihood of success is increased to the extent that these factors have been carefully thought about and accounted for. (There is some support for the view that these factors are significantly related to the success or failure of the curriculum innovations.[12]) This kind of diagnostic analysis is clearly a leadership responsibility and it may be naïve to suppose that it can be effectively carried out by classroom teachers. (Opinions on this were clearly divided at the third international curriculum conference, the English favouring the idea that classroom teachers could take many more responsibilities than the Americans thought possible. The work of Rudd at Manchester and of Kerr at Leicester involving teachers in responsible tasks illustrates the English approach.[13] On the functions to be expected of heads, directors of study and other key personnel in initiating curriculum change there is a substantial American literature.[14])

But there is another question arising out of that cluster of issues I raised a little while ago. By asking 'whose view of the curriculum is the right one?' I wanted to draw attention to the point that whoever in fact *does* control the curriculum it is fitting to ask who *should* control it. Is the curriculum simply a professional instrument or, for instance, do parents, employers and the pupils themselves have some rights in its determination? A thorough analysis of this question goes far beyond the limits of this paper. I shall try very briefly to show that these three groups legitimately can claim certain rights. But this demonstration rests on acceptance of the view that the curriculum is a vital factor in the development of children and of the wider society: that educational content makes a significant difference to experience: to values, ideas, skills, attitudes and understandings. Conceptions of the curriculum which express this set of ideas are part of the idealist tradition, e.g. R. Ulich's definition:[15]

> A curriculum or a programme of studies represents an attempt on the part of educational institutions to provide a learning person with a coherent sequence of impressions, exercise and cognitive subjects by virtue of which he can participate consciously, conscientiously, and productively in the cultural development of the nation and of mankind as a whole.

This generalization should serve as an invitation to ask more precise questions. May I mention some of them. What concept do we have of a 'person'? What is learning? What subjects should be taught? What is the relation of education to society?

We can hardly claim, I think, that any one cultural subgroup, e.g. the teachers, have proprietorial rights over human experience. What is worthwhile in life is, it seems to me, a genuinely open public question to which the whole community should be invited to contribute. The translation of agreed answers to this question into pedagogical programmes is a professional skill, but we should ask, I think, at what point in curriculum making does the public in our society participate? Perhaps heads should be doing rather more than is common at present to involve a wider public in at least the discussion of the basic qualities, values and experiences to be emphasized in the school curriculum. (Perhaps the most ambitious efforts along these lines have been the Illinois Curriculum Programme and the community school movement.[16])

Now the pupils. The same arguments I have just adduced apply here but the manner of the operation would of course be rather different. Instead of general discussions of broader questions of educational policy, the specifics of actual curricula should be discussed, and at all stages, with children. This is not only because children have some fundamental rights of self determination and a genuine and vital stake in the question of which significant experiences they should undergo. It is also because there are important motivational issues at stake here. It does not, perhaps, require much in the way of research evidence to suggest that learning best proceeds when children are interested in what they are doing, have some say in determining the nature of the activities they are to be engaged in and understand, however incompletely, the purpose, significance and outcomes of their studies. (Karl Mannheim long ago forcibly argued this point with particular reference to adolescents in *Diagnosis of Our Time* and *Freedom, Power and Democratic Planning*. University students have been making this point in a more practical and vociferous way since the Berkeley and Paris uprisings of the mid sixties.) So the active participation of children in curriculum making is worth considering both on motivational grounds and in terms of the more abstract question of by what right the teacher decides which experiences children are to undergo. A strategy which intends to take into active account the participation of pupils in curriculum making will be very different from one which proceeds on the assumption that the class teacher is the proper sole determinant of curriculum, and this in turn will be very different from a strategy deployed by the head to transform, say, science teaching in his school, with or without teacher and pupil participation in policy formation. (The argument applies no less to teachers than pupils in relation to proposed changes in their work patterns. Confirmation of some of the tenets of 'progressive education' concerning participation by teachers comes from unexpected sources. An article in *Sociology of Education* reports a study, derived from industrial, commercial and voluntary agency research, of the relationship of teacher satisfaction to perceived influence on decision-making.[17])

What emerges from this is that the nature of the strategy will itself vary with the material constraints and opportunities presented by different situations, and with kinds, numbers and status of the participants. (Participating and nonparticipating models of change may usefully be employed here to study particular situations . . . The mechanistic–organismic model of Burns and Stalker was used by Dines in studying curriculum change by participating methods in a large comprehensive school.[18]) For example, Joslyn Owen referred to the Schools Council as a forum where strategy is hammered out.[19] This is doubtless true and for some indication of how this works, so far as committee structures go, it is instructive to read the Council's newssheet, *Dialogue*. But it is also true that many school staff meetings are 'forums where strategy is hammered out'—but the level and the whole nature of the operation is different, and what might work or indeed be required for the Schools Council in the way of committee structure might hamstring change if anything like so elaborate a committee structure were set up in a school or even a local authority. (This is not to question the value of committee procedures in initiating change within schools. Relatively little published material is available on the work of such committees in English education.[20])

It may nevertheless be felt that behind the admitted diversity of situations to which strategies of change must be directed, there must be some common factors. Is there a process for directing curriculum change which might at least have wide applicability for classroom teachers? Are there some questions which must be answered? Is there a sequence of such questions? Are there common pitfalls? Are there some practical tips and some ideas about machinery? These are questions that may be answered positively but at the risk of going well beyond what experience and research have to offer. I shall conclude by outlining some of these positive answers, but I hope it will be noted that my remarks here are very tentative.

I should like to consider the classroom teacher as a change agent. (The change agent concept derives from the helping professions.[21]) An agent of whom? First, of the concept of education itself, as we understand it, of the tradition of values and experience evolved through thought, inquiry and experience. Second, of society, especially of those identifiable forces to which the school owes allegiance: parents, the educational administrative framework, the polity, the economy and so forth. But this is or should be a critical and not a subservient allegiance. Third, the teacher is an agent of his own pupils, of their 'best interest' to learn and to grow through education.

As a change agent, the teacher has a situation to consider, a situation which he wishes to change or to develop and structure in certain ways. I have already outlined some of the relevant factors in this situation, and I have tried to indicate that, whether he wills it or not, the teacher is now faced with an ongoing, external pressure for change, and what I am proposing is that he should, as far as he may, take a direct hand in guiding these changes insofar as they affect his own work. As an agent, wishing to change a situation, the teacher will have certain objectives or desired outcomes in mind. Or, at least, he will be conscious of certain criteria, or procedural principles against which he will test his particular actions as a teacher. These objectives, or criteria, are themselves constantly developing, as the teacher compares his actions with them and as he thinks more about his work. They are not, like the canons of the classical tradition or the imperatives of a single strategy, fixed and dominating.

The objectives or criteria the teacher has in mind should refer explicitly to pupil learnings. The teacher's objective is satisfied when the pupil learns something, in a certain way. It is not sufficient to have an intention which does not issue in any discernible change in the pupils, although such intentions are not altogether rare in education. (Teaching 'by objectives' is hotly contested.[22])

For the teacher to have an intention which results in discernible and desired changes in pupils implies that he will have some procedural means for bringing about these changes. These means consist of content, as it is commonly understood in the form of skills to be acquired, knowledge to be developed, beliefs and attitudes to be challenged and so forth. Also the means consist of forms of activity for pupils to engage in. Now the teacher needs not only ideas about content and forms of activity, he also needs some plan of campaign, and he needs some means for ascertaining whether his plan of campaign has been effective—that is he needs a scheme of implementation and he needs a scheme of evaluation.

These points may be summarized into a simple model of the teacher, as change agent, diagnosing a situation, preparing objectives, designing schemes of work, devising implementation procedures, implementing and evaluating the effects of his treatment. My contention is that he should be able to argue out each of these steps or stages, to show how they interrelate and to have means for changing what he does in relation to each stage in accordance with his experience of particular units of work.

But I have been in danger of overlooking the pupil's contribution. Let us take a few examples. Diagnosis of a learning situation is improved to the extent that pupils are encouraged to contribute their views on what they get and what they need. Objectives are better when understood and appreciated by pupils. In one sense, unless they come to be understood and appreciated over the course of the learning enterprises, then the teaching has failed. Similarly evaluation is better to the extent that pupils contribute to the evaluation of their own work—i.e. come to apprehend its value in terms of their individual performances and of the significance of the kind of activity they have been engaged in.[23]

Does all this constitute a strategy of curriculum innovation? By my own argument it ought not to do so! Yet it may be that some foundations for a discussion of curriculum strategies have been suggested. These foundations could be set out as a list of suggestions:

1 Strategies will differ according to the situations for which they are intended.

2 The question of *who* participates in the determining of curriculum content is fundamental.

3 Curriculum change characterizes contemporary education and teachers need to develop ways of coping with the pressures for change to which they will be increasingly exposed.

4 Research and experience can be drawn upon, but they do not provide conclusive answers, rather they serve to remind us of the dangers of panaceas and simple solutions.

5 The classroom teacher in our system has a vital part to play

in curriculum innovation and can come to grips with the problem of *how* to change the curriculum by using a simple change model which has been outlined.

6 Teachers could help enormously the understanding of change processes by keeping records and diaries, by making written observations on their own curriculum innovations, by trying to justify their objectives and by using more systematic methods of evaluating the results of their teaching.

All of this of course adds greatly to the demands being made on teachers. The concept of a strategy reminds us of the need to plan and organize our experiences and work situations in a period when inputs in the form of ideas, possibilities and pressures have greatly increased. Current arrangements in school in the form of teaching loads, contact time and timetables will require drastic revision if teachers are to gain the time and freedom to participate actively as curriculum developers and change agents. It is the responsibility of heads of departments, inspectors and others in the administrative branches of education to implement and sustain new forms of support, to enable teachers to contribute effectively to curriculum development.

References

1 See for example R. W. Heath, *New Curricula* (Harper & Row, 1969); P. Rosenbloom (ed.), *Modern Viewpoints in the Curriculum* (McGraw Hill, 1964); S. McLure, *Curriculum Innovation in Practice* (HMSO, 1968).

2 J. Bruner, *The Process of Education* (Harvard University Press, 1960).

3 For the relationship between Bruner's and Piaget's ideas, see D. B. Harrison, 'Piaget, Bruner and the teachers', *Manitoba Journal of Education*, vol. 4 no. 1 (November 1968).

4 See R. D. Archambault (ed.), *Dewey on Education: Appraisals* (Random House, 1966).

5 R. M. Bar, 'The role of colleges of education in curriculum innovation' in R. M. Bar (ed.), *Curriculum Innovation in Practice: In Relation to Colleges of Education* (Edge Hill College of Education, 1969).

6 'The curriculum mongers: Education in reverse', *New Society*, 6 March 1969.

7 There are of course various conceptual schemes for the analysis of strategies. Several of these are discussed in E. Hoyle, 'How does the curriculum change?' *Journal of Curriculum Studies*, vol. 1 nos 1 and 2 (1969); R. L. Foster, 'The search for change', *Educational Leadership*, vol. 25 no. 4 (January 1968); M. Miles (ed.), *Innovation in Education* (Columbia University, 1964). On some problems in the concept of strategies see D. Gorwin, 'Defects in the doctrine of educational strategies', *Educational Theory*, vol.

14 no. 2 (1964). Some of the dangers ('dogmatism' and 'overprecision') in seeking models of the change process are discussed in K. Hansen, 'Design for decision', *National Association of Secondary School Principals Bulletin*, vol. 51 no. 322 (November 1967). Weaknesses in recent research and theorizing on educational innovations are discussed in N. Gross, J. B. Giacquinta and M. Bernstein, *An Attempt to Implement a Major Educational Innovation: A Sociological Inquiry* (Harvard University Press, 1968). The literature of management contains many efforts to schematize change strategies, e.g. A. L. Delbecq, 'The management of decision-making', *Academy of Management Journal*, vol. 10 no. 4 (December 1967).

8 McLure, *op. cit.*

9 Details to be published in a forthcoming book edited by Jack Walton (Oxford, Pergamon Press).

10 P. Levy, 'New research for new curricula,' *Journal of Curriculum Studies*, vol. 1 no. 2 (May 1969).

11 For a discussion of some of the problems arising in team teaching, see J. Kemp, 'The Formulation of an Organizational Strategy for Team Teaching', unpublished M. Ed. dissertation (University of Bristol, 1969).

12 Gross, Giacquinta and Bernstein, *op. cit.*

13 McLure, *op. cit.*; W. G. A. Rudd, 'Curriculum innovation: regional and local effects' in R. M. Bar (ed.), *op. cit.*; 'Progress Reports on the Work of Curriculum Study Groups' (University of Leicester School of Education).

14 J. P. Jones, 'Changing patterns of leadership', *Personnel*, vol. 44 no. 2 (March–April 1967); A. F. Brown, 'Research in organizational dynamics: implications for school administrators', *Journal of Educational Administration*, vol. 5 no. 1 (May 1967); H. Seymour, 'The principal as the instructional leader', *NASSP Bulletin*, vol. 51 no. 322 (November 1967); F. T. Willhelms, 'The principalship on the spot', *NASSP Bulletin*, vol. 51 no. 322 (November 1967); G. W. Angel, 'Leadership for transformation', *NASSP Bulletin*, vol. 52 no. 332 (December 1968).

15 B. Burnham (ed.), *New Designs for Learning* (University of Toronto Press, 1967).

16 K. D. Benne and B. Muntyan (eds), *Human Relations in Curriculum Change* (Dryden, 1951); E. G. Olsen, *The School and the Community Reader* (Macmillan, 1963). For the community sides of the equation in a British city today, see E. Midwinter, 'Educational priority areas and the community school', *New Era*, vol. 51 no. 7 (July–August 1970).

17 H. A. Hornstein, D. M. Callahan, E. Fisch and B. A. Benedict, 'Influence and satisfaction in organizations: a replication', *Sociology of Education*, vol. 41 (fall 1968); see also J. H. Johansen, 'The relationship between teachers' perceptions of influence in local curriculum decision making and curriculum implementation', *Journal of Educational Research*, vol. 61 no. 2 (October 1967). The importance of teacher understanding of proposed changes is underlined in Gross, Giacquinta and Bernstein, *op. cit.* and in J. B. Lunn, *Streaming in the Primary School* (NFER, 1970).

18 T. Burns and J. Stalker, *The Management of Innovation* (Tavistock, 1961); P. Dines, 'Curriculum Change in Comprehensive Schooling', unpublished M. Ed. thesis (University of Bristol, 1968).

19 McLure, *op. cit.*

20 Dines, *op. cit.*; R. E. Copeland, P. D. Holland and W. L. Lewis, 'Curriculum planning in a large school', *Forum*, vol. 10 no. 1 (autumn 1967); and E. Richardson, *The Environment of Learning* (Nelson, 1967).

21 W. G. Bennis, K. D. Benne and R. Chin (eds), *The Planning of Change* (Holt, Rinehart & Winston, 1969); R. Lippitt, J. Watson and B. Westley, *The Dynamics of Planned Change* (Harcourt Brace, 1958).

22 J. Dewey 'Progressive education and the science of education', *Progressive Education*, 5 (1928); R. W. Tyler, *Basic Principles of Curriculum and Instruction* (Chicago University Press, 1949); E. W. Eisner, 'Educational objectives: help or hindrance', *School Review* (autumn 1967); D. R. Krathwohl, 'The taxonomy of educational objectives – its use in curriculum building', *Defining Educational Objectives*, C. M. Lindvall (ed.), (University of Pittsburgh, 1963); J. D. McNeil, 'Concomitants of using behavioral objectives in the assessment of teacher effectiveness', *Journal of Experimental Education*, vol. 36 no. 1 (fall 1967); M. Haberman, 'Behavioral objectives: bandwagon or breakthrough?' *Journal of Teacher Education*, vol. 14 no. 1 (spring 1968).

23 On student involvement in assessment, see M. Skilbeck, 'Assessment in general studies', *The Vocational Aspect of Education*, vol. 21 no. 50 (autumn 1969).

4.3 Teaching with the urban environment

Eric Midwinter

The child: the significance of his environment

The Malayan rubber plantation syndrome: a case history
A social environment course for teachers was once begun by
asking them to inspect and then comment on a well-constructed
model of a Malayan rubber plantation. They examined it very
critically, lifting up the huts and looking closely at the sap cups on
the trees. They admired it technically noting, presumably for
future reference, tips about how this or that piece of material was
utilized. Not one asked why it had been done. Not one said that
this was a travesty, albeit a rhapsodic travesty, of the rubber
trade, failing as it did to depict the nastiness of exploitation,
colonialism, racialism or whatever. No one said that the primary
child's (perhaps even the teacher's) conceptual development was
inadequate to cope with the validity of the rubber plantation,
hence its unconsciously dishonest reduction to a level compre-
hensible to the child. No one pointed out that the art and craft
work was essentially third-hand, so remote was it from the experience of the child or indeed from that of anyone in contact with
the child.

In short, there was a concentration on the method. Over the
last score or so years, there has been a remarkable and welcome
change in method, but unluckily some educationists have seen
this as a fundamental revolution. It is far from being this. Indeed,
the wondrous attractions of new methods have sometimes hidden
the sterility of the old content on which they've been practised.
What was rubbish when rote-learnt still remains rubbish when
'discovered'. If 'doing' Richard the Lionheart is a relative waste of
time, no amount of ribboning, scissoring and mounting of assaults

Source: Eric Midwinter, *Social Environment and the Urban School*, Ward Lock
Educational (1972), 10–14, 16–19.

on the colour supplements will save it. Where once children copied it down from the blackboard into their books, they now copy it out of other books into their books. But unless the substance is different, it is much the same exercise. Arrant nonsense on a stencilled handout remains arrant nonsense despite its transfer to a tape recorder.

College history tutors can always do a bit of magic with students preparing for school practice. 'I'm doing the manor,' says the student. 'Ah,' says the tutor airily, 'you have an eight-plus class'— simply because the historical eras can be neatly geared to the junior school chronology. Ancient Britons and Anglo-Saxons in the first year; monks and manors in the second; Tudors and Stuarts in the third; and other denominations in the fourth, to say nothing of another whirl around the mulberry bush in the secondary school. This cannot be right. It must make one of two cardinal errors. The topic must either be done properly and correctly, in which case the child couldn't understand; or, as usually happens, it must be done via stories at the child-level. This has produced a nation with a seven year old view of the Anglo-Saxons. An HMI once tidily completed the argument by suggesting that we did the Anglo-Saxons first because theirs was a simpler society to understand. There have been few less complex societies. It had of course been oversimplified, i.e. falsified, for his childlike delectation.

This cannot be altered by making it 'social' rather than 'political', along the lines of Egbert the swineherd's son or Tobias, the boy who knew St Paul. Nor can it be justified, as it so often is, in terms of 'interest'. 'Interest' is about method; while agreeing wholeheartedly that a child must be interested to be educated, the reverse is not true, otherwise a diet of television serials might suffice. It is equally the teacher's function, not only to opt easily for what is evidently interesting, but to make professional judgments about what is valuable, and then by shrewd deployment of methodology to make it interesting and tempting.

Unlike other areas, such as maths or reading, the teacher's traditional wisdom seems awry in the humanities, where the pupil is forcefed huge chunks of indigestible and often worthless knowledge. It is rarely developmental, as we offer our massive helpings of Masai tribesmen, Good Samaritans and Francis Drakes. It is the equivalent of starting the infant reception class reading with *Pickwick Papers* or first year juniors with quadratic equations. In social studies or humanities, as in other fields, the children need to develop awareness and sensitivity in the temporal, spatial, moral and spiritual, scientific and logico-rational aspects of their life.

A checklist of five criteria

In presenting the urban child with work in the social environment, five criteria must be satisfied as perfectly as possible.

1 Is it understandable?

Is the work too far removed in time or space or whatever other concept for children to understand, with the result that it is simplified to the point of distortion?

2 Is it useful?

Will the children benefit in knowledge or have their development nurtured by the work, or is it so distant from their experience as to be superfluous?

3 Is it interesting?

It is the teacher's task to make the work interesting, once it has been decided that the work is valuable.

4 Is it first-hand?

Even when the activity is practical and craft-like, it can still be faulted. In the classic lesson of the teacher telling the tale of the monks or the Masai tribe and the children drawing a picture or making a model, the felony is compounded. The art is just as second-hand as the history or geography.

5 Is it developmental?

Does the work sharpen the children's awareness of the social environment, as opposed to merely presenting them with chunks of indigestible information?

Familiarity breeds response

All this is desperately important because empirically one sees (and not only in downtown areas) many people with social troubles. Many people are faced with myriad social difficulties of all kinds with only the ability to recite *Cargoes* or to catalogue the symptoms of the Black Death as their educational stock-in-trade. Thousands of our children are living in our town centres and in our municipal redevelopment estates. Some will be educated to the standard where they can legitimately and fairly expect to move to more salubrious and affluent surroundings. Some educationists seem to think that all our education should be directed to this Laramie-like policy of 'git 'em up an' move 'em out'. Unhappily,

the city centres and corporation estates are not going to be de-
populated. We must prepare our children not only for the life
that they would like to lead but for the life that they are likely to
lead. Thousands of children will continue to live in these kinds of
urban conditions; soon they will be citizens and parents in these
areas. Will they have been any better equipped than their parents
to handle the day to day pressures of the life-issues that inevitably
face them?

The teacher's task should be to acquaint these children as pro-
foundly as possible with the context in which they live. From this
they might just reach out past a resigned acceptance of their lot, or
a crude, negative reaction against it, to a clear articulation of
their needs and to positive responses to those needs. Eventually a
community must save itself, and education could be one of the
keys to the necessary self-awareness on which reconstruction
might be built. We must (to exchange an old for a new cliché) not
so much move from the known to the unknown, as make the
known more knowable. The emphasis is on the 'now', on bringing
in the new and the external to illuminate the immediacy of the
child, rather than constantly reaching out for the new and the
distant which is often completely alien to the child's reality.

The urban curriculum

Three more points must be made. First, this is not (as has been
complained) inward-looking, designed to nurture a ghetto
mentality, or a soporific to stop the peasants from being revolting.
It is an attempt to open the eyes of urban children dynamically
and critically to the locality as a secure base for educational
advance. It means a curriculum more social and less academic
than hitherto but, by the same token, it need be no less creatively
and intellectually exhilarating. Teachers talk of *widening* horizons
when, by zooming off via telly, coach or book to New Zealand,
the Holy Land or the countryside, they are frequently *exchanging*
horizons and running the risk of producing social schizophrenics.
Because of the ostensible drabness of the city environment, well-
intentioned teachers have indulged in escapism, either by creating
a culturally alien air-raid shelter in the classroom or by passion-
ately pursuing the arcadian idyll of rurality for an hour or two—
unfortunately, as many a battery hen could testify, this is now an
empty dream of yesteryear. Rather should we begin by helping
children to face up to their own reality competently and imagin-

atively, looking for the stimuli in the rich potential of the urban culture.

Second, a community-oriented or environmentally-based curriculum is more likely to engage the involvement of parents and other members of the community. So much is now known of the imbalance of home and school in socially different areas that it becomes imperative to take a step or two toward the parents. Many didn't get much out of school when they were there and now, with the added mumbo jumbo of ita, modern maths and so on, it must look desperate to them. If we believe in the need for a harmony of interest between school and home, and thus a stable balance of support for the child between school and home, then it is urgently necessary to harmonize the cultural content and values between them, and these are at their most crucial in curricular terms.

Third, with a reappraised curriculum, it is sometimes argued that the slender minority who at the moment do manage to scramble out and head for the white picket fences of suburbia might take a tumble. Briefly, it is equally arguable that by rooting the work of children in what is real and immediate, traditional attainment norms like reading and writing are unlikely to decline and conceivably could rise.

These three points seem particularly firm subsidiary reasons for the emphatic inclusion and sophistication of social environmental study as the principal element in the junior school. But there is yet another more delicate issue. Much of what has been said is, in portion, accomplished by many teachers who colourfully and vitally use local pointers as guide-lines for their work. Indeed, the only major innovation suggested so far is in the scale of the enterprise which bids for a large share of the syllabus. The investigation of the urban environment requires, of course, to be tolerant and open-minded. It necessitates that very dangerous examination of varying values, standards and codes of conduct. Teachers have traditionally been seen as the guardians of the status quo, the planks of the establishment and high sounding cultural and other virtues. Occasionally there may be a teacher who in school hours fights to the death for British law and order and the virtues of saving, before speeding home at fifty through a built-up area to fill in his football pool, or who preaches Tennyson by day and watches *Coronation Street* by night. Most, none the less, would probably feel that they had certain set patterns of behaviour and beliefs which they should communicate to children for the children's own good. It is difficult to spot which of these have controversial aspects; it is difficult to replace them with the creation of an outstandingly high standard in the nobility of open-endedness. It is perhaps unfair to ask teachers, given their background of upbringing and training, to take on this function of equipping the parents and citizens of the future with well-defined powers of social criticism and action. But this is possibly the largest blank in the picture of environmental teaching at the moment. For example, teachers in urban areas who continue to teach about avuncular policemen under the heading of 'people who help us' are doing no kindness to the children, the police or themselves. It is as unfair to the policeman as anyone to dress him in this sentimental image.

This, in broad outline, is the significance of the urban environment in the education of the child. No apology is made for pitching it at a sort of philosophic level which may seem to lack those practical tit-bits teachers adore. There must be social purpose and overall social goals in our teaching. Whatever the pseudo-realist, nursing his mug of tea in the staffroom easy chair, may say about airy-fairy (that favourite adjective) nonsense and getting your feet on the ground, there is nothing so far from down to earth, nothing so unpractical and unrealistic and unprofessional, as teaching without an aim and a vision. Some will say this is an alarming, risky prospect for the teachers. With these we sympathize; you have understood and you are correct. Others will say 'We've been doing this for years'; to these I say: 'Look out of the window; why is it still like that if you have been producing positive, radical actionists for so long?'

The child: his concept of the social environment

Understanding the town
How much of the town or city is incomprehensible to the urban child?

In recent years we have learned a great deal about conceptual development in the child. We know (from the work of Piaget) about the growth of understanding. But understanding of what?—speed, weight, volume, space, time, density, cause effect, geometry, distance, velocity and number. We know that every one of these concepts is built up slowly and laboriously. Take the concept of time for example. Primitive man uses phrases like 'three more sleeps'. The egocentric child talks about playtime, bedtime, home-time. In one piece of research by Sturt and Oakden children were asked 'What day of the week is it?' Having given the right answer they were then asked 'What day of the week is it in another town?', which one-third of them were unable to answer.

But what of more difficult or less relevant concepts? What about patriotism or race or tolerance or 'your neighbour', or the unification of Italy, or the economic growth of Brazil, or the conversion of French francs into pounds and new pence? Much of our thinking about concept development has been specialized enquiry into mathematical and scientific intellectual abstractions. It is perhaps time we knew a little more about social and human concepts.

In fact we do know a little bit about some of the more human concepts which might influence the growth of the child. We know, for example, that he is slowly accumulating an image of himself. We know that he needs reassurance. Piaget has shown us that the child gains in reciprocity in a complex way. He slowly learns how many other people there are in his family. He slowly learns how to sympathize with other people. He slowly learns how to take another child's point of view. He learns how to distinguish between humans and animals. The confusion which precedes this kind of social maturity is often very great. How do children develop knowledge of rules and justice? How do they learn what proper behaviour is? Piaget has described how rules in the game of marbles developed, how the children proceed from expiation and vindictiveness—a sort of an eye for an eye philosophy—to a stage of forgiveness and understanding and a recognition of equality. How does the city child play the game? How does the city child behave when he loses? It's not always a question of not playing to win, or playing for the sake of the game, or losing graciously, or keeping a stiff upper lip, or being generous in defeat.

Let's consider some of the moral and spiritual concepts which might be developed by the child in the town or city. What does the child understand by cheating? What are the norms of the street? What is the difference between them and us? What does the child really know of the values which are placed before him by many of our colleagues? What does he understand by thrift or industry or punctuality or honesty? What does he learn about right or wrong in his home? Wrong is what is punished and when his mum says 'Shut up or I'll hit you.' We know too, particularly through the work of Basil Bernstein, that language is of crucial importance in the development of the city child. We know that words are understood precariously. They are frequently a smoke screen camouflaging ignorance and the language used by the urban child may be more restricted than it is liberating.

There are so many illustrations of how easily the teacher or other adults can mistake a child's conceptual grasp. The conventions of our society are frequently intellectual fabrications relating to the prevailing social climate. These adult notions are not so natural nor so organic that they occur spontaneously in a child. For example, many authorities are worried about vandalism. How many children in our city centres have watched hundreds of homes (possibly including their own) demolished and swept away by men well-equipped with machines? The subtle distinction between large scale legal and small scale illegal destruction is not always an easy one for a child to grasp. But perhaps the best instance is to recall how many howlers crop up in the 'social' subjects like history, geography and religious education. Children 'learn' bits and pieces of information for which they do not have a conceptual structure and they attach these to their own most approximate item of reality. Hence the difficulties over guerilla warfare, the Diet of Worms or, in a child's illustration of *Silent Night, Holy Night*, a jolly fat man in a brown jerkin sitting comfortably in the nativity stable; on questioning, the child said it was 'Round John Virgin'.

Some pointers might be mentioned as a guide to the sort of skills or faculties that need to be strengthened so that children might better understand their social environment. Children need to learn to place facts or events in time and space and to put them into context and perspective. They need to be able to work out the logic of cause and effect sequences, so that they can read in explanations and anticipations. They need to assess facts, not only in terms of accuracy, but in terms of their relationship one to the other, their relevance and their value. They need to develop their ability to express and communicate with regard to social materials. These are some of the main conceptual skills that need experience and exercise.

Anthropology at home

One of the depressing features of modern social life is the vast differences in the environment and experience of our children. Under a mantle of anthropology we find it easy to appreciate cultural relativity. We know that Aboriginals south of Darwin are very good at rubbing sticks together and making fire. We know that Eskimos in the Arctic are extremely competent and understand the properties of snow; if they don't their houses drip on their heads. We know that Bantus in Africa have highly sophisticated ways of categorizing and recording and tallying cattle. These different kinds of expertise and behaviour are different because they are determined by the needs of the environment. Aboriginals, Eskimos and Bantus are different because they adapt to different circumstances. What is less apparent is the subcultural relativity which exists in our own society. One trouble with educationists today is that they haven't studied the environment in which they work thoroughly enough. We know more about New Guinea and Samoa than we know about the East End of London. Margaret Mead has suggested that 'If fish were to explore their environment the last thing they would discover would be water.' Our society teems with dualisms and contrasts—the sheep and goats, the haves and have nots, class differences, middle versus working, regional differences, towns versus country. There are also economic differences between rich and poor, sex differences, family size differences, and so on.

Our literary heritage also teems with examples, such as *Two Nations, North and South, Culture and Anarchy*. At these extremes there are two nations and two cultures. Perhaps slum and suburb would be a better contrast, since 90 per cent of our children live within built-up conurbations. In fact there will be many different environments to which urban children will be exposed. Because human development is a slow, building up process of increasing complexity, which operates in response to widely different environmental stimuli, children's concepts of the town will vary enormously. The child will relate to what is relevant to him. His growth will depend on *his* conceptual development of *his* city, street, gang, environment. He will be bombarded in school perhaps by new concepts which are foreign, remote, bizarre, irrelevant and unrealistic in terms of his backgound. He will reject these or distort them into some more palatable form. This is precisely the fate of masses of scholastic information, standards and ideals presented to city children in our schools.

The law of the asphalt jungle or the urban desert is adapt or die —survival of the fittest. By fittest is meant those best equipped to adapt to the environment in which *they* live, i.e. the conurbation.

4.4 The question of black studies

Charles V. Hamilton

Several years from now, when historians studying race and
politics in the United States look back on the 1960s, they will see a
decade of innumerable phrases and labels. They will see such
terms as *integration, bussing, nonviolence, violence, freedom now,
law and order, black power, community control, white racism,
institutional racism, separatism, black nationalism, revolution,
black studies.* Hopefully, those historians will realize the intense
political environment out of which these terms came. These terms
were abbreviated ways—and therefore dangerous because of the
great possibility of oversimplification—of explaining or projecting
complicated phenomena. Arising out of an emotional, intense
political struggle, these terms became less the subject for pene-
trating, in-depth analyses and more the basis on which a polemical, momentarily dramatic debate was engaged.

The black studies issue is one example of this sort of treatment.
The term rose out of the protest demands of black students on
college campuses in the late 1960s. The demands generally were
summed up in another phrase: 'a relevant education.' The black
students wanted their exposure to higher education to be 'relevant'
to them as black people. They were dissatisfied with the nature of
the college curriculum as it existed in most places around the
country—and they were specific in their criticisms, with particular
emphasis on the humanities, history, and the social sciences. They
pointed out major substantive gaps in American academia, and
many of them concluded that these gaps were as much a function
of a value system that deliberately chose the kinds of subjects to
include in the curriculum as they were simply the result of scholarship yet to be done. In other words, the failure to depict the true
role of black people in American history, or the exclusion of black
writers from the reading lists of courses in American Literature,

Source: *Phi Delta Kappan* (1970), 51, 362–4.

for example, was a clear reflection of the values of American academia. Law schools and other professional schools were vehemently criticized for offering a course of study which did not 'relate' to the developmental needs of a depressed black community.[1]

Thus the students began to demand black studies as an academic mechanism to overcome these normative and substantive problems. One has to understand that these demands were *political* precisely because they reflected—explicitly and implicitly—a feeling among the students that the colleges and universities were not 'legitimate'. That is, the students were demanding that the institutions change in many ways: in how they recruited black students, in what they did with the black students once they were on campus, in how the schools related to black communities, in the recruitment of black professors, in the kinds of courses offered. Therefore, as *political* demands for *academic* innovation, the demands were subject to negotiation and compromise. At all times, the demands were focal points of a political struggle. The struggle was political in the sense that the right of the college and university to rule unchallenged in the traditional ways was being questioned. *This was the central question: the question of legitimacy.*

Most schools readily admitted that changes (in curriculum, recruitment, community relations) had to be made. But then ensued an unfortunate period when many of the specific alternatives—which had to be understood as products of a political struggle—were taken as absolute academic ends. And before there was time to examine perceptively the kinds of *academic* changes that could be made, many people began to join the polemical debate. Black studies were called 'soul courses'; they were seen as places where a cadre of revolutionaries would be trained; respected scholars admonished that black students needed 'higher education' in order to compete, not something called black studies.

If one examined closely some of the black studies proposals, there is no question that he would find many of them being concerned with issues of ideology and what might be called subjective matters. This is so precisely because the proposals were trying to—and in many instances did—articulate a new system of legitimacy. The proposals were rejecting, for example, traditional and widely accepted political science literature that argued in favor of the virtual inviolability of a two-party system. The proposals in that field called for courses that attempted to explore new ways to approach socio-political change in modern America—at least from the vantage point of black Americans. Perhaps those courses were aimed at 'getting ourselves together' and at developing political power among black people. Why are these 'soul courses'—in the catharsis-serving and demeaning sense of that phrase? Have not some political science courses traditionally been dealing with how groups operated 'effectively' in the society? Have not many of the economics courses not only dealt with mere descriptions of the existing economic order but also with ways to strengthen and make that order more viable? Are we unaware of the mass of research carried on on the college campuses by scholars under contract with the government in the natural, physical, and policy sciences? Indeed, virtually all of American education (and surely this would apply to any educational system) has served as a socializing process.

The black students—perceiving blatant weaknesses in that process vis-à-vis their own lives and experiences—were calling for a substantive alternative. They no longer believed in the myth that higher education was value-free, objective, above the social turmoil. Traditional American scholarship has been geared to maintenance of the status quo. The black studies proposals were out to alter that orientation. Professors Seymour Martin Lipset and Philip G. Altbach—who cannot be accused of being generally and unequivocally sympathetic to the black student demands— made an interesting observation on the nature of the university:[2]

In the developing countries, there is an intrinsic conflict between the university and the society, thereby creating a fertile ground for student political awareness and participation. The university, as one of the primary modernizing elements in largely traditional societies, necessarily finds itself opposed to other elements in its society, and must often fight to protect its values and orientation. Students are often involved in these conflicts and are key protectors of the modern orientation of the university. . . . In the developed nations, on the other hand, no such conflict exists. The university is a carrier of the traditions of the society, as well as a training agency for necessary technical skills. It is a participant in a continuing modernizing development, rather than in the vanguard of such development. University students are not called upon to protect the values of their institutions against societal encroachments. In most cases, they are merely asked to gain the qualifications necessary for a useful role in a technological society.

This is an interesting observation because the black students *are* asking their universities to be in the vanguard of development.

The black students and the black studies demands have a valid *political* point. If this is generally accepted, as very many thoughtful people have conceded, it would appear that the next step would be to begin to work out the kinds of *academic* changes those demands call for. Clearly, the students who have served as the catalyst for this should not be expected to come up with the final answers. Those people who style themselves scholars have the burden of proceeding to try to develop new knowledge consistent with a new orientation.

Much of the empirical work has yet to be done, because the questions have never been asked. What is the feasibility of massive economic cooperative ventures in rural and urban black communities? What is the nature of and significance of the black culture vis-à-vis new forms and styles of political action in the black community? Is it possible to talk about a peculiar 'black experience' that has relevance to the way black Americans organize themselves and conduct their lives? What is the impact of the oral tradition on social, economic, and political phenomena? Black Americans have a heritage, a black experience of abrupt cultural transformation to traumatized conditions of slavery in a distant, alien land with a different language and different life styles; to legal freedom from legal slavery in the same place and economic position; to an urban atomized, technological environment from a rural, intimate, agrarian environment. What is the meaning of this heritage and experience in terms of new adaptive cultural characteristics, characteristics that can sustain black Americans as a viable people? What does it mean for the kinds of effort made to bridge tradition and modernity in the black community? What is meant by the 'crisis-oriented' nature of the black political experience? What is meant by 'political traumatization' (as opposed to 'political apathy') that makes this distinction relevant to one trying to understand and deal with the problems of black community development?

These are some of the kinds of questions that their proponents want black studies to deal with. Are these 'soul courses'? Are they 'separatist,' 'violent advocacy of revolution,' 'catharsis-serving' courses? Do they take one *out* of 'higher education'?

I believe that, *if these courses are carefully thought out, they will be the epitome of higher education.* They will prepare the student to engage the total society, not to withdraw from it. One is not going to know much about how to proceed with black economic development without knowing a great deal about the total economic, educational, and political systems. And if one listens carefully to the major thrust of the student arguments—rather than focusing on particular polemical sentences here and there— this point will come through clearly.

One must understand that the demands made in a particular environment—political, suspicious, hostile—have many functions: They serve to wrench an entrenched, closed system into a new awareness; they serve to state specifically a rejection of old values and to state generally a framework for new values. The new directions *cannot* be very specific; they are new programs for experimental times. All answers are not known. There is a tendency on the part of some people to require certainty of results and consequences before they are willing to innovate. In social dynamics, this is hardly reasonable. Of course, there is the possibility of unanticipated consequences. But if those who led the fight in the American colonies to break with England in the 1770s had waited until they knew the precise consequences, they probably would not have moved. Or, to take a less 'ruptured' case, those who began to implement New Deal measures in the crises of the 1930s could not wait until they had definitive answers about results. They were faced with crises, and, hopefully bringing the best judgment to bear, they had to act.

American higher education faces a serious series of crises. The demands for black studies simply point up one area of intense concern. It is unfortunate, but understandable (if one agrees with Lipset and Altbach) that some *so-called* culturally disadvantaged black students had to take the lead in pointing out serious educational weaknesses. And precisely because *they* had to assume the role of innovator in an area traditionally felt to be in the province of 'experts,' it is quite possible that many people in power positions have forfeited their claim to authenticity. Many of them have been lax and unimaginative and listless for so long that many black students now view them as anachronisms.

If all the colleges and universities now rushing to set up some sort of black studies department are sincere in agreeing to the validity of their moves, then why—the black sudents ask—did they not recognize the need before now? Why did they have to be prodded and poked and seized? (If they are acting now simply to avoid another sit-in or disruption, then they should be exposed as spineless hypocrites!) The point is that the credibility of many of the schools in the eyes of many black students is so low—the students, indeed, in some instances, question their integrity—that the students do not trust the traditional administrators and faculty to set up and implement a viable program. And this is the crux of the control problem. *The students do not want control because they want to insure easy grades, but because they want to insure a quality program.* They ask: How can the people who have been so negligent and value-oriented in harmful ways now be *trusted* to administer this exciting, vibrant new educational innovation? These are important questions.

In a sense, it is the *pride* of established academia that is hurt. And frequently their vanity requires its representatives to call for assurances that 'high standards' be maintained—in evaluation of class work, recruitment of professors, etc. It is rather strange to hear such calls issue from a group that has admitted its own failure and ineptness. How could a scholar in American intellectual history, for example, not recognize the genius of W. E. B. Du Bois? What sort of standards must have prevailed that permitted such a scholar to assume a position of authority?

Let us consider proposals for black studies submitted by black students. Do the black students have the answers? Obviously not; they are still in the early stages of their formal education. But they have enough insights gleaned from their black experience (a term which some people have come to see as delightfully mystic or just quaint) to know that much of what has been taught is inconsistent with—indeed, irrelevant to—the lives they lead as black Americans. *And it is this recognition that accounts for a great part of the thrust for black studies.* Many of the proposals may sound, and in fact are, extreme and farcical. But one should not be too quick to dismiss the entire 'movement'.[3]

A Harvard University faculty committee on African and Afro-American studies made the following statement: 'We are dealing with 25 million of our own people with a special history, culture, and a range of problems. It can hardly be doubted that the study of black men in America is a legitimate and urgent academic endeavor.'[4]

Is American academia seriously prepared to embark on such an important intellectual pursuit? Or will there continue to be nit-picking and polemics and energy-wasting efforts over momentarily glamorous and dramatic issues (kicking white students out of black studies classes, separatism, etc.)? The black students have performed an invaluable educational service by raising in a political context the hard academic questions—a political context, incidentally, which many students perceived to be absolutely necessary, given the arrogance, smugness, and entrenched nature of many sources of power. The question now becomes whether higher education can be perceptive and intelligent enough to deliver the empirical goods.

American professors and deans are not unfamiliar with political struggles on their campuses. Campus politics has a long history in this country: interdepartmental rivalries; personality clashes; competition for promotion and tenure; faculty-wife gossip and clashes; at times, in some places, vindictive vetoing of each others' Ph.D. candidates; bitter maneuvering for fewer and smaller classes (and larger office space) at choice (i.e., not 8 a.m.) hours of the day and week.

But the demands and the criticisms leveled by many black students today will make those perennial squabbles seem like tea parties—or perhaps one should say panty raids. The demands of the black students are not nearly so frivolous. The black students are raising serious politico-academic questions that cut to the core, to the very nature of the university and college systems. The black students are political modernizers vis-à-vis higher education in a way never before experienced on American campuses. And traditional American academia may well flunk the test (a metaphor not entirely unintended) if it does not do its homework (hard, empirical, relevant research and teaching).

Notes

1 See mimeographed newsletter issued by Harvard Black Law Students Association, spring, 1968.
2 Seymour Martin Lipset and Philip G. Altbach, 'Student politics and higher education in the United States', in *Student Politics*, Seymour Martin Lipset (ed.), New York, Basic Books, 1967, p. 242.
3 One writer made the following observation: 'To recruit thousands of young blacks into hitherto restricted American universities and to fill their heads full of something called black studies is to prepare them for nothing.' Arnold Beichman, 'As the campus civil war goes on, will teacher be the new dropout?' *The New York Times Magazine*, 7 December 1969, p. 84.
4 Report of the Faculty Committee on African and Afro-American Studies, Harvard University, 20 January 1969, p. 14.

4.5 Some guidelines for instructional strategies

Hilda Taba and Deborah Elkins

. . . It is recognized rather generally that conventional instruction does not reach adolescents with cultural and educational deficits who have already established a negative attitude toward their own capacities, school learning, teachers, and the rest. The kind of experiences that are offered, the motivational devices used, the content, as well as the approaches to teaching, seem somehow to miss the mark, either because they are incompatible with the needs of such students and therefore represent meaningless drudgery to them, or because some links in their education are missing. The severe retardation of such students that shows up in the junior high* is an eloquent testimony to the lack of success of such programs.

This suggests also that remedial measures on higher grade levels that only repeat what these students have already failed at are not the best answer. Perhaps a qualitatively different program is called for. . . .

Basically, of course, there is no difference in the way in which culturally disadvantaged students learn. Their learning processes are subject to the same general principles of learning as are learning processes of the normal run of students, but with a difference. For example, all need to proceed from the concrete to the abstract, but there is a difference in what is abstract and what is concrete to students who have gaps in their cognitive and verbal development and whose life experience may be limited in certain areas. Possibly, less verbal students need a different kind of concreteness than do those with normal linguistic equipment. Verbal explanations may communicate more to the latter than to the for-

Source: Hilda Taba and Deborah Elkins, *Teaching Strategies for the Culturally Disadvantaged*, Chicago, Rand McNally (1966), 65–87 (extracts).

* [*Editorial footnote:* American school grades 7–8 or 7–9; age-group 12–13 or 12–14.]

mer. All students need certain basic cognitive tools to process information and to develop insight into relationships between facts and concepts. But the students from limited environments may lack the concepts which children in a normally stimulating environment have already acquired. Some of these now in the sixth or seventh grade may be working with the intellectual motor of a seven-year-old, at least in certain aspects of their encounters with school materials and the world. All students need to be motivated to learn anything at all. But *what* motivates them may be totally different. All students need to practice skills, and all learn these skills more easily and more willingly when such practice avoids rote drill, concentrating rather on repetition in a new context, but culturally deprived children may require more numerous repetitions in a more visible and inviting context.

What then, are the requirements for the instructional patterns?

A continual diagnosis

A continual diagnosis of these needs and gaps and a continual appraisal of progress are almost an absolute necessity ... diagnosis must be made integral to the very process of learning and teaching; otherwise it would absorb an unreasonable amount of instructional time and possibly provide less effective guidance to teaching.

Diagnosis also needs to be comprehensive: assess the background of experience, the way students feel about school and themselves, the values they hold, their basic, emotional, human needs which are not met and which therefore retard learning, the interests and areas of concern which offer clues to motivation for learning, the ideas and concepts they have, and how they think. The list is endless, and each teacher can extend the diagnosis to what seem to be the most urgent requirements for her particular group and the program. If the teacher, for example, wishes to make a transition from walls as material objects to the abstract concept of walls as psychological barriers, she needs to know whether her students can make the transition. She needs to know who is ready to examine a situation deeply and who can only scratch the surface, who can express ideas with ease and who finds it extremely difficult. Diagnosis via feedback thus becomes part of every teaching act and a basis for planning the next learning experience. This daily feedback and diagnosis are especially needed to help a teacher reared in one subculture to tune into the learning process of children in another subculture and, thus, to permit her to translate what is to be learned into appropriate experiences, instead of being forced to bend the students to conventional learning patterns.

A simultaneous pursuit of multiple objectives

It is a widely accepted fact that acquiring knowledge and skills is not the only objective of education. Balanced instruction must provide also for increasingly effective ways of processing and thinking with that knowledge for attainment of desirable attitudes and sensitivities. If instruction is to be effective, these four areas of objectives—knowledge, thinking, attitudes, and skills—need to be pursued simultaneously. . . .

It is important for all students to master certain cognitive processes and intellectual skills because they are a cornerstone for many other types of achievement from reading to solving mathematical problems. This need for basic conceptual tools has been obscured because the life experience of so-called normal children usually provides them with sufficient practice of these skills to enable them to succeed in the ordinary school tasks.

The case is different with the educationally disadvantaged youngsters. They come to school with a severe deficit in ability to abstract, to see relationships and other cognitive processes. It is not uncommon, for example, for the sixth- and seventh-graders in disadvantaged areas to operate with the cognitive motor of a seven-year-old: they cannot restate sequences of events in a story, have not yet acquired even the simplest forms of categorizing, do not have a model for connecting causes to consequences, etc. These deficiencies prevent success in all kinds of learning tasks. Students who lack the concept of similarity have no idea what to do when workbook directions call for putting commas between similar words. Inability to restate or even to recognize sequences of events renders meaningless certain passages in novels or historical accounts in texts. . . .

Because there is a serious deficit in the development of cognitive tools in their earlier socialization, emphasis on developing a capacity to conceptualize, to generalize, and to abstract is an objective of prime importance for students from culturally deprived homes. Their low academic performance is not necessarily an indication that they cannot master these processes. Students who currently show low academic performance can learn many of the cognitive skills, provided a beginning is made where they are, and provided account is taken of the existing level of their cognitive tools. . . .

Sensitivity training and the development of attitudes toward self, other people, and to the gamut of democratic values and human relations are another important area of emphasis. These qualities and powers are the necessary ingredients of self-development as well as of school learning. . . .

The lack of ordinary skills, such as reading and writing, among the culturally deprived has been subject to so much comment that it requires no elaboration. Name an academic skill and you locate a deficit. But there are other less frequently noted, but perhaps even more crucial, skills, such as the complex of skills related to impulse control, solving interpersonal conflicts, and listening to each other or to directions. Because the problems of interpersonal relations, especially those of handling rebuff, misunderstanding, and criticism, are a regular part of the lives of these students, the skills relevant to coping with these situations are important aspects of becoming a person in their own eyes and of preventing a sense of failure. . . .

Implementation of the platform of multiple objectives described above sets several new requirements for instructional planning. First, it is important to keep in mind that selection of content implements only one of these areas of objectives, namely the acquisition of information. The kind of content one deals with does not help develop thinking, attitudes, or even particular skills; these are learned from the type of learning experiences that are provided. This means that the planning of learning sequences must proceed on two tracks simultaneously: planning content and planning the learning experiences and activities. In planning instruction, teachers must think of the scope and the sequence of the learning experiences, as they now think of the scope and sequence of content.

Teachers must also be aware that a different learning strategy is needed to achieve each of the four areas of objectives noted above. The way of learning facts (knowledge) does not automatically produce a way of thinking with facts. For one thing, facts are learned instantaneously and can be acquired by passive absorption. Thinking is learned only by active process, by doing it, and it takes time and repeated performance to master the skills that are part of it. Learning of attitudes usually requires experiences and materials which have an impact on feelings. Skills are learned primarily through practice and, if possible, repeated practice in different contexts.

A depth study of concepts and ideas

... Because of the many deficits in content background, in reading and language of these students, their power to absorb new content is slow.

A better program for such students is one which emphasizes a number of important concepts and ideas and which judiciously limits the coverage of detail in order to provide time for depth study of these ideas and concepts. If the program is to be productive of learning, these ideas should be both significant generally and capable of being made important to these students. This approach amounts to emphasizing fewer aspects of durable knowledge on behalf of a wider coverage. A clearer understanding of an idea can emerge from studying a few instances in depth than it can from covering many lightly. This way of organizing content and learning experiences should be especially suitable to students with a host of learning difficulties. ...

In order for the depth study of a concept or an idea to be productive, certain requirements have to be met in organizing the instructional plan. First, the central organizing idea or concept of any topic or area of study must be one which can be translated into learning experiences that are within the capacity of the particular group of students. In other words, the ideas and the details necessary for understanding them must be both significant and learnable.

Constructing a psychologically valid sequence of learning experiences is another, and a rather crucial, requirement. Learning experiences need to be organized in a sequential order in which each preceding step develops a basis for the subsequent one, and each subsequent step capitalizes and builds on what preceded. This continuity and sequence are especially important in the development of abstract ideas and concepts and of the skills required for processing information. These are learnings which cannot be acquired instantaneously in one lesson or sometimes even in one unit. However, as long as the interest span remains short, the sequences to develop a concept or an idea must also be short. But they should build upon each other so that the depth study represents an accumulation of shorter sequences. In other words, it is necessary to plan learning sequences both in terms of short-term and long-term goals. . . .

Providing for heterogeneity

The learning experiences or activities must also allow for and even capitalize upon heterogeneity of ability, skill, and background of knowledge. Perhaps the greatest stumbling block to learning in the traditional scheme of instruction is the lack of individualization of learning: the imposition of standardized expectations regarding performance, the uniformity of materials and of pacing. Planning for heterogeneity implies more than individualizing the rate of covering a given topic. It requires provision of varied activities related to the same topic, such as self-selection of diverse books to be read to find answers to common questions, and opportunity for different students to find their own way into new content and ideas. Primarily, though, it involves an organization of instruction around ideas and concepts large enough to permit an open-ended and varied approach (Elkins, 1963) so that each individual can respond to the task in terms of his particular concern and according to his level of perception, performance, and skill. . . .

Part of the strategy of providing for heterogeneity is the use of a greater range of materials and of means of learning, such as stories, pictures, films, and tape recordings to supplement or even to supplant the textbooks, and of observation, manipulation, and experimentation to extend the means of learning beyond reading. The teacher needs to assemble a variety of such material, and much of it will have to be produced by teachers. Some can gradually be produced by students and then used by subsequent classes. Fortunately, the textbook stranglehold is being broken, and a greater variety of study materials from short selections of raw data to maps and pictures are becoming available. . . .

Pacing of learning

Just as the content of instruction moves from topic to topic, so it should also move from one cognitive skill to another. Both movements need to have an appropriate psychological sequence, and the movement of both must be in accordance with the readiness of students and the level of difficulty. The teacher needs to know whether the students can handle the new concepts and the processes required by the new task.

Of special importance to students with learning difficulties is the adjustment of pacing to their performance level. While the sequential steps in learning sequences must be incremental in the sense that each step requires performance on a higher level than the preceding one, the crucial problem is to determine how long a group must remain on one level of performance before a transition is made to a more demanding level. However, the successive learning tasks must be 'bite-size,' namely, they must require a performance that students can manage on their own, challenging enough to require them to improve, but not so difficult as to ask more than they are capable of at that time. For groups with meager skills, this programming of bite-size steps which are at once appropriate to the task and to a given group of students requires of teachers a great deal of awareness and judgment. Each learning step must match the powers of the students. When the task is too complex for them to master on their own, not only do they lack a feeling of success, but learning tends to be less autonomous and effective. To calculate what is bite-size for a given group and to break the learning tasks down accordingly, it is necessary to take into account not just content facts, but also the difficulty of the concepts that organize these facts and the intellectual processes with which to process the data. Decisions must therefore be made regarding the time needed to master the content, concepts and cognitive processes before transition can be made to the next and more demanding steps. This is conceivably the problem of pacing (see Taba & Hills, 1965). . . .

Creating appropriate motivating devices

. . . Too many students have already acquired a negative or an indifferent orientation toward learning by the time they reach the upper elementary grades and junior high schools. Therefore, motivating devices are needed (1) to break this orientation and to engage the students in the learning process, and (2) to keep them learning once the process has been started.

To engage students with an already weakened or nonexistent drive for learning, the use of experiences with strong emotional impact is an almost essential device. . . .

Another important device is the use of the novel and the unexpected, in place of the usual media, at least for the time being. For example, to immobilize the previously acquired negative attitudes toward books, teachers, and directions, such devices as reading stories to the class instead of having students read them, or better still, recording them on the tape recorder for students to listen to either individually or in groups, are useful. As transitional devices to break established responses, such reversals of the usual with the use of the unexpected are quite successful. Whatever the nature of these initiatory experiences, their content must have a close bearing on, or connection with, the experiences and concerns of the students if these experiences are to evoke a response from them. . . .

For a continued energizing of learning, other devices are needed. Knowledge of the characteristics of lower-class students who are educationally and culturally deprived suggests certain necessary features for these devices. For example, tangibility, concreteness, and overt activity are necessary ingredients of the learning experiences if curiosity is to be kept alive and the habit of short attention span is to be overcome. The learning experiences also need to include overt activities, which in themselves are either intriguing or rewarding to students. Writing in order to develop a booklet is such an activity, because being authors of a book is considered an accomplishment, the requirements for developing the ideas that go into it and the making of it set the pace, and because peers will read what they have to say. . . .

Finally, learning experiences must allow success to be experienced fairly immediately. This suggests that long-term sequences must be broken into smaller units which can be punctuated with some tangible, rewarding product or outcome, and which are selected so as to contain the possibility or even the certainty of success.

All this is not to suggest that the possibility of eventually capturing the intrinsic motivation is to be overlooked. Even the more retarded, deprived students have a potentiality for curiosity in learning per se. They *do* want to know something, to feel masters of some processes. They *can* be intrigued with performing such intellectual processes as discovering the causes and consequences of events, of putting facts together and making inferences from them. The problem is how to get them started so that they can experience the pleasure of performing these processes. The devices described above must be seen as transitional measures. Eventually the motivation of the students must spring from the task itself, and from the satisfaction that comes from being able to manage, to perform, to cope with, and to master things which hitherto had defeated them.

The use of literature

... Literature can serve many purposes in the education of the culturally deprived. First, it is a means of sensitivity training, a way of extending their limited experience with human behavior and the problems of human relations. Cultural isolation and alienation are the chief facts of life of the culturally disadvantaged. Each individual grows up in a cultural shell because his immediate socializing group, the group in which he grows up, is culturally unique and hemmed in. The avenues to the mainstreams of culture are usually further closed by segregation of residence areas, by a marginal existence, and by social isolation. ...

These limitations impose on schools a special task of acculturation, of filling in the gaps left by defects in family life and the neighborhood. The use of literature is one means of filling this gap. Fiction is a potent source for extending experience, for internalizing values, for creating identification with people and problems unlike one's own. ...

Reading and discussing stories that are relevant to their life problems also give them a perspective on their own feelings, help them see the universality of emotions and something of their causes and consequences. Literature also helps them identify with other human beings. In other words, literature takes a student out of his own limited and confined existence and helps him to become acquainted with the larger world. The chief contribution of literature, however, lies in its use as a motivating device to focus attention, and as a way of engaging students in the study of an idea, a problem, or a topic. ...

Rotation of intake and expression

... Studies of cognitive development have established the idea that the dynamic growth in intellectual operations is produced by a systematic rotation of (1) assimilation of intake of new information with (2) demand to synthesize the information and to express it in some way that is different from that in which it was acquired. The principle on which this rotation is based is that whatever the students assimilate, they organize and interpret according to the concepts they have at the time. If these concepts are inadequate, defective, or misleading, the meaning students get from information is also bound to be defective or misleading. Since it is impossible to 'give' a student a new concept, it is necessary to use devices that force him to alter, reorganize, or stretch the 'filing system' in his head. This is usually done by introducing a discrepant event, a question that raises a new issue or proposes a different angle.

Dramatization, play-making and role-playing

... The 'play' is a way of creating, identifying, and clarifying conflicting views and feelings. Because the performance of a play means having an audience, pupils will practice endlessly in order to make a good showing. This gives them an incentive to acquire the necessary skills of reading in a fraction of the time it would take in a remedial reading session. They will, for example, practice reading lines with appropriate expression over and over again. The process of trying out plays also requires much discussion before and after each attempt to discover what the central meaning of the story line and of the character is and how to convey this meaning most appropriately. After the character is established and events discussed, the students can read the lines with far greater insight. Meantime they gain in understanding human behavior.

The same is true of poetry. ... Ballads and other narrative poetry ... can be dramatized and they lend themselves to choral reading, which adds another element of interest. Should the voice be that of a girl? Why? What is there in the poem that makes you feel this way? Should the whole class say *these* lines? Why do you think several voices are necessary? Should the chorus be male voices only? Why? Pupils learn interpretation because they *need* it for their performance. Analysis made in this manner seems meaningful and exciting.

Making up plays from stories is another intriguing and useful device for infusing reading with meaning and purpose, and for practicing skills in writing. ...

Role-playing has similar virtues but serves still other purposes. It creates a situation in which immediate problems can be tackled directly, without putting individuals on the spot. Students can express personal feelings and deal with sensitive personal problems under the guise of representing someone else, of 'taking a role.' Shy and reticent individuals, who rarely take part in a large group, can find a place in the endeavor of a small group involved in sociodrama. Since role-playing usually focuses on real life situations, the discussions of the scenes provide ample material for analyzing problems, for assessing motives and values, and for discovering the causes of human behavior. As such, these discussions are also a rich source of diagnostic information.

Role-playing is also useful for skill-training. For example, the pitfalls and problems of small-group work can be acted out by having one such group conduct its first meeting in full view of the rest of the class. Their procedures can be then analyzed by having the entire class discuss such aspects as how the decisions were made and who made them. Such skill sessions usually improve the planning of the subsequent group meetings. . . .

Observing and interviewing

For students who find reading a relatively meager source of information because of reading difficulties, observation and interviewing are important additional sources of information. . . .

The content of observations also lends itself to scientific treatment and thus affords first lessons in such processes as tallying in order to discover patterns, and comparing and contrasting. For example, tallying ways in which young people, babies, and adults react to certain situations or to people in general and comparing the results bring home the need for considering behavior in terms of developmental sequences and differences according to the maturity of the individuals.

The results of observations thus treated provide the content for class work and help students to see the connection between school and the other aspects of their lives. . . . Observations of human behavior also enhance the meaning of the stories, plays, and poems they read, and help them to interpret the various activities that surround them with more insight. . . .

The interview serves many of the same functions. There are, however, additional reasons for using the interview as a learning technique. It brings young people in direct communication with peers, adults, and younger children. To sit down with an adult and hold a conversation, in which he finds out pertinent facts about his life or what he believes, is an experience few of these students have ever had. To them, adults, by and large, are creatures to avoid. In an interview the student functions in a positive relationship and discovers more often than not that adults are flattered by the attention.

Of course, to have interviews function this way requires careful preparation in school. Methods of asking questions need to be practiced in role-playing sessions. 'How do you put the adult at ease?' 'How do you give him the background and reasons for your questions?' 'How do you thank him?' 'What do you say to him?' 'Do you merely throw question after question at him?' 'How do you take notes?' Young people thus prepared usually return to school with glowing reports about the experience. Things that didn't go well need to be subjected to more role-playing and analysis. The results of interviews can also be used in many ways: they can be written up and tallied and the results used again and again for comparison with literature, newspaper items, and historical events.

Organizing the class for study

Any reasonably broad topic can be studied in a variety of ways. Some matters require the participation of the whole class, such as planning the main issues to tackle, converting an aggregate of information into usable ideas, interpreting new facts, and making generalizations. Other matters can be studied more effectively in smaller groups; for example, several committees may undertake to study a number of ethnic groups in order to marshal a wider array of facts and insights for the final comparing and contrasting of similarities and differences between the groups. Other matters are best studied individually.

Combining ways of learning in this fashion extracts the maximum value from the study and uses both the individual powers and the resources of the group to advantage. Such a marshalling of the ways of working also increases the array of skills any one student can acquire in connection with any one learning activity and avoids the necessity of individuals repeating the same routine over and over again after it has ceased to provide new learning for him. This saving of unnecessary routine work is especially important to students whose absorbing powers are slow and whose time, therefore, must be saved for productive activities rather than being spent on routine ones.

References

Elkins, Deborah (1963) *Reading Improvement in the Junior High School*, New York, Bureau of Publications, Teachers College, Columbia University.

Taba, Hilda, and Hills, James L. (1965) *Teacher Handbook for Contra Costa Social Studies Grades 1–6*, Hayward, Calif.; Rapid Printers & Lithographers.

Index